Acknowledgments

I would like to thank my parents, Trudy and Jerry Bohland; Bettie and Lou Lopez;

the Lopez family; my friends at the *Rocky Mountain News, The Detroit News, The*

Daily Iberian, Kaiser Permanente, Lee Reedy Design, Scott Group, Johnson Printing

and Johnson Books for making this project possible. There are so many others who

have given me their kindness and support. I thank you all.

KATHLEEN BOHLAND

Copyright ©1996 by Bohland Publishing Company.

All rights reserved.

Printed in the United States of America.

First edition

ISBN 0-965469-5-0-6

Library of Congress Catalog Card Number 96-079445

Cover Design: Heather Haworth, Lee Reedy Design

Layout: Barbara Scott

Articles in this book have been reprinted with permission from the *Rocky Mountain News, The Detroit News* and *The Daily Iberian.*

Printed by Johnson Printing on recycled paper with soy ink.

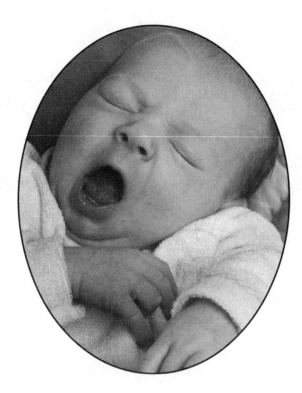

For Calla

Born October 18, 1996

This collection is dedicated to you in memory of your father.

"What's going on?" Stories of Life

by Greg Lopez
Rocky Mountain News columnist

Edited by Kathleen Bohland

Table of contents

Foreword by Gene Amole

It isn't possible to hide behind a newspaper column. A column isn't written from Olympus. It isn't a parallel life, or a routine or an act, or a performance. The column is really a mirror that accurately reflects who the writer is, warts and all.

When Greg Lopez was killed, people asked me what he was really like. I would tell them that the Greg Lopez they enjoyed in the *Rocky Mountain News* was the real Greg Lopez. His honesty, his fun, his compassion, his curiosity, his warmth, his devotion to hard work; all of these things were revealed in his columns.

Being burned out is an occupational hazard in this game. How tempting it is to retreat into a seen-that, done-that state of mind. The numbing repetition of events seems to suggest that there really isn't any news at all but only the same things happening over and over, but to different people.

Just how many drive-by shootings are there? Or, how can I write about yet another bureaucratic foul up? Or, is any one unwed mother's story very different from thousands of others? Or, if you have seen one hit-and-run accident, have you seen them all?

No. The one that killed Greg was different because Greg was one of us. His death served to remind us that what we do here is not about statistics but about people. Greg certainly understood that and always found uniqueness in each person about whom he wrote.

The reason Greg's language seems to jump from the page and into our hearts is because he was such a good listener. He didn't bring bias to work with him. When he interviewed people, he listened from their perspective, not his own. What a rare skill that is.

He had great writing skills. His copy was clean, clear and to the point. Greg chose his words carefully. He never wasted the reader's time with a lot of linguistic flummery.

This is a book you'll want to keep because it is such a wonderful companion, as was Greg. In reading his work again — or for the first time — you'll become better acquainted with him. You'll also feel the presence of his wife, Kathleen Bohland. Like Greg, she is a journalist, and she selected her favorite columns for this anthology. It was truly a labor of love she will always feel for him.

I have been hacking away at this kind of work for 55 years. What keeps me going is the association I have every day with young journalists like Greg. They don't make me any younger or smarter, but they elevate my spirits and make each day worthwhile.

Greg worked right across from me in the newsroom. Every morning he would sit down and clear the top of his desk, then look up at me and smile, and then he would ask, "What have you got going today?"

I miss that very much.

Introduction   by Kathleen Bohland

"What's going on?" said a familiar voice on the other end of the phone line.

It happened four or five times a day. My husband, Greg Lopez, was checking in.

He didn't bother with pleasantries or greetings. Like his writing, he spoke with a brevity that got to the point.

He also hated to talk on the phone.

"I gotta go, I'm really busy," he would say about 15 seconds later.

And he was the one who called me.

The first time I saw Greg, it was June 1987. He wore a shiny blue suit that looked like a hand-me-down from a big brother. It had lapels that were about five inches wide and framed one of those fat ties that managed to survive the '70s.

Nolan Finley, day city editor at *The Detroit News,* told me Greg was there to interview for a reporting job. He asked me to take him to a Tigers game.

"You're kidding," I said. "I'm not your babysitter."

We got to be friends working as general assignment reporters on the night shift. I worked 2-10 p.m. Greg worked 4-midnight.

Despite my first impression, when the clock rolled around to 3:55, I looked to the end of the newsroom waiting for him. Like clockwork, he came in, his first look and smile for me. It didn't take us long to get together.

Greg always wanted to be a columnist — his job at the *Rocky Mountain News* was a dream come true. He often called himself a dinosaur, because he had been doing what he wanted for 14 years, and he still loved it.

He knew his writing was good, but he didn't have a big ego. He was happiest when people read his stories two or three times to get more out of them.

He wasn't the most conventional husband. On our wedding day, he discarded the patent-leather shoes in favor of black cowboy boots with his morning suit.

One Valentine's Day, he argued with a florist for 30 minutes about how he didn't care that a dozen yellow roses cost the same as a half dozen — six were more accurate for the number of years we had been together. Then he forgot and left them in the car overnight where they froze.

For my 30th birthday, he got a tattoo of a heart with my name scripted on it on his right arm.

He owned 96 Hawaiian shirts, 54 pairs of jeans, 10 sets of cowboy boots and one suit.

He lived his life the way he wanted. His stories were more outrageous when he had a couple of beers in him. He chewed tobacco and sneaked cigarettes outside when he thought I wasn't paying attention. He had a stash of Camels hidden behind a box of Miracle Gro on a shelf in the garage.

He could throw himself into a temper and drove me crazy with his obsession with perfection. He used a ruler to measure the exact amount of digging he needed to plant a rosebush and measuring cups to get the precise mix of peat moss to soil. A home-remodeling project was left in limbo for six months because he couldn't stand the fact he didn't lay the tile perfectly.

We finally decided hiring someone is cheaper than divorce.

He would stagger into the emergency room two weeks later rather than admit to anyone he broke four ribs after being thrown from a bull during a media event.

He always told me, "You're the most loved girl in the world."

It's hard to sum up nine years of knowing someone, especially when I learned something new about him every day.

I do know no one brought more joy or fun into my life. He always said we were a team and we should keep it going. And we did.

Whatever we could we did together. We brought a child into the world and buried her together. We planted 1,000 flowers in our gardens each summer. We went whale watching with a group of transvestites in Cape Cod, snorkeled in Cancun, discovered grizzly bears in Montana and hung out in an IRA bar in Northern Ireland. We put tens of thousands of miles on a series of cars on road trips, singing along to Johnny Cash, George and Tammy and Hank Jr.

On our last trip, we flew to Tampa, drove to Key West, went on to Mardi Gras in New Orleans and wandered back to Florida by way of Selma, Alabama — 2,400 miles in two weeks.

We packed a lot into that trip. One day we went snorkeling on Key West's coral reef then hopped on another boat to try parasailing. We drove three hours up to Miami to see jai alai and went on to Fort Lauderdale that night.

It was a great day. I remember Greg saying, "You know, most people don't know how to have fun, it's actually hard work."

Greg found fun in work and in life.

The stories in this collection tell you a lot about Greg.

They also tell you what's going on.

A letter Greg sent to a *Detroit News* editor in 1987 asking for a job. The letter tells about his life as a columnist in New Iberia, La. Greg joined *The Detroit News* in July 1987 at age 26.

Mr. Fancher: The place to start, I think, is the night Robert Mendoza walked into Papa Joe's with his ear in his stomach. I was there.

This is a long story, especially to begin an autobiography, but I think it explains a lot. It helps explain why I am here, what I am like and how I think about things. I think it's a funny story.

Besides, this is the only chance I will ever get to write about this, because Mendoza doesn't think it's funny.

About two years ago, he broke up with his girlfriend, and when he went to try to straighten things out he got in a fight with her new boyfriend. Somehow — the ex-girlfriend and her new boyfriend both say they didn't do it — the top of Mendoza's ear got bit off.

At the hospital, the doctors said they might be able to sew the ear back on, but they couldn't do it right away. To keep it fresh, they cut him open and put the bit-off part in his stomach. I don't know the medical reason behind any of this, but that is what they did.

Two days later, Howard Derouen, Papa Joe's son, went to visit Mendoza in the hospital. Papa Joe's bar is in Lydia, which is on the other side of New Iberia on the way from Detroit. Everybody at Papa Joe's had heard that Mendoza's ear was in his stomach, but nobody believed it.

Right here, you should know that Mendoza is the same Mendoza who came into Papa Joe's one night with the same look he had the night he came in with his ear in his stomach, but without the bandages. Howard asked him what was wrong. You also should know that the circus was in town that week.

Mendoza said, "I was driving down Johnston Street, and all of a sudden this truck pulls out in front of me and I ran into it and wrecked my car. But that's not the worst of it."

Howard asked what was the worst of it.

Mendoza said, "You should've seen that old boy chasin' those monkeys."

Anyway, Mendoza asked Howard to sneak him out of the hospital to Papa Joe's for a Coke. When they walked in, William, who is another long story, walked over to Mendoza. He bent over to look straight into Mendoza's stomach and shouted, "How... are...you...doing?"

The point in all of this is not just that I think the stories a person likes tells a lot about the person.

The point isn't even that this could only happen down here, although the odds in favor of that are pretty high.

The point in all of this, of course, is I was there the night Mendoza walked into Papa Joe's in Lydia with his ear in his stomach.

I grew up in Englewood, Colo., the son of an anesthesiologist and a housewife who used to be a reporter for *The Denver Post*. I am and always have been close to them.

My father was born in Maxwell, N.M., population about 400. His mother died when he was seven years old, and his father put him and his blind brother in boarding school in Raton, N.M. He went to Colorado College on the G.I. bill and put himself through medical school by gardening at a home in the neighborhood where I grew up.

I admire my father more than anybody I know.

When I was 13 or 14, I read the autobiography of Gene Fowler, a reporter for *The Denver Post* and several New York newspapers. A reporter seemed like a great thing to be, and this was before I learned how to drink. Later, of course, it would all fall into place.

After that, I never had to worry about what I wanted to do, only how to do it.

I got by in Cherry Creek High School. I made a lot of friends who still are my best friends. I developed a talent for fun, which is more of a talent than many people realize.

At the University of Missouri, I refined that talent. The journalism school has a good reputation, and it probably deserves it. I thought and still think that journalists spend too much time with other journalists, so most of the friends I made majored in forestry.

More important than anything else, I learned how to recognize good writing — or what I consider to be good writing.

I told you in my last letter that I always wanted to live and work in a small town in the South, and I still don't know why. The story about Mendoza probably explains part of it. I have learned it isn't fair to try to psychoanalyze people I write about, and I won't start here.

Here, though, is a good place to tell you some basic things about myself.

I avoid verbs that end in "ing."

I wear socks to work since the memo came down. I have never missed a day of work. I don't want to be an editor — to me, that is like a young girl who wants to grow up to be Angela Lansbury.

I don't write stories to show how people are different. I try to show how people are the same.

In New Orleans for Mardi Gras last March, a waiter in a restaurant told us we couldn't just sit there and drink beer, we had to order food. I made a comment about a liquid diet, and he turned around and walked away. About two minutes later a cop grabbed me, told me I was under arrest for disturbing the peace. I said I thought that was the whole point of Mardi Gras.

It cost me $175.

The Mardi Gras before that in New Orleans, I broke my left hand in three places when I fell off a mechanical bull.

I am a Catholic. Religion can't count for me or against me, but it is important enough to me to be a necessary part of my autobiography. At least, I hope it is.

I don't hit and run. After I write about somebody, I try to call or go to see them. I don't use people for a story.

There was the time I was in a buffet line behind Gov. Edwin Edwards, when a man in a cook's hat, standing behind the roast beef, smiled and said, "Roast beef, Guv'nor?" The governor smiled back and shook his head — he is good at that — and moved on. The man in the cook's hat smiled at me and said, "Roast beef, Guv'nor?"

There was the time I interviewed a seven-year-old boy with cerebral palsy. He had just received a computer that talks for him, and I asked him how it would change his life. It took him a full minute because he was just learning how to operate it, but finally the computer voice said, "That's a stupid question."

There was the time Roland "Hobo" Landry and Arthur "Wheel" Louviere jammed the corner of the gunnysack into their hubcap to cure a dog of chasing cars, and both of them ended up with teeth marks all over them.

There was the time in Jackson Hole, Wyo., when Scott Heiserman tried to jump over a rented Buick Park Avenue and went through the back window. We had to take him to the hospital because he had a hunk of glass stuck in his leg. The doctor said, "Let me get this straight — you got hit by a car?"

Scott said, "Well, sort of."

All these stories say something about me, too.

A year ago, the two-year contract I had signed here expired. I decided to move on, after I worked my way through a list of people I wanted to write about. A year later, I had written about all of them, but the list was longer with new names.

So I am still here, in a town that looks like you tried to type New Orleans with your fingers on the wrong keys. It has been great. The only thing I regret is the time I fell off the mechanical bull, and I only regret that on cold, damp mornings.

I don't know how all of this leads to Detroit, but I hope it does. I do know that a lot of this might not be considered proper material to send to a person I am asking for a job.

All I can say is that's what happened.

Chapter one

Street Life

"Greg

Lopez

touched

my family's

life."

— OLLIE PHASON,
BRODERICK BELL'S MOTHER

Summer's for Fun

DENVER — Broderick Bell was on the seesaw Friday with his younger brother, DeVaun, talking about what he's going to do now that it is summer again.

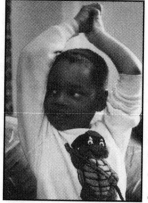

BRODERICK BELL

Broderick was shot in the head two years ago Friday. He is a victim of random gang violence who helped convince politicians that random solutions to gangs won't work. Broderick is 8, and DeVaun is 5.

He went up, and DeVaun went down. "It's summer again, so we got to be careful," Broderick said.

He finished the second grade at Smith Elementary School on Wednesday.

He still can't open and close his left hand and can't lift his left arm above his neck. He has trouble concentrating and following instructions because the bullet went through the part of his brain that controls non-verbal skills. Still, all of his grades were either "satisfactory" or "excellent," and he came home from his field day with blue ribbons in the beanbag toss, the goal kick and the 50-yard dash.

A child's natural recovery from a brain injury continues for two years, and now it is up to him.

"You hear a gun go off, we get inside," he said.

He was shot on the way home from his first karate class. His sister, Anika, picked him up in their mother's car and went to see a friend who lived on Jasmine Street. He sat in the back seat in the driveway, and a car that was shiny and green drove past, a girl in a blue bandanna leaning out the passenger window firing two semiautomatic guns for three blocks.

A 9mm bullet went through the windshield of his mother's car and hit him in the forehead.

"You see an older kid, it looks like they got their pants falling down, don't go up and ask why don't they get a belt," he said. "Mom gets mad."

He came out of a drug-induced coma six days after the shooting and asked his mother when he could go back to karate. The bullet stopped at the back of his skull and remains there. His mother led a march against gang violence, and the state legislature had a special session to pass stronger laws against kids and guns.

DeVaun watched his older brother get all the attention and told his mother, "I wish I got shot."

"We can't be fighting with each other all the time," Broderick said. "We're supposed to be brothers."

He wants to do something to get rid of the dent in his forehead and the scars from the incisions so people won't think he is different.

His teacher gave him math books so he can practice subtraction over the summer. He goes to physical therapy every other Friday. Sometimes, he keeps his right hand in his pocket so he has to use his left.

In Kmart a couple of weeks ago, he took a toy gun up to his mother and asked if he could have it, and then he laughed so hard at his own joke he almost fell over.

"You got that?" Broderick said.

"I think so," DeVaun said.

Now it is summer again.

His mother hears him talking to himself sometimes, saying "I got to get better, I got to get better fast." He had his first karate lesson two years ago Friday. His second is Wednesday.

He went down on the seesaw and stopped, and he looked up at DeVaun.

"The main thing you got to remember about summer is it's for fun," he said.

Rocky Mountain News
June 11, 1995

Cyrus McCrimmon/Rocky Mountain News

BRODERICK BELL, 9, TRIES OUT HIS NEW BICYCLE WITH THE HELP OF ANTHONY TROXELL.

Nothing Average about This Statistic

DENVER — Jose Diaz was chosen by a computer.

The newspaper had put in three months of statistics on youth violence in Denver, and the computer said Jose was the average victim. He was a Hispanic male, 17.7 years old, and he was attacked on a street by another Hispanic male. All of those statistics made him the average victim.

I met him in October.

"I'm not exactly an innocent victim," he said.

He said he had been in a gang and had been beaten by three members of another gang. The beating was revenge for an earlier fight he had started. He had pleaded guilty to assault for the first fight and was on probation.

He didn't have to tell me this: as a juvenile, his record wasn't public.

He also said he had stopped hanging around with the gang, and he had moved with his mother, two younger brothers and younger sister to get away from it. He had gone back to Lincoln High School after a year as a dropout and had a 3.2 grade-point average. He worked weeknights as a janitor, weekends on construction jobs and was trying to find a job to fit in between to help support his family.

In October, he already had bought two baseball mitts, a basketball, a football, six tickets to a Denver Nuggets game, a necklace and a bag filled with games for them for Christmas.

"I don't feel average," he said. "I've got ideas, like I want to go to Greece, but I knew the homies would just laugh at me if I said that. Man, I have dreams, like graduating from college and going to the restaurant on the sixth floor of the Radisson Hotel in downtown Denver and ordering lobster and crab.

"I never had lobster or crab before — I don't even know if they have a restaurant on the sixth floor of the Radisson Hotel, but it's a tall building. "If you've got dreams and ideas like that, how can you be average?"

This summer, Jose worked a construction job during the day and the janitor job at night. He was trying to find a weekend job for when school started. He had bought new clothes for his final semester of high school, and Monday morning he was supposed to buy a pickup.

Last Sunday evening, while his family was at a church carnival and two friends were with him in his basement, Jose shot himself in the right temple with a .22-caliber revolver, Denver police said.

He was pronounced dead early Monday morning at Denver General Hospital.

He left a family that now is trying to find a way to fly his body back to San Luis Potosi, Mexico, where he was born, and to pay the hospital for trying to save his life.

His mother, three of his teachers at Lincoln and his former probation officer all called and said the same things. They talked about how they never would have believed Jose would have killed himself. They said the things people always say after a suicide, and they were right.

"I kept the story about Jose up on the wall in my office to show other kids they could straighten out, too," his former probation officer, Chris Quintana, said. "I thought he'd made it. Now, what do I tell them?"

He was chosen by statistics, and then he chose to make himself a statistic.

Statistics are the only way a person can be called average.

After the story about the average victim of youth violence ran, I told him I would take him to the restaurant at the Radisson Hotel.

"I've been thinking about that crab and lobster," he said. "For now, how about if we just go to Wendy's, and I order a lot?"

Rocky Mountain News
August 21, 1994

Measuring Life by a Fifth of Thunderbird

DENVER — The door at Denver CARES detoxification center opened at 2 p.m., and Bobby Broshears walked out into the afternoon to begin the process of getting back in.

He checked his pockets and found 27 cents and four cigarettes from yesterday. He was two fifths of Thunderbird wine from tomorrow. Today would be like yesterday for Broshears, who has been in Denver CARES 1,569 times.

A Denver CARES bus token later, he was at East Colfax Avenue and York Street, where he has spent most of the past 40 years, and he held up his hand to stop a woman walking in the opposite direction.

"With respect, ma'am," he said. "I'm an old young 'un, and may I ask you, not being nasty or facetious or under the discombobulation of intoxication, if you could help an old tramp coagulate enough recompense so's I could get myself a taste?"

This is how he begins most days. A day is $5.24 to buy wine to get drunk to get back into Denver CARES to sleep. A day in the life of Bobby Broshears usually doesn't last all day.

He is 61 years old, with a white beard down to his chest and clear blue eyes that seem to reflect today's sky, which he hadn't bothered to notice. He wore a blue suit jacket, a white button-down shirt with the initials MJM monogrammed on the pocket, blue dress pants and Rockport shoes from the Salvation Army thrift store. On his wrist, he still wore the orange band that said he was assigned last night to bed No. 96. He doesn't have any other identification.

The woman took three quarters, a nickel and seven pennies out of her purse, and he was 87 cents closer to tomorrow.

"Get yourself a sandwich or something," she said.

"With respect," he said. "I'm a connoisseur of the contemplation of the grape. Would you like a refund?"

She shook her head and continued in her direction, and he walked down Colfax in his. In November 1988, he was involuntarily committed to Denver General Hospital to be evaluated, and the report said his wide, irregular gait possibly indicates neurological damage from drinking. The psychiatrist who evaluated him concluded that his history of drinking for the previous 40 years was "remarkable."

"If I had done that for this long — if just about anybody else had done that for half as long — they'd probably be dead," said Rich Berry, director of Denver CARES. "A lot are dead. He's not getting away with this, but in a negative way what he has done has to be considered an achievement."

Broshears went into The Upper Cut barbershop, where Walt Young has cut hair for almost as long as Broshears has drunk, and sat in a chair under an oil painting of himself.

"With respect, Walt," he said. "I fell through the cracks of society again."

"Bobby," he said, "as long as you're not falling on my floor, you're welcome in here."

Young draws and paints the people who walk past his shop. He has done nine portraits of Broshears.

Young keeps a copy of *Best Tales of the Yukon* by Robert W. Service for Broshears, who can recite *The Cremation of Sam McGee* from memory.

Young cut hair, and Broshears read *Reader's Digest* until he was ready.

He cleared his throat, and Young stopped.

There are strange things done
In the midnight sun
By the men who moil for gold
The Arctic trails
Have their secret tales
That would make your blood run cold

Broshears grew up in Boonville, Ind., where he lettered in football and track in high school. The yearbook said he was "popular, funny and knows how to use big words." His senior year, he won the school's poetry contest.

He graduated from high school to drinking the same night.

"Wine and beer," he said. "It worked. I didn't start out intending to be a chronic alcoholic, but I guess I never really intended to do anything else, either."

He drove to California with a friend but didn't like it, so he turned around and ran out of money on East Colfax. He lived in an apartment across the street from Young's barbershop. He served two years in the Army, worked as a cement finisher, got married and had two daughters and a son.

He isn't sure when his wife divorced him and moved to Nebraska, but he hasn't seen her or the children since then.

After he had finished the poem, he pulled up the sleeve of his coat and looked at the orange name band the way other people look at their watches.

"Looks like I ought to be moving on," he said. "No time to waste."

Outside, he walked down Colfax. One time, he stopped a man carrying a sign that said "Free Croatia" and said, "I'm not sure what it is, but if you're giving them free, I'm taking." Another time, he saw a man harass a couple into giving a dollar, so he gave the couple a dollar he had panhandled and said, "We're not all like that."

He has done this for so long that some people on Colfax give him money before he asks.

"I show respect and tell the kind people the truth instead of lying and saying I want money for food or coffee or something like that," he said. "A lot of folks give me something. Others just give me a glare, and others get specific."

Three kind people later, he was behind a dumpster behind Paul's Liquors with a bottle of Thunderbird in a paper bag. Thunderbird is a white wine fortified to raise the alcohol content to 18 percent. He switched to Thunderbird from Night Train, a fortified red wine, because when he drank Night Train and vomited, he couldn't tell whether he had lost any blood.

He twisted the paper bag around the neck of the bottle and unscrewed the cap. "The Thundering Bird," he said.

He was admitted to Denver CARES the day it opened Jan. 15, 1975. He has been in the center almost twice as many times as the person with the second-highest total, Billy Palmer, who was admitted 861 times. Palmer was sober for a year before he died in December. The living person with the second-highest total, 742, now lives in a nursing home.

Broshears also has been arrested at least 151 times in Denver and Aurora for misdemeanors ranging from public intoxication to begging. This does not include the bench warrants issued after he failed to appear 27 consecutive times in 1987 in Denver County Court to face begging charges or the 22 consecutive times he failed to appear last year to face loitering charges.

Sometimes he sleeps on the streets or at a friend's apartment on Broadway, and sometimes he stays an extra night at Denver CARES because he can't get out early enough to get back in.

The only time during the past 20 years he has been off the street for an extended period was two months in a nursing home with a broken leg after he was hit by a car, and another two months in another nursing home after 80 percent of his stomach was removed because of a perforated ulcer.

Three gulps and half a fifth later, he screwed the cap back on the bottle and put it down the sleeve of his coat.

"When you don't have a taste, it's the lonesomest feeling in the world until you get one," he said. "You can taste its potentiality. I tell you, though, you get a taste and you think you're on Cloud Nine, but in actuality, you're under Cloud Five, and it's raining on you."

He walked down Colfax, and the afternoon started to take effect. His resistance to alcohol has been lowered by the years until the first drink has a noticeable impact. The hand didn't shake, and the movements got larger.

He met Craig Tait, walking the opposite direction for the same reason.

"Bobby, I'm feeling mighty lonesome for a drink," Tait said.

"If you'd care to step down this alley, young 'un," Broshears said, "I might be able to arrange a taste."

They went behind the dumpster behind the Satire Lounge, and Broshears drank from the bottle, then handed it to Tait.

Tait drank and handed it back.

"Bobby, I got a bed at my brother's who's trying to get me off the streets," he said. "You oughtta sleep there tonight."

"No disrespect intended," Broshears said. "But I don't like to feel compelled to stay in a place where it isn't compulsory."

Broshears drank and passed the bottle to Tait, and then they were lonesome together.

"With respect," Broshears said. "Young 'un, you wouldn't happen to have a taste on you, would you?"

Tait pulled a pint bottle of Thunderbird out of his pocket, drank and handed it to Broshears.

Two drinks later, they were back on Colfax, walking in opposite directions for the same purpose.

The next day, he would not remember anything that happened after this.

He sold his bus token for 30 cents. He ate the half of the peanut butter sandwich he had wrapped in a napkin at lunch at Denver CARES. He panhandled enough for a second bottle of Thunderbird, and a pack of L&M cigarettes.

Three dumpsters later, he was at Clarkson Street and East Colfax, where Robert Payson pulled over in his 1989 Oldsmobile 88.

"Bobby, get in the car," he said.

Payson hasn't had a drink since Jan. 23, 1983, when he woke up with his face frozen to a puddle in an alley off 23rd Street and Broadway. He is a construction foreman, and he plans to get married in May. He was going home from an Alcoholics Anonymous meeting.

Broshears got into the back seat.

"Colfax and York," he said.

"OK, but you've got to listen to me," Payson said. "Bobby, you've got to quit this drinking."

"With respect," Broshears said. "You're right."

Payson drove, and Broshears watched the rearview mirror to make sure he wasn't looking. He pulled the bottle out of his sleeve. He watched the mirror and drank.

"Bobby," Payson said. "Look at what I got after I quit drinking. I got me a 1989 Oldsmobile."

"With respect," Broshears said. "You're right."

"Bobby, you've got to get back your respect for yourself."

"With respect. You're right."

They continued up Colfax, Payson talking about not drinking, and Broshears respecting and agreeing and drinking.

Payson pulled into the 7-Eleven at York Street.

"Here we are," Payson said. "Colfax and York."

Broshears leaned forward over the front seat. He squinted. He was trying to read the digital clock in the dashboard.

"So," he said. "How much do I owe you, driver?"

Back on Colfax, he walked in the direction he had just come from. Afternoon became night. Colfax is the kind of street that gets brighter as it gets later.

He took a step forward, but before he could get his foot to the ground he had to take two steps back. A parking meter appeared, and, trying to avoid it, he bumped into Popeye's Fried Chicken. Headlights glared, and neon lights got specific.

He fell to the sidewalk. He rolled over and reached into his coat to check the bottle. He might have slipped through the cracks of society, but he also has tripped over cracks in a lot of sidewalks.

"Got to find a situation to re-evaluate my prerogativeness," he said.

He stood and staggered to the steps of the Holiday Chalet Hotel. He sat and stared straight ahead, seeing nothing. He didn't see the van from Denver CARES pull over in front of him five minutes later.

John Bruno, an emergency service technician, got out and stood in front of him.

"Bobby," he said.

Broshears looked up, and recognition spread across his face.

"What are you doing?" Bruno said.

"Flabbergasting," Broshears said.

In the receiving room at Denver CARES, attendants guided him

Dennis Schroeder/Rocky Mountain News

IN A TYPICAL DAY BOBBY BROSHEARS CONSUMES TWO OR THREE FIFTHS OF THUNDERBIRD WINE.

to a bench. He slid off and laid on the floor. As David Twohorse used to tell Broshears before he was found dead in an alley off Larimer Street two Octobers ago, "You can't fall off the floor."

It was 7:30 p.m., and Broshears was finished with today.

"Young 'un," Broshears said.

"Yes?" Frederick Marsh said.

"Young 'un," Broshears said.

Marsh, who has admitted Broshears into Denver CARES for nine years, had pulled him up to sit in a chair. Marsh was getting the same answers to the same questions.

"Yes, Bobby," Marsh said.

"Young 'un."

"Yes?"

"With..." Broshears said. "With...with..."

"With respect?" Marsh said.

Broshears winked and leaned forward to slap Marsh on the back, and he fell to the floor. A man who claimed he was the late Keith Moon was trying to prove it by pounding on the bench. A man who was in a padded "quiet room" had lain down to urinate under the door to show everybody how much trouble they were in.

Marsh cut off the old orange wristband and put on a new one that said Broshears was assigned to bed No. 16.

Nancy Bingham took Broshears into the room with the Intoxilyzer and put a tube in his mouth.

He took it out.

"Darlin'," he said, "you folks in here always treat me with respect, so I appreciate coming here. If you ever need somebody to do a commercial or something..."

The Intoxilyzer showed his blood-alcohol content to be .287, nearly three times the legal limit for intoxication for driving.

The highest blood-alcohol level he remembers was .397 a couple of years ago, but he can't remember what led to that.

Broshears was given a hospital gown and led to bed No. 16, where an attendant pulled up the rails on the sides because he has had at least two withdrawal seizures.

He lay on his side and started to speak:

The Northern Lights
Have seen queer sights
But the queerest they ever did see
Was that night on the marge of Lebarge
I cremated Sam McGee

At 6 a.m., Broshears mumbled at the attendant who woke him. He lay in bed through breakfast. At 10 a.m. he got up and walked in his bare feet to the smoking area in the corner.

He sat next to Tait.

"Three-twelve," Tait said. "You?"

"They said I was .287," Broshears said. "That feels about right."

At lunchtime, he ate half his turkey sandwich. He wrapped the other half in a napkin. He went back to his bed with a *Reader's Digest* and read *Life in These United States.*

"I don't know," he said. "Folks in this country sure do some zany things."

At 1 p.m., he was called for his counseling session. It is mandatory for a counselor to ask him the same two questions. He was asked whether he thought he had a drinking problem and whether he wanted to seek treatment.

"I know I want to stop drinking," he said. "I'm just not so sure about tonight."

In 1969, he joined Alcoholics Anonymous. He rented an apartment across the street from the meeting place at 1411 York Street. For 14 months, he worked and didn't drink.

"One day, a fella just starting out in AA says to me, 'I respect what you've done and how you've got your life all back together,'" he said. "That did it. I just couldn't handle that kind of respect, and I went out and had a drink and walked into a police car at Broadway and Colfax, and that was that."

He got his clothes back at 1:30. He was given two bus tokens. The door at Denver CARES opened at 2 p.m., and Bobby Broshears walked into the afternoon with $1.14 and two cigarettes.

He has been released 1,569 times from Denver CARES, so he already knew what today would be.

"It's always nice to have the opportunity for a confabulation of my proclivity," he said. "But I gotta catch a bus."

Rocky Mountain News
April 4, 1993

She's Not Homeless

DENVER — Pat was reading *Bonfire of the Vanities,* and Bill was sleeping when a voice outside called "Anybody home?"

Home is a shack next to the South Platte River, and the light inside was from three votive candles a Catholic church gave to Pat. The light was dim, because votive candles are for hope, not reading. Pat opened the door to the sunshine and a worker from a homeless shelter.

Even when Pat used to sleep under a bridge, the shelter workers always called "Anybody home?"

"Hello," the shelter worker said.

"You want me to move into your shelter, but I know I'd have to say I'm mentally incompetent and hear voices, and I'd have to give up my pets, wouldn't I?" Pat said. "Well, the only voices I hear are when you people come down here, and I'm certainly not going to give up my pets. I've got a door I can close and lock, and that's all I need in a home, so goodbye."

Pat closed the door and went back to *Bonfire of the Vanities.*

Pat had lived on the streets and in shelters for three years before a photograph of her with her cat and two dogs appeared in October on the front page of the *Rocky Mountain News* under the headline "Homeless up 68 percent in Colorado."

She had grown up in southwestern Wyoming and worked as a nurse's aide in Wheat Ridge before back problems forced her to quit three years ago. The dogs and the cat were already living under the bridge when she moved in. She refused to go into shelters because they don't allow pets, and she fed them by collecting cans and anything else she could sell.

The day the photograph appeared in the newspaper, people gave her 14 bags of dog food, 12 bags of cat food, sweaters for the dogs, toys for the cat and offers of jobs and homes.

"I think it was all because of Tasha, the cat," Pat said. "She's extremely photogenic."

Two days later, Step 13 moved her into a $220-a-month Capitol Hill apartment that waived its policy against pets.

Her father wrote her from Wyoming, but she didn't write back because he was abusive and once killed her dog, she said.

She turned down every job she was offered. Sometimes, she said they weren't interesting enough. Other times, she said the dogs barked when she was away.

Two months ago, she left the apartment to move in with Bill, whom she had met when they both were sleeping in the same field.

"I guess other people would say we're homeless," Pat said. "But when I had a home, I didn't have all the things I have here. Neither one of us drinks or smokes, so we don't have to put up with a bunch of neighbors drinking and smoking.

"About the only thing I don't have is anybody saying what I can and can't do."

The Indians named the spot Buffalo Crossing, and it was home for as many as 50 homeless men until they were burned out by skinheads three years ago.

Bill built the shack out of plywood, two-by-fours and anything else somebody didn't want — an afterthought with two bunks, shelves, linoleum and no leaks.

A separate room is the outhouse.

"I thought about digging a hole and putting ashes in there for the outhouse," Bill said. "But we're within 150 feet of a waterway, so it wouldn't be legal. So we just have to use a bucket."

Three other men live in shacks around them. A Raggedy Ann doll that was in a garbage receptacle is nailed to a willow.

Carlos, who lives in one of the other shacks, comes by to borrow a rake to clean up some garbage somebody dumped here.

"I find out who dropped that here, I'll take it and drop it on their front lawn," he said.

"People," Pat said. "They're probably the ones who wonder why I wanted out of the city life."

Bill and Pat get water from a faucet behind a warehouse, vegetables that aren't fresh enough for stores from a distributor and fish that is two days old from a shop on Larimer. They have planted leeks, onions, potatoes, a yam and what is either squash or a weed. They have adopted a chipmunk.

She is down to the last 25-pound bag of dog food and 10-pound bag of cat food people gave to her after the photograph appeared in the newspaper, so she will have to go back to saving cans and anything else she can sell.

"I'm grateful for all the things people tried to do for me, but I've learned there's always strings attached," she said. "Before I got the apartment, one lady pulled up by me in her car and said, 'You're going home with me right now.' When I said I wasn't sure, she said, 'You ungrateful bitch,' and drove away.

"I want to thank everybody for trying to help me back then, but I'm happier now."

She went back inside, where the votive candles still burned.

The homeless are up by 68 percent in Colorado, but she doesn't consider herself one of them.

She has a door she can close and lock, and that is what she did.

Rocky Mountain News
April 26, 1992

Greg did some stories about me, a former homeless woman living with her pets on the South Platte River. He helped me a lot, and I considered him a friend. I feel so very bad he died I can't express it in words.

PATRICIA MYERS

Michigan Avenue

DETROIT — At the beginning of Michigan Avenue, Davis Moser sells carnations.

Up the street, there is American Coney Island and Lafayette Coney Island — whatever you want. The Cadillac Building is empty, with a brass plaque for its past and no sign of a future. The statue of Gen. Thaddeus Kosciusko points the way to the suburbs.

Carnations are six for $3. "I've been doing this for 19 years," he says. "It gets any slower, I'm gonna sell lilies."

This is the beginning.

At the other end, 292.4 miles away, is Michigan Avenue in Chicago — the Magnificent Mile, Woodward Avenue to Lakeshore Drive, from where the United Shirt used to be to The Drake Hotel. And all that is in between.

When the road was completed in 1924, it was the longest paved street in the world.

Now, it's the long way.

Tiger Stadium, and Detroit is warming up to play the Minnesota Twins.

"It's another beautiful day here at Michigan and Trumbull," Ernie Harwell says on the radio.

Pawnshops, Coney Islands, bars, punctuated every couple of blocks by a church.

Topless! Bottomless! And what is in between wears white boots and tries to hitch a ride toward Chicago.

Andy's Avenue Bar, where Robert Worley's dog got shot three years ago, is the first of three bars, a party store, a grocery store and an antique shop on U.S. 12 that are named after an Andy.

Worley's dog, a black pit bull named Red, had stumbled out of a corner of the bar, foaming at the mouth. Three customers pulled out guns, and one shot the dog dead. Worley came out of the corner, looked down at Red and the foam that had dissolved into a puddle on the floor.

"The dog liked beer," he said.

Tour the detour.

U.S. 12 was the main Indian route across the territory, the Great Sauk Trail. It was the stagecoach line — eight days to Chicago if the road was dry — then the Chicago Turnpike. When Interstate 94 was completed in 1961, traffic dropped more than 25 percent.

Dearborn, Wayne, Canton, Ypsilanti, Hallelujah Beauty & Barber Salon & Gospel Records — let Hallelujah Do You.

The road narrows from six to four to two lanes. Birds on the lines, like measures of music. The Renaissance Center disappears in the rear-view mirror, and the skyline is silos.

A rock the size of a Volkswagen sits in a cornfield outside Saline, spray-painted every color, every emotion: " '89 Forever," "No War," "Scott loves Naomi."

Scott Terryman, 18, of Saline does not love Naomi anymore.

"We broke up two weeks before prom," he says. "That was just something I did last February. My dad says us kids have it easy — when he was my age they didn't have spray paint so they had to use brushes."

Weller's, the mill Henry Ford used to make soybeans into paint and steering wheels, is an antiques store.

So is Brick Walker Tavern, where the novelist James Fenimore Cooper wrote notes for one of his least-known poems, "Oak Opening."

Michael S. Green/The Detroit News

MICHIGAN AVENUE

Antique if you sell it, old if you sit on it.

Arjay Pederson, 72, sits in his grandfather's rocking chair on the porch of his mobile home outside Clinton and points at where his barn was. He built it with his father when he was 11. Last May, a woman from Franklin paid him $4,000 for it to panel her living room.

"I was gonna tear it down anyway," he says. "Then she comes, says it's quaint and offers $6,000 for it. I talked her down to four.

"I wish somebody would think this old trailer is quaint."

Up into the Irish Hills, the road rolls and carves around the lakes. Everything seems bigger. Except the golf, which is miniature.

"New & Improved Prehistoric Forest." Dinosaurs made of fiberglass, trees made of fiberglass. It will be worth the wait 10,000 years from now, when the archeologists dig this up.

Cement City — the towers of the cement company are crumbling. The clay ran out, and Consolidated Cement left in 1961. A sign buried in the bushes: "Let's change the town name. We don't make cement no more."

Somerset, Moscow and Jonesville. The road becomes Main Street in towns big enough to have their own water tower, not too big to put their name on it. Portable signs with arrows that flash: "Ye ! We Ha e R a os!"

Allen, population 266, has 24 antique stores. Bill Pengelly, owner of the Michiana Antiques, says he has been in the business the longest, since 1965 except for a couple of years in Indiana. Three antique shops down, Andy Bailey says his shop is the oldest because it has been open continuously since 1971.

Anyway, Pengelly points at an old Philco with dials, wires and tubes.

"I've sold this thing three times," he says. "Each time it gets cheaper. Next time, I'll be giving it away."

At the intersection of Halfway Road, 146.2 miles from Chicago and Detroit, Jacob Albert has lived for 79 years. He never has been to either end of the road.

He has the Tigers on a 1952 Zenith that three antiques dealers have tried to buy.

"Some days I'm a Tiger fan," he says. "Some days I'm a Cub fan. Depends on which one I get better on the radio."

When the Tigers fall behind, 13-0 in the eighth inning, he turns off the Philco and Ernie fades away.

"I heard a joke the other day," he says. "What do you call a nun that wears men's clothing?"

The Great Sauk Trail curved along Fawn River, but when it was paved, it was straightened to go a mile north, and the town died.

Judy Disney lives alone in her house with an electric plant on Fawn River. She is 57, has pigtails, master's degrees in ecology and psychology, and prunes plants in a nursery. The foundations for the former dance hall, bar and post office are in her front yard.

The plant produced electricity that was sold to Sturgis from 1905 until the flood-gates up the river broke last May. She has a $100,000 turbine she bought for $2,000 from a plant owner in Bangor who had cancer and didn't want to leave anything to his children, but it has begun to rust. She needs about $50,000 to fix the floodgates.

The plant can generate about $400 a month in electricity.

"This is what I have left," she says. "If nothing else, I just want to keep the idea alive. It's too late to give in now."

Back on U.S. 12, the road goes straight through Sturgis, where the sixth annual Toy Run will start and end in September.

Last September, 2,500 bikers came from as far as Arizona, California and Rhode Island. The line stretched seven miles down U.S. 12, and bikers each had a toy strapped on the seat behind them. For the party in the field afterward, door prizes are tattoos.

Bob Harrington dyes his beard white, tucks in his ponytail into his leather jacket and leads it all as Santa.

"You ever look back and see seven miles of bikers following you?" says Harrington, a welder and bartender at the B&W Tavern. "If it wasn't for a good cause, it'd be scary."

The road tiptoes along the Indiana border. Irrigation lines draw circles Crayola green. Cows stare. Truckers bypass the scales on the Indiana Turnpike.

"I don't give a damn about history or scenery," says Richie Parton, who is hauling jeans and books from Baltimore to Utah in his 18-wheeler. "This way saves time and money. Unless you get behind some old folks or a buggy."

Traffic is held up a quarter of a mile by Aaron Stander in his buggy.

Stander, who is Amish, farms west of Sturgis. At night, he carves heads and bodies, and his wife and children make clothes for dolls without faces. Images are against their belief.

A man in Sturgis trades him grain and livestock for dolls. On some of them, his wife paints eyes and a beard or lips. At the flea market 15 miles south in Shipshewana, Ind., he sells them for $10 to people who need a face.

"We follow our beliefs," Stander says. "What is important is that we do what we believe. I don't worry about the people who honk their horns at me when I'm in my buggy, either."

By the time Stander gets to White Pigeon to buy fabric for the dolls, the line is half a mile long behind him.

Wahbememe Chief White Pigeon ran here from Detroit in about 1830 to warn settlers that Indians planned to massacre them, and then he died.

Around the corner from the last U.S. Government Land Office still standing, Alta Roy has run her grocery store for more than 50 years. She knows what everybody wants, and if she doesn't stock it, they don't need it. She had cataract surgery, though, and couldn't drive to Kalamazoo to get Pillsbury Biscuit Dough for Jane Miles.

"I'll get over there this week," Roy says to Miles. "You'll just have to have toast till then."

Seven dead raccoons and one dead cat in one mile — what good are nine lives to an 18-wheeler?

Just south of U.S. 12 in Niles, Waylow Foods sold more lottery tickets in 1988 than any place in Michigan.

Michigan Welcomes You at the edge of the parking lot. When the jackpot is big enough, three employees sell tickets full time, and the line winds through 10 aisles and out the door. Three Lotto winners bought their tickets here.

Bob Hettinghouse, who owns Waylow, plays a couple of times a day. He Easy Picks and plays his birthday, his wife's birthday and the date his father died. He never has hit more than three numbers.

"I've sold millions of tickets — enough to figure out a system if there was one," he says. "I've seen people play every system, every date, even the telephone number on this 'For Sale' sign across the street. The only system I can figure out is to just play a lot."

Three Oaks still has the cannon President William McKinley gave it in 1899 because the 1,844 citizens contributed $1,400 — more per capita than any town in the United States — to remember the Battleship *Maine*.

"Hams Bloney Ed Sez Try Our Cheeze Thank U Folks Pleeze Combak Soon."

Ed Drier, the owner of Drier's Butcher Shop in Three Oaks, gets a new personalized license plate every year for his car, the last Checker Cab made in Kalamazoo. The plates are nailed to the wall of the shop. Around the corner is a deer head with the sign: The buck stopped here."

Drier, 70, and his two daughters smoke the hams and make the bologna and liver sausage. He took over from his father, who bought the store in 1913. Author and poet Carl Sandburg, the first Chicago Mayor Richard Daley and actor Larry Hagman all have been customers.

"We've learned recently that most of what we sell is very high in cholesterol," Drier says. "Of course, the average age of the customers is about 80. You can draw your own conclusions."

Into Indiana.

Mount Baldy, 123 feet high, one

A CHICAGO WOMAN CHASES PHOTOGRAPHER MICHAEL GREEN. GREG IS IN THE BACKGROUND.

Michael S. Green/The Detroit News

of the highest dunes on the shore of Lake Michigan, is moving four to five feet southwest a year. It buries trees and anything else in its way. It also is the best place in the area to hang glide.

The wind comes off the lake, up the dune and lifts the wings straight up from the sand. Up 40 feet, the skyline of Chicago appears 50 miles across the water. Up 60 feet, the wind seems to die, and everything flows past.

And then it doesn't, so it is a mile walk with wings, like a flustered hen.

Back on U.S. 12. Through Gary and mile after mile of steel mills. It looks like the inside of an old radio.

The road is rerouted up onto the Chicago Skyway, then back down into the South Side of Chicago.

Men watch from the front porch of the row houses, their faces almost erased. Buildings have no back wall, like a dollhouse. Lester Michaels, 71, moved from Detroit in 1959, and now he sits all day on a rocking chair that was here before he was.

"I figured it would be a nicer place to paint cars," he says. "Now look at it. Is it any better than Detroit?"

Michigan Avenue widens to 10 lanes and becomes the Magnificent Mile, the busiest street in Chicago.

According to city and company records, Consolidated Cement of Cement City, Mich., made some of the cement for the sidewalks.

The Billy Goat Tavern is down a flight of steps, under Michigan Avenue. This is where *Saturday Night Live* got "Cheezborger, Cheezborger. No Coke. Pepsi." It is the only place along the Magnificent Mile where anybody looks like they would know what to do with a sober dog.

Mike Royko, the syndicated newspaper columnist, sits at the end of the bar and delivers the punch line.

"A trans sister," he says.

The John Hancock Building, Neiman-Marcus, Tiffany's, Bloomingdale's. Anything you can't find in the pawnshops at the other end of Michigan Avenue, you can find here. Sunlight reaches the street two hours a day.

Finally, The Drake Hotel, 999 Michigan Avenue. A night here is a month at the other end. Valet to bellboy to concierge to elevator operator to chocolate on the pillow.

The lights up Michigan Avenue get less specific until they become a line.

"All the way to Detroit?" says the concierge at the Drake, Michael Raynor. "Then why didn't they call it Illinois Avenue?"

Michigan Avenue curves to merge into Lakeshore Drive, where Suzie Perlman sells carnations.

The Detroit News
May 8, 1989

Thief Turns a New Leaf

DENVER — At 6:30 Thursday night, Mary Wilson opened the front door, and a 20-year-old man was standing on the porch.

"You get home all right, Miss Wilson?" the man said.

"Darrien," Wilson said. "I told you, you don't have to worry about me."

Darrien, who did not want his last name used, just got off work and is studying to get his general equivalency diploma and comes over two or three nights a week to study. Wilson is 47, a hair stylist in Aurora. Darrien lives with his grandmother, three houses down from the house behind Wilson's.

They never met before Darrien stole Wilson's purse.

"I told you I could give you a ride," Darrien said.

"In the kitchen, boy," Wilson said. "You got work to do."

One night three years ago last October, Wilson was walking up Downing Street from the bus stop, home from work. She has lived alone since her son graduated from Metropolitan State College and moved to Colorado Springs. Darrien and a friend ran up behind her.

There was $22 in the purse.

A man who lives on the other side of Downing recognized Darrien's friend, the friend told police it was Darrien's idea, and the police found the purse and everything except the money in the garbage can behind Darrien's neighbor's house. It was Darrien's second offense. He got 18 months on probation.

Two years ago in February, Darrien knocked on the door and asked if she needed somebody to shovel her sidewalk. She recognized him first. When he didn't deny it, she asked him the only question she ever has asked about the night three years ago in October.

"That $22 was three days' tips — it was a Wednesday night, and I don't get paid till Fridays — and I asked what he spent his part on," she said. "He said he took the bus to the Bennigan's in Aurora and ordered two hamburgers with avocado. He said he always wanted to go to a Bennigan's."

After the first 11 snows, she has given him $2 each time he shovels her sidewalk. She and his probation officer pushed him to get his general equivalency diploma. She asked him to study in her kitchen because his cousin, who also lives with his grandmother, plays music too loud.

She bought books she thought he should read and a yellow highlight pen.

"Let me see that book," she said.

Darrien slid the *Norton Anthology of Short Fiction* across the kitchen table. She flipped through the pages. She stopped at *The Scarlet Letter*.

"It's all yellow," she said.

"It's all pretty important," he said.

At 8:30, Darrien closed his books. He sweeps an office building from 9 p.m. to midnight.

He just made the last payment to buy her son's 1975 Toyota.

Out on the front porch, he turned around.

"Lock it up, Miss Wilson," Darrien said. "Don't open it for any strange peoples."

"I tell you, boy," she said. "Why would I do that?"

Rocky Mountain News
January 8, 1995

A Bus Ride to Freedom

DENVER — The bus is light blue with "Department of Corrections" on the side, and at 11:12 a.m. it stopped at the corner of Potomac and East Colfax to drop him off.

He followed a guard off the bus. He had a Toastmaster Citrus Juicer box under his left arm. With his right hand, he signed a piece of paper on a clipboard the guard held, and the guard gave him an envelope and two bus tokens and got back onto the bus without a word.

The light blue bus pulled away to go back to Canon City.

"Got to avoid verbal confrontations," he said.

He is 37 and just finished seven years for aggravated robbery of a liquor store in Lakewood.

The envelope had a check for $100 in it, and he folded it and stuck it into his back pocket. The citrus juicer box had letters and birthday cards in it, from a woman he never met who lives in Fallon, Nev. He wore a yellow button-down shirt, dark blue polyester pants that dragged on the ground and a jacket made from the same material as the pants, all made by inmates.

He didn't want his name to be used, which doesn't matter because the light blue bus drops off men wearing the same clothes and carrying cardboard boxes at the corner of Potomac Street and East Colfax Avenue every Monday, Wednesday and Friday.

"Can't be thinking old ways, old associations," he said.

He got onto the first bus that pulled up. He asked the driver what to do with the bus token. He looked around and sat on the right side, halfway down the bus, next to a woman wearing a Popeye's Fried Chicken uniform.

He turned and watched the signs pass: "Budweiser, $13.49 a case," he said. "Makes me feel old."

The woman in the Popeye's uniform got off.

In pre-release, they talked about things such as how to manage a budget and how to buy a used car and how to fill out an application, but he didn't pay attention. He had a nine-year sentence. Good behavior got him out now.

He got up and sat on the left side of the bus and turned so he could look down at the women in the cars that passed the bus.

"Got to get me that money," he said.

One of his cellmates at Territorial Prison said a bank won't cash the check in the envelope unless you have an account there. He didn't have any identification except his prison identification. His cellmate said there was a bar near 21st and Larimer streets that will cash the check for $10 and give him his first beer free.

A woman walking on East Colfax waved to him, and he waved back.

"Definitely got to get me that money," he said.

The bus came into downtown, and the bus driver said this was the last stop.

He got up and picked up the citrus juicer box. He asked the driver which way to Larimer Street. The bus driver turned to look at him, a man in the dark blue polyester jacket and pants that don't fit, holding a cardboard box, who gets on the bus every Monday, Wednesday and Friday at the corner of Potomac and East Colfax.

He got off the bus and walked the way the bus driver had pointed.

"Nobody got to worry about me," he said. "I'm free."

Rocky Mountain News
December 17, 1995

Living Under a Bridge Too Far

DENVER — It is rush hour on Speer Boulevard bridge, and Steve Kyser sits under it watching the 5 p.m. news.

On the bridge, the driver of a new Porsche that is black and sleek like an oil slick is honking and yelling at the driver of a Chrysler who is big and square like a Chrysler.

On the news, there is a bar graph showing that the economy is down.

Kyser lives under the bridge with his 19 cats, and he turns off the television so the only light comes from two candles.

He has piled rocks in Cherry Creek so the water flows over them and drowns the sounds of the world.

"I can't stand to hear all the time about that economy — up and down and up and down," he says. "Down here, at least everything's one level. I just sit here while everybody's honking and screaming at each other, and all the cats and me hear is shhhhh."

On one side of him is Cherry Creek and the bike path crowded with joggers, bicycle riders and roller-bladers. On the other is the tee for the 14th hole of the Denver Country Club. An RTD bus stop is directly above him.

Kyser, 40, has lived here for four years in two rooms he built, carpeted and furnished.

Everything he has is something somebody else threw away. A mattress and box springs are in the bedroom area, and the kitchen area has a camping stove, pots, pans and dishes. He has an 8-inch television that gets a fuzzy picture but works on batteries, three radios, hundreds of stuffed animals and shelves filled with souvenirs from places he hasn't been.

The golf course workers sometimes yell at him because his cats use the sand traps for litter boxes, but nobody else seems to notice him.

"I know people who pay to live in some house with noisy neighbors, and here my cats and me have a bridge that probably cost five million dollars," he says. "I never did understand why people would just throw a cat out on the street like it's just disposable.

"People can take care of themselves, but cats need love and attention."

He grew up in Alabama and came to Denver in 1983. He lived under the Larimer Street bridge until he was arrested for a parole violation and sent back to Florida to finish his sentence on a marijuana charge.

Then he came back but moved out from under the Larimer bridge because the other men who lived under it drank too much.

He lived under the Washington Street and Downing Street bridges, where the men also drank too much, then found the Speer bridge. It is the suburbs of bridges, too far from food lines and liquor stores for most of the other people who live under bridges. His only neighbor is a skunk that comes in at night to eat cat food.

When it gets dark, he crawls out from under the bridge and pulls out his bicycle to make his rounds. He got the bicycle in a trade for a stack of pornographic magazines.

He rides down the bike path along Cherry Creek.

Under the Lincoln Avenue bridge, drunken men are standing around another drunken man, telling each other not to move him. The man on the ground had fallen from the space where he lives under the bridge. One of the men realizes they are making enough noise to bring the police, so he says, "Shhhhh."

Then everybody tells each other "Shhhhh," until they drown the sound of the water flowing over the rocks they piled in the creek.

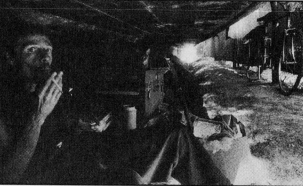

One of the men steps away from the group and waves to Kyser.

"Steve, you sure you don't have any openings under your bridge?" he says. "I gotta find me a better bridge to live under."

"You know I don't allow drinking under my bridge," Kyser says.

"Yeah," the man says. "But I forgot."

The man blends back in, and Kyser starts his rounds.

STEVE KYSER HAS BEEN LIVING FOR FOUR YEARS WITH HIS 19 CATS UNDER A SPEER BOULEVARD BRIDGE.

He goes through the garbage receptacles in the alleys behind the apartment buildings on his route. An apartment manager comes out with a bag of empty cans for him. A Denver police officer he knows stops and gives him two doughnuts.

The sun comes up, so he starts home. The basket on his bike is filled with empty cans, 12 pornographic magazines, four pieces of pizza, four AA batteries that might still have some power and a souvenir ashtray from Council Bluffs, Iowa.

The silhouette of downtown becomes visible in the dawn. From here, it could be a graph of the economy.

Kyser gets back to the Speer bridge and crawls inside. He lights the two candles. He looks at a painting of the Golden Gate Bridge at night.

Traffic has picked up on the bridge, and under it three cats climb into his lap.

"Sometimes, I wonder if anybody lives under that one. Can you imagine what it would be like to live under the Golden Gate Bridge?" he says. "I'd rather have a whole bridge to myself, but it's something to think about, at least."

Rocky Mountain News
September 1, 1991

The Youngest Inmate

CANON CITY, Colo. — Juan Villapando was talking about how it is to be turning 16, and you're in prison, and you just had a fight with your girlfriend.

She said he treats her like a kid. He turned 16 on Saturday. He was in his cell in Unit 5, third tier, at Territorial Prison, the Department of Corrections' youngest inmate.

An inmate in another cell was calling to him with a soft voice, "Juanito, Juanito..."

"My lady, she said she'd write me every day, but then she goes, 'I had to go over to my sister's,' " he said. "So I go, 'You weren't the first, and if this keeps up you won't be the last.' I don't have time for that kind of stuff.

"Well, I guess I do, but I'm not going to tell her that."

Villapando is serving 12 years for manslaughter for shooting River Thomas, 22, in the heart March 4, 1994, in Denver.

He will be the youngest inmate until Gilbert Gonzales, 14, is sentenced June 29 in Denver District Court for second-degree murder for shooting Joseph Green, 15, in the head.

Villapando was charged as an adult, and he is treated as an adult.

"Yeah, I already got in a fight — a guy came into my cell — but I don't want to talk about that," he said. "The food's greasier than the stuff at the juvenile detention centers, but they got better books here. I just finished another Jackie Collins' sex novel, *Hollywood Husbands* — it's about the fifth book by her I read since I got here. And when I'm finished with her I'll go on to Harold Robbins.

"And besides, I always did hang around with older guys."

The first time he was arrested, he was 10. He and a friend broke into the friend's aunt's house and stole her jewelry. Before that, he only broke into cars, he said.

They sold the jewelry for $40, but before they could spend the money somebody told the police.

He has been convicted of burglary and auto theft twice. He has been in Lookout Mountain, Montview and Gilliam juvenile detention centers. He dropped out of Merrill Middle School in the eighth grade.

"See, I'd already joined a gang when I was 11 and got my first gun when I was 12," he said. "Even if I was out, I wouldn't get my driver's license until I'm 18 since I got caught driving my brother's car when I was 12. So 16 is just another birthday."

He had a .22-caliber rifle, the barrel and the stock sawed off, stuck down his pants when he and other members of his gang went to a party at a house near 25th and Lawrence streets.

River Thomas was a freshman at Community College of Denver, and he went to the party with his cousin to pick up his cousin's girlfriend, according to police reports. He asked somebody why so many people were wearing shirts the same color. The members of Villapando's gang chased Thomas and his cousin outside and started to beat him.

Villapando told police he didn't hear what Thomas said but started hitting him with the barrel of his gun. It fired. He said he didn't remember hearing the gun fire, but seven members of his gang told the police he pulled the trigger.

He was charged as an adult because of the crime and his record. He pleaded guilty to manslaughter to avoid more serious charges. He was sentenced March 20 by District Judge Morris Hoffman.

"A guy was telling me you're supposed to say you remember you didn't do it, but it's too late for that, I guess," he said. "Besides, my homeboys were supposed to stick by me and keep me from getting sent down here."

In his cell, he has styling gel, a pack of Marlboros, Kool-Aid and photographs of his girlfriend and their son, Juan Jr., four and a half months.

He has a scribble of a mustache and a beard. He has been lifting weights. He still lets the nails on his pinkies grow out, like he did when he snorted cocaine off them.

He has the symbol of his gang tattooed on both hands and below his elbows. He has "Danny" tattooed on his right forearm, because his nephew was born while he was in Lookout Mountain. He has "Mi" tattooed below that.

He was going to tattoo "Mi Vida Loca" — My Crazy Life — but he got caught by a guard before he could finish.

"My boy, I'm going to make sure he doesn't do the things I did," he said. "I just have to wait till I get out and get things straight with my lady."

His girlfriend before this one is Gilbert Gonzales' older sister.

Gonzales pleaded guilty to second-degree murder last week. He faces a sentence of 30-48 years. He wrote Villapando a letter, asking what it is like in prison. "I wrote back and told him we get two and a half hours visitation a week, five and a half hours out of our cell a day," he said. "The rest of the stuff, I didn't want to talk about that."

He is eligible for parole in 2000. He wants to be a construction worker or an auto mechanic.

Whenever he is released, he will be an adult.

"It's weird, but before I came down here, I felt grown up," he said. "I slept as late as I wanted, ate when I wanted, kicked back with the homeboys when I wanted. Now, I sit here, and they tell me when to sleep, when I can eat, when I can go out of this cell.

"They treat me like I'm a kid."

Rocky Mountain News
June 4, 1995

Gang Members Lost after Losing Their Leader

DENVER — It was almost night again, and the one they call Bangers was sitting around the house trying to figure out what the one they call Little O would do if he were there.

Before Little O was convicted of murder, they didn't have to think about what to do at night. Prosecutors say Orlando Domena was the "undisputed leader of the notorious Rollin' 30s Crips gang." The members of the gang agree, which is why they still were sitting around the house in the 3400 block of Fillmore Street when it was almost night again. Bangers is 15, and Domena is the only gang leader he's ever had.

"O used to say, 'You sittin' around here, you ain't someplace else,'" Bangers said. "See, people just didn't understand O."

Police understood well enough to arrest Domena for killing Charles Baker, 21, and for shooting Mikecail Edlow, 21. A jury understood well enough to convict him of first-degree murder, attempted first-degree murder and first-degree assault. He was sentenced Friday to life without parole and 20 years.

"He used to say, 'You free, you do what you want,'" Bangers said. "I used to didn't have to think about what it was I want, 'cause he knew."

Bangers grew up around here, and for as long as he can remember, Domena was the one he wanted to be like. Domena was the one who started calling him Bangers after he drank two 40-ounce bottles of Olde English two years ago and ran into a lot of things. Domena is the one he showed his gun to after he got it. "He said, 'You got a strap, you got power,'" Bangers said. "You do what you want. You decide what you want."

After Domena was arrested this time, Bangers wrote him a letter in jail and said he would go to his trial every day. It turns out every day is a lot. He and some of the others did go two afternoons, but it also turns out that court is boring if it isn't about you.

Instead, he used a needle and ink from a pen to tattoo an "O" on his right arm.

"O always say they ain't gonna touch him," he said. "He'll get outta this some way."

Since Domena was convicted, there are other people who want to be what he used to be, but nobody is sure which one will. Some of them wanted to go and drive around. Some of them wanted to get some 40-ounce bottles of Olde English and stay here because it was cold out there.

"He says we all got to stick together for life," Bangers said. "It'll take a while, though."

Domena is 20 and will spend the rest of his life in prison. Bangers is 15. The last time Domena sent a letter to the house on Fillmore Street, he said to never forget him.

Until Bangers starts the rest of his life, that's something to do. "He never said what's all of us supposed to do when he ain't around?" he said. "That's one thing O never did say."

Rocky Mountain News
March 10, 1996

A Grandmother Understands

DENVER — The woman is sitting in the dark in her living room, talking about gangs and her grandson, when somebody knocks.

The curtains are closed across the pieces of plywood she nailed over the picture window after somebody shot it and threw an empty 40-ounce Olde English malt liquor bottle at it.

She doesn't know whether the bullet and bottle were meant for her or for her grandson. Her grandson is 15 and a gang member, and now she doesn't know whether the knocking is for her or for her grandson.

She waits until it stops.

"I tried to talk to him about this, about what he's doing, but he says, 'You don't understand,'" she says. "Maybe I don't. I'm not sure what's worse — thinking I don't understand or thinking I really do."

She is 67, and her grandson has lived with her for nine years, since his father was murdered and his mother dropped him off for an afternoon that never ended.

Now she lives the life Louise Brown lived in northeast Denver with her 17-year-old nephew, a suspected gang member, before she was shot and killed last month.

Her grandson was supposed to be home for supper two hours ago.

"My grandson and the boy down the street, Bobby, they grew up together and were best friends, but last summer I told Bobby's mother to keep him away from my grandson because I saw Bobby hanging around with gang members," she says. "She says 'My boy? It's your grandson that's in a gang.' We look at each other, and we both know."

Her grandson and other gang members sat in the living room this afternoon, drinking beer, smoking marijuana and deciding what to do next.

There is a bullet hole she noticed a few weeks ago in the ceiling of the living room. She asked her grandson about it. He said he didn't know how it got there.

She lay in her bedroom until she heard them leave.

"He put this lock on his bedroom door, so when I hear him lock that I know it's OK to come out," she says. "I used to have to keep on him to clean up his room. Anymore, he carries around this big bunch of keys — a 15-year-old boy worrying about a bunch of keys."

She has called the police. Sometimes, the police come immediately. Other times, the police don't get here until they have left.

She doesn't know which is worse.

"They come when the boys are here, and the boys come back later and yell and throw stuff," she says. "So mostly I go back in my bedroom and just lie down when they're here. Then when they leave, I can come out here and sit."

She is sitting in the dark in her living room when the front door opens, and her grandson stands in the rectangle of light.

They squint at each other.

"You all right, baby?" she says.

"I'm home, ain't I?" he says.

He closes the door and walks past her to his bedroom. He takes a ring of keys out of his pocket. He finds the key for his bedroom and unlocks the door.

"You want me to heat up your supper?" she says.

He turns around and looks at her. He is her grandson and 15 years old. He is a gang member.

They look at each other, and they both know.

"Got to go out later," he says. "You don't understand."

He closes the door.

She sits in the dark in her living room, the curtains closed across the pieces of plywood.

"Yes," she says. "I'm afraid I do understand."

Rocky Mountain News
June 20, 1993

Angels, Knuckleheads and Herkimerjerks

DENVER — Sebastian Metz was walking in formation with eight of his Guardian Angel recruits at 9 p.m. on East Colfax when the two in the front saw an argument between a man and a woman.

The two recruits in the front stopped. The two recruits behind walked into them, and the two recruits behind walked into them. Metz stopped and looked down at the pile of his Guardian Angel recruits.

The man and the woman stopped arguing to see what was going on.

"Another situation defused by the presence of the Guardian Angels," Metz said. "But we need to work on technique."

Metz, 30, has been a Guardian Angel for 11 years and has lived in Denver since October. He will graduate the first class of recruits today. Next month, he will stuff everything he owns into a carry-on bag and fly to San Francisco to start over again.

This is what he does, and this is how he talks:

"Take knuckleheads, for example," he said. "Knuckleheads are between herkimerjerks and kukulamongas in my vocabulary. Maybe my contribution to society will be defining the difference between knuckleheads, herkimerjerks and kukulamongas the way J.R.R. Tolkien defined the difference between dwarfs and elves, elves being the ones with pointed ears, drinking wine and working on their Macintosh computers, while dwarfs run around with wooden mallets.

"Maybe defining the term 'knucklehead' and improving the American vocabulary will be my ultimate contribution to society."

His parents lived in Manhattan until he was five, then drove across the country in a milk truck and threw their wedding rings into the Pacific Ocean because the trip had proved they shouldn't be married. They lived in a commune, and the kids earned their allowance harvesting marijuana. When he was 13, he threw away his marijuana pipe and enrolled himself in high school.

"Basically, my parents spent the 1970s trying to pretend it was still the '60s, trying to deny the existence of John Travolta," he said. "I'm the black sheep. People ask me why I don't become a cop, and I say it's because I wouldn't want to have to arrest my own family."

He joined the Guardian Angels in 1983 in Vancouver, and today he is the international coordinator. He gets no money from the Guardian Angels, and his income is $40 a week for a talk show 4-6 p.m. Sunday on KTLK AM-760. The last time he made a deposit in his bank account was in 1990.

He has helped to start about 18 chapters as far away as Stockholm and London. He has built a reputation. He has tried to break down fears about the Guardian Angels.

And somewhere along the way, he also picked up a Brooklyn accent.

"Well, you don't survive very long in New York when you sound like you're from Vancouver," he said.

He knows what the Guardian Angels can and can't do.

Curtis Sliwa, the founder of the Guardian Angels, admitted two years ago he had faked six incidents in which he claimed the Guardian Angels had stopped a crime.

Metz doesn't make claims like that. In 11 years of looking for trouble, he says, he has been cut by a prostitute with a box knife, shot with a pellet gun, hit by a car and beaten with bottles. He thinks he has thrown fewer than five punches and helped make about 30 citizen's arrests.

"Some people want to join because the cops wouldn't take them," he said. "You get some who want to join to get over on people. We have to weed them out.

"The ones we want are the ones who just want to be out there to do something positive, the ones who aren't just attracted by the glamorous lifestyle I lead from my penthouse apartment."

The apartment is on East 14th Avenue, half a flight of stairs down from the street, one room with two bunk beds, a couch, a weight-lifting bench and a stack of martial-arts magazines.

He lives here with Shredder, Bouncer and Roadblock. He has a pair of Reebok high-top

Linda McConnell/Rocky Mountain News

SEBASTIAN METZ IS HEAD OF THE GUARDIAN ANGELS, WALKING THE STREETS OF DENVER.

shoes, a pair of Doc Martens boots, eight pairs of black socks, four pairs of combat pants, 10 Guardian Angel T-shirts, three berets and the book he just finished, *Leadership Secrets of Atilla the Hun*. Everything else he owns, mostly parts of old two-way radios, is in a gym locker in New York.

The kitchen cupboards are filled with food people have donated — cans of soup and vegetables stacked six high and boxes of six kinds of macaroni and cheese, including three different generic brands. They finished the Christmas cookies last week. He held up the last two slices of bread to make sure they still were the right color, put two pieces of lettuce and a hunk of cucumber between them and ate dinner.

"In New York, we had this deal to get doughnuts in the afternoon and leftover Popeye's fried chicken after they closed," he said. "My body went through more changes in a month than puberty."

Since he came to Denver, 170 people have signed up to become Guardian Angels, and today 30 to 35 will graduate. He has taught them how to restrain other people. He has taught them how to restrain themselves.

He calls them racial slurs, personal names and everything else he has been called on the streets — "Charlie's Angels," "Guardian Anal," "Nazi." Everybody, including him, is frisked, and their breath is smelled whenever they enter the headquarters. They give up all rights to privacy, and in return he gives them a nickname and the chance to wear a beret and walk in formation.

That, and an improved vocabulary.

"I used to think the world revolved around the Guardian Angels — when people would ask me why I'm out here, I'd say, 'No, the question is why aren't you out here,'" he said. "Now, I realize we're just a part of it all, and I'm just a part of that part. I know there's more to life than the Guardian Angels, but I've chosen to make the Guardian Angels my life...

"Now, I don't want to sound like a knucklehead, but that's me."

Rocky Mountain News
March 20, 1990

Violent Crime Rules at Complex

AURORA, Colo. — The knocking came while she was watching television with the sound turned down, and she put her hand over her baby's mouth to wait for it to stop.

It was 7:15 p.m. Monday night in the Windsor Court Apartments. She is 21, and her baby is seven months. She waited.

She heard the knocking on a door down the hall.

"He said he'd give me $20 just to use this place sometimes," she said. "I forgot to ask, was it $20 every time or just whenever."

The Windsor Court Apartments are six buildings, stucco and angles, the kind that look modern until they are built. They are across East 16th Avenue from Garrett Park. The park is the center of the area with the highest violent-crime rate in Aurora.

Preston Hill, 17, was selling drugs out of somebody else's apartment last week, and when he tried to run from police he was shot and killed by an undercover officer chasing him.

"Either way," she said. "$20 is pretty good. If I was to do it, I mean." The lamp is in front of the window so she doesn't make shadows they can see from the street. She leaves it on all the time. Another girl down the hall taught her that.

On the sidewalk, people had left half-burned candles, and somebody spray-painted "R.I.P. Preston." The summer before last, Jovan C. Mills, 16, was shot and killed in an apartment. The year before, Herlend Brother, 17, was shot and killed on the sidewalk, but the spray-paint wore off.

Police have concentrated on the area around the park for seven months and have lowered the violent-crime rate 10 percent.

Kids with hoods pulled over their heads stood on the corners down the street, nodding to the drivers in the cars that passed on East 16th Avenue.

"They can't see my shadow," she said. "They can't hold it against somebody if they're not home. Can they?"

She moved in here two months ago because there was an apartment open and the rent is subsidized and it is close. She works days at an auto parts store on East Colfax Avenue. She wants to go to school to learn how to do manicures.

The second time she saw a fight across the street, she called the police. The first time, she had thought somebody else would. The problem with calling the police is the police come.

The next night, a guy was at the front door when she got home and said, "Don't be calling no police on us." She wondered how he knew. Then the girl who lives down the hall told her the guy said that to everybody when they came home.

The same people paid the girl down the hall $10 to push a baby stroller up and down the sidewalk.

"She had to borrow one," she said. "She doesn't even have a baby."

It was 8 on a Monday night. The knocking usually comes again. She sat in the apartment, holding her baby, not making a shadow anybody could see.

"I'm gonna have to give them an answer sometime," she said. "I can't not be home forever."

Rocky Mountain News
November 1, 1995

Keeping Out of Trouble

DENVER — Norman Johnson is 18 years old and doesn't remember being in trouble since he was in the ninth grade and left his new winter coat at a Denny's restaurant.

"I got to keep out of trouble," Norman said. "I promised my mom."

After his mother died three years ago, he lived with his older brother until his older brother was sent to prison again. He lives with an aunt he pays $300 a month. He graduated last year from an alternative program and wants to go to Emily Griffith Opportunity School.

When he isn't working at Taco Bell, he takes the bus or rides his bike to shopping centers and asks people if they want him to help them. "Some people, they give me money if I help," he said. "Other ones can't. The ones that can't give me money are the ones I really help, and they help me keep out of trouble."

He carries bags to cars, takes back shopping carts and runs errands. One woman in the JCRS Shopping Center called police, but the manager at Albertsons explained that Norman was trying to stay out of trouble. One of the officers asked him to watch a rack where bicycles had been stolen.

About a year ago, he went into Frank Le's Laundry on South Federal Boulevard.

"I don't know why, but I gave him a chance," Le said. "Maybe it's because he asked. I gave him a $50 bill this lady gave me for a couple of shirts and told him to get change, and a couple of minutes later he came back with three tens, two fives and the rest in ones.

"I offered him a dollar, but he said he only wanted 69 cents for a soda."

After that, Norman came in twice a week. He picked up lunch for Le, washed windows and took lunch money to Le's daughter at school. Sometimes, Le saved large bills in a plastic pouch with a zipper so he would need change.

About a month ago, Le gave Norman the pouch with two $20 bills in it. Norman was gone for almost two hours. When he got back, he gave the pouch to Le and said he had to go.

In the pouch, there was $50. Norman didn't come back for a week. When he came in, Le said, "Norman, there is a problem."

Norman said, "They wouldn't tell me how much they took."

He said he was almost to the bank when two boys he knew from his neighborhood stopped him. They asked what was in the pouch, so he opened it and showed them the money. They grabbed the money and pushed him down.

"So I got back on my bike and went to the bank where they have my money and got out $50," Norman said. "I just got paid at work. I thought it was enough."

Le tried to give him $50.

Norman would take only $10.

Norman has gone into Le's laundry once since then but said he was busy and couldn't help Le.

"I don't know what my mom would say," Norman said. "But I'm not going to take any more chances."

Rocky Mountain News
May 25, 1994

A Family Affair

GREELEY, Colo. — Michael Taylor sat at the kitchen table and studied the original colonies, and Lejon "Boogie" Vivens sat next to him and studied the directions on the back of a box of Rice-a-Roni.

It was 6:30 p.m. and they were in family student housing at the University of Northern Colorado. The chicken was frying. They had finished school and football practice and playing basketball in the parking lot, and they were home.

They are family.

"You know how the original colonists got by, Boogie?" Michael said.

"By sticking together, Michael?" Vivens said.

"How'd you know that, Boogie?"

Vivens is 21, a redshirt sophomore wide receiver who is fourth on the UNC team in receptions and majoring in computer information systems. Michael is 11, a sixth-grader at Brentwood Middle School with size-10 feet and hands big enough to palm a basketball. They are cousins, and Vivens is Michael's legal guardian.

They sat at the kitchen table, each of them two years from being teenagers, and this is the way they are a family.

"Michael," Vivens said.

"Boogie," Michael said.

They grew up in Five Points, their families never more than six blocks apart. Their mothers worked to support them. Their fathers were somewhere else.

Their grandfather is Clarence Lucas, a minister at Community Church of God in Christ, and their grandmother is Ruth Lucas, who worked at Red Shield Community Center for 25 years and is called "Mama" by everybody except her 12 grandchildren.

"My grandmother, she could let you know what was up just by the way she said your name or just by the way she looked at you," Vivens said. "No matter what happened, she was there to let you know what was right."

The summer when Vivens was 15, he was walking home after a Joint Effort basketball game when a car full of gang members from the other side of Colorado Boulevard pulled up next to him. Three got out and one put a gun to his head. He looked in the car, and his eyes met the eyes of another cousin.

"Man, that's Boogie," the cousin said. "Get back here."

Vivens got an athletic scholarship to Mullen High School. He got there on 4.5 speed and the 5:30 a.m. bus. He had six close friends he didn't see as much.

Since then, four have been killed, one is in jail and the other just was released.

Last summer, Michael's mother was saying she wished she could afford to send Michael to a private school. Vivens said he was planning to move out of the dormitory. For a month, Clarice Taylor told him reasons he wouldn't want to take Michael, and then she signed the papers making him Michael's legal guardian.

"It's not impossible to get out of the Points," Vivens said. "I did. But I'd look at Michael, and I'd wonder whether they were going to catch up to him."

A week after Michael moved to Greeley, he was playing outside with other kids when he hit his head on a stairwell and needed 13 stitches.

"I guess I was out of practice for playing outside," Michael said. "I used to have to stay inside all the time because of the drive-bys."

They live in a two-room apartment with Earnest Collins, a cornerback on the football team. Collins helps pay the rent and watches Michael when Vivens goes to
the library. Vivens sleeps on the couch.

"Like, I'll go over to a female friend's house, and we'll sit on the couch and watch television, me, then Michael, then her," Vivens said. "It's not always easy. I have to
be a football player, too. I have to be a college student, too.

"But there's always friends and coaches and parents of players to help, and Michael is always there when I need to remember why I'm doing this."

When Vivens dropped a pass that might have been the touchdown that won the game against Western State, Michael ran up to him and said, "Keep your head up, Boogie."

When Michael played outside 10 minutes past curfew two weeks ago, Vivens grounded him, which meant they both stayed inside for a week.

"I hug him and tell him I love him at least twice a day," Vivens said. "I never hugged, because men never hugged me, but one day I decided a kid should feel like it's OK for a man to show a kid he loves him. So I do."

After school, Vivens or one of the girlfriends of his teammates gives Michael a ride to practice. The head coach, Joe Glenn, made him the ballboy. Practice ends at 6 p.m., and by 6:15 each night, Michael has said he wants fried chicken for supper.

Vivens had made the batter and started to fry the chicken, and after he read the directions on the Rice-a-Roni he decided green beans would be better. He set a plate of chicken and green beans on the table. Michael said grace.

"I didn't bring up the green beans on purpose again, Boogie," he said. "I don't want the lord to think I'm ungrateful."

"Michael," Vivens said.

By the time Vivens came back to the table with a plate for himself, Michael's plate was empty. He set his in front of Michael.

After Michael finished eating, he went into his bedroom to iron his clothes for school the next day. Vivens made a tuna sandwich. Michael called him.

Vivens checked the pants, then the shirt, and then he looked at Michael.

"Why iron the back when you're already going to be gone by the time they see it?" Michael said.

"Michael," Vivens said.

While Michael ironed the back of his shirt, Vivens ate his sandwich and got out his own books. He has a 3.6 grade-point average. He is on schedule to become the first member of his family to graduate.

The light went out in the bedroom. Vivens went in and kneeled next to Michael. They said their prayers, and Michael got in bed.

"Boogie," Michael said.

"Michael," Vivens said.

Vivens hugged Michael. He went out of the bedroom. He closed the door and sat down at the kitchen table to be a college student, too.

Rocky Mountain News
October 30, 1994

A Car to Dote On

DENVER — The car is a 1989 Grand Prix, yellow with gold rims, and his mother says she'll lend him the money for it if he promises to not cause her any more trouble.

He will be 17 in March. He is a junior at North High School. He is the father of three babies by three mothers.

"It's got a stereo. You can't turn it up all the way," he said. "It'll make you cry."

A study released Thursday said 38 percent of new mothers in Denver aren't married, which means there are that many unwed new fathers.

He wants his name in the newspaper, which is why it isn't.

"You don't care for them, they go bad," he said. "The rims, you got to keep them polished. I promise you, I'll take care of them."

The babies are Kanisha, 14 months, Krystal, 5 months, and either Tarin or Taren, 7 months. All girls. He wanted to name one of them Whitney, but none of the mothers would listen to him.

If his mother doesn't give him the money for the car, he says, he'll have to get it some other way.

"I need a car if I'm gonna go see my babies," he said. "I'm not going to take no babies on no bus."

One of the mothers is in his American History class, but she's mad about something and doesn't even look at him. Another dropped out of school and moved in with her brother somewhere in Thornton. The other one lives a couple of blocks from him, so he runs into her and the baby all the time.

He thinks the reason the other two mothers don't talk to him is that their babies were born two months apart.

"Last time I saw the one that's not all mad, she goes, 'You don't even care,' so I go, 'I do, too,'" he said. "She says, well then why don't I come and see her more? I go, 'I would if you wasn't all the time on my back, I might give you rides when I get the car.'"

He lives with his mother and his two sisters, 5 and 7, and sometimes his mother makes him go with her to see her granddaughters. His older brother is 18 and lives with a girl who already had two kids. He has a friend who is 19 and has four or five kids, and two other friends who are 16 and 17 and have two.

He knows how it will be for his children to grow up without a father, because he did.

"I didn't have no father giving me things," he said. "Right now, I got to beg my mother just to use her car to take out my lady. I just want something to call my own."

The car has gold seats and a steering wheel that looks like it's made of wood. It has a tear in the back seat he'd have to cover with a blanket or something. It also has lights that flash across the back window like they're crawling across it.

If he does promise to not cause his mother any more trouble, he will finally have something he can call his own, he said.

"I do take one of the kids in the car, they're gonna be trained," he said. "Nobody's gonna mess up my car."

Rocky Mountain News
December 3, 1995

A Code of Honor

DENVER — At 8:15 a.m. Wednesday in the parking lot of the Taco Bell at East Colfax and Williams, Gary Askew got into his uncle's Blazer, his right hand inside his coat.

His uncle is Dean Askew. For six years, Dean has run Street Smart and Street Beat to keep kids off the streets. For two hours, Dean would drive up and down streets and try to decide whether to take his nephew to police to be charged with killing his pregnant girlfriend.

The next morning, Dean would sit on a bench outside a courtroom in the Denver City Jail, waiting for his nephew to be charged with murder, and wonder whether he did the right thing.

"First thing he says when he gets in the car, he says, 'How's my baby?'" Dean said. "He had his right hand inside his coat, and I could see the shape of the gun pointed up at his chin. I said his baby was fine, had the Askew fat cheeks and her mother's little ears.

"I said I'd get him a picture."

Dean drove west on Colfax.

Police say Gary, 19, dragged Tiauna Quarles, 20, out of the house where she lived with relatives and shot her in the head just before midnight Jan. 12. Witnesses said Gary and Tiauna had argued about her drug use and drinking. The baby was due in five weeks.

The baby was delivered by Caesarean section at 12:22 a.m. Jan. 13 at Denver General Hospital, and Tiauna died two hours later.

Dean turned right onto Downing.

"I just wanted to talk to him, like about when we got him his first pair of football shoes to try out at Manual (High School)," Dean said. "Before football started, he got jumped by some gang members because he wouldn't join up, and they broke both his hands. He laughed when I talked about how I had to turn on the shower and soap him up and feed him and tie his shoes."

There are 311 kids in Street Beat. Dean, 40, grew up in Five Points, and he started Street Smart, then Street Beat. The program offers counseling, sports and classes. Any kid who wants to stay out of trouble can come in.

Dean turned right onto East 17th Avenue.

"I thought about Utah," he said. "I could have taken $500 out of the bank and taken him to Utah. I could have thrown the gun in the lake at City Park. "And then I could come back here and send him money and pictures."

Gary never knew his father. He lived with his mother and spent most of his time with his uncle and the kids his uncle was trying to keep out of trouble. Two years ago, he got involved with drugs and kids who weren't part of his uncle's program, and he and his uncle didn't see each other as often.

Dean drove past City Park.

"I told him to never think he had let me down," he said. "That he's family. All those things I'm always talking to other kids about, responsibility for their actions and all that — I told him there's what's right morally and what's right family.

"Then we drove past some kids we know, kids who ought to be in the program."

Gary and Tiauna met at Street Smart.

Tiauna was the best dancer in the dance class. After she got involved with drugs, Dean used to drive past her on the street and honk and wave. A couple of weeks ago, he stopped to give her a ride home, and he talked all the way about how she had to take responsibility for her actions.

Dean drove around the park and turned west onto East 20th Avenue.

"It was quiet a while," he said. "He took out his hand and gave me the gun."

The first five days after the killing, the phone would ring, and Dean would hear silence. He talked about how he would love his nephew no matter what happened, about things they had done, about taking responsibility for his actions. Then he would hear his nephew say, " 'Bye."

When the phone rang Wednesday morning, his nephew asked him to come to the Taco Bell.

"After he gave me the gun, I called two friends to come and follow us," Dean said. "I didn't want

DEAN ASKEW SPEAKS TO A CROWD.

Frank Kimmel/Rocky Mountain News

to be able to change my mind. I had him empty out his pockets and asked if he had clean underwear."

Dean went to the homes of Gary's aunt, then his uncle, then his mother. His friends Winston Hill and Herman White followed in their cars. Gary went into the houses, came out a few minutes later and got back into the Blazer.

Dean drove down East 14th Avenue to the police station.

"Four years ago, I walked into the police station with another kid who'd told me he'd killed somebody," he said. "That was hard, but I knew I was doing what was right. Gary and I, we walked in there with our arms around each other, guiding each other."

That afternoon, Gary confessed to the killing, police said.

That afternoon, Dean coached practice for the Street Beat Heat girls and boys basketball teams at Gove Middle School. He went to Denver General and saw the baby. That night, he ran a counseling program for 26 kids.

The program is called Choices, and all the questions the kids asked were about the choice Dean made that morning.

"I did what I want you to do," he said. "We all have to take responsibility for our actions. We all know what's right and what's wrong."

Rocky Mountain News
January 22, 1995

Greg, you are surely missed...
I miss the phone call — checking
to see if I'm OK and have I gotten
some sleep lately. Greg was a good
friend for writing the truth about
a bad situation. Greg knew I was
going to quit working with kids
and maybe stop living all together.
So Greg became more than a
writer, he became a support, a
friend. He helped me see the light
in a dark room. Greg helped me
fight for what I believed in...truth.
So Greg you will be missed, but
not forgotten. I never got a chance
to say thanks, so I hope you
hear me.

DEAN ASKEW

The Right Lane

DETROIT — It is 10 o'clock on a Wednesday night and Walter Polidor is riding a city bus up Woodward, facing his reflection in the window.

Polidor always sits behind the driver. He is 69, a retired Ford worker who lives alone. Some nights, he gets on a bus at the State Fairgrounds and pays a dollar to ride to Cadillac Square, then a dollar to ride back.

Life in the right lane.

"Sometimes I go someplace," he says, as if talking to his reflection. "Sometimes I just go. Instead of sitting at home watching the world pass, I just get on a bus and pass it all."

He passes Woodward with one other passenger in a well-lighted Detroit Department of Transportation bus: party stores, hotels, bars, buildings with iron grates closed for the night. Fluorescents glare.

A man gets on at Erksine, sits between Polidor and his reflection and talks to himself.

"First," he says, "we attack and seal off their southern flank..."

It was about this time of night, May 21, when Derrick Rollins, a bus driver on the Linwood line, was stabbed three times and seriously injured. Drivers say that they are threatened almost every night. The City Council has asked Police Chief William L. Hart to put plainclothes officers on buses at night.

DOT and police officials said they do not keep records on the number of incidents on city buses.

Cora Etherington, 63, sits alone in the back seat, holding her purse in one hand and a rosary in the other. She works in her brother's party store on Jefferson and is going home.

"Usually, I finish the whole thing before I get there unless somebody bothers me," she says. "One time, somebody tried to grab my beads — I guess they didn't know they were just plastic — and they broke. Most of the time, though, I think it works."

She closes her eyes and prays.

On Woodward, men lean against buildings. Women stand with their thumbs out until they see the bus. Public transportation is the only kind they don't want. People wave down the bus for a ride to another spot on Woodward.

Craig and Arden Vilton get on at Warren. They had been at a sociology discussion at Wayne State University. They sit near the middle of the bus, close together, like something fragile packed for a trip.

"We, both of us, believe, regardless of whether you have your own personal form of transportation or not, that people should choose public transportation whenever it is feasible," Arden Vilton says.

The drivers have radios to call police. One driver says he radioed police that a group of teen-agers was smoking and yelling, and the police came and took the kids off the bus. On the driver's next trip up Woodward, somebody threw a brick through the bus windshield.

A man gets on at Chicago, sets a bottle of Night Train wine in a paper bag on the floor and tries to find the dollar in his pockets. He drops $1.37 in the slot, picks up the bottle and walks to the back seat.

He sits next to Etherington, who doesn't open her eyes.

"Pasadena," he yells and he takes a drink from the bottle. "Fast."

A driver on the other bus saw a bulge under a passenger's coat his second day on the job and told him he couldn't bring an intoxicating beverage onto a DOT bus. The passenger said it wasn't a bottle, and they argued. The passenger opened his coat and showed the driver a gun.

The driver apologized and drove.

A kid who looks old enough to throw a brick through a windshield gets on at Burlingame wearing a Chicago Bulls cap. He sits in front of the Viltons. He turns around and looks at them.

Craig Vilton leans across his wife and they both look out the window. They are on the bus because they had gone to a discussion about sociology. They don't want to actually see something sociological happen.

Three seats behind the Viltons sits a kid in a Los Angeles Lakers cap.

"Bulls?" the Lakers kid yells. "Bull ——."

The Viltons keep looking out the window.

Polidor looks out the window at the front of the bus.

"Sometimes, I go to get on the bus, and in the window it looks like a Wild West movie in there," he said.

Etherington doesn't open her eyes.

The Lakers kid steps past the Viltons, grabs the Bulls cap and throws it on the floor. The two stare at each other until the bus stops at Pasadena. The man who had finished the Night Train at Tyler, three blocks back, gets off.

The Lakers kid looks out the window.

"Pasadena?" he says and he grabs the Bulls cap off the floor and runs. The other kid chases him off the bus. The Viltons watch them disappear down Woodward.

At the front of the bus, the man across from Polidor has changed the subject: "Some of the berries that look so juicy and delicious are so poisonous..."

He still is talking when he gets off at Hilldale.

Etherington, who had finished the rosary before she got to Palmer Park Municipal Golf Course, gets off at Larchwood.

"I guess it worked again," she says.

The Viltons get off at Wellesley, and the bus turns into the fairgrounds.

Polidor and a man asleep in the back of the bus are the only passengers. Most nights, drivers wake up a couple riders at the end of the line and get another dollar to take them back to where they were supposed to get off. Sometimes, a rider will sleep up and down Woodward all night.

Polidor stands up to walk home.

"Another night," he says. "Right back where I started."

The Detroit News
June 16, 1988

The Pay Phone

DETROIT — The kid on the phone has a bad connection, so he has to talk loud.

"No, no, no," he says. "Baby, you got the whip."

Byrtha Sherard, 62, looks at her watch. It is 7:21 on a Monday night and she has been here since 7, standing apart from the men waiting in line to make calls. Her son, William, calls her here at 7:30 p.m. almost every Monday.

"He's a good boy, my son," Sherard says. "He's not hanging around some corner all the time. Last week he said he might have something important for me."

The pay phone is on a wall painted yellow with an orange sign that says "Play Lotto Daily." Above that, it says "Grandy Market, Beer and Wine." It is at the corner of Medbury and Grandy, two blocks from a Total gas station that has two phones.

Louis Walker, who is waiting to use the phone, taps the kid talking to his girlfriends.

"What the hell you mean, lover boy?" Walker says. "The whip?"

The kid holds up his hand for Walker to be quiet.

"Nobody baby," he says into the phone. "It's just better when I can actually see you in person."

The kid hangs up and Walker picks up the phone.

"I've got two women I call every night," Walker says after he goes into the store to buy a quart of Colt 45. "I tell them I got an unlisted number. It's a bitch when it's cold."

The two men make calls, and it is 7:27.

ARTHUR PETERSON OF DETROIT USES THE PHONE AT GRANDY MARKET.

Steve Haines/The Detroit News

Sherard lives in a room in a house down Grandy. Her husband died in 1963 and her son moved to Flint in 1972. William lost his job in 1985, so once a week, she sends him $2.65 for a six-minute call from a pay phone down the street from his apartment. Waiting at the phone is better now that it is spring and daylight savings time.

She walks over and stands between the next man in line and the phone.

"Don't you know it's almost 7:30 at night?" Sherard says. "You gotta get up and go to school and work tomorrow, don't you?"

"I got business right now," the man says and steps around her.

"Do it with quickness," Sherard says. She gets in line.

A man who just finished a quart of Stroh's and a woman who walked up Grandy carrying two babies make their calls. Then a white 1988 Park Avenue with a red leather interior stops on Medbury. A kid who looks old enough to get up and go to school tomorrow gets out and stands behind the woman holding the babies. The kid, who has two beepers on his belt, may not realize it's almost 7:30 at night because he is wearing sunglasses. When the woman with the two babies hangs up, the kid grabs the phone, dials.

"It's at the main spot," the kid says into the phone. He puts in another quarter, dials again, repeats. "It's at the main spot." He gets back into his car and drives away.

At exactly 7:30, Carlton Fulton picks up the phone to call his wife.

Sherard stares at the Monday turning yellow and orange above a row of burned out houses on Medbury. The men leaning against the wall of Grandy Market don't notice. Fulton hangs up and goes inside to buy a quart of Stroh's.

"It don't matter what I tell her," he says. "Gonna catch hell at home anyways."

Sherard steps up to the phone and waits. William told her he doesn't know the number of the pay phone in Flint because somebody scratched it off, so she can't call him. A couple of times he hasn't called, the next week telling her he had to use the money for something else.

There is one man waiting, and after about two minutes, he notices Sherard has not picked up the phone.

"You want me to show you how to use that, lady?" he says.

"I waited in line to use this phone and I can use it how I want," Sherard says, and she waits.

At 7:43, Walker finishes his Colt 45 and gets in line, and Sherard steps back from the phone.

It is 7:53 and Walker is finishing up a call to his second woman.

"Baby," he says, "you got the whip..."

After he hangs up and goes back into the store, nobody is waiting to make a call.

At 7:58, the phone rings.

Sherard picks it up and turns her back so she can hear better.

At 8:04 she hangs up and starts to walk down Grandy.

"He said he's moving to San Diego, Calif., with a friend of his to try and find a job," she says. "He took so long trying not to say it, there wasn't time to try and say anything to him about it. He said he'd write."

The Detroit News
May 1, 1988

The First Time

DENVER — The first time she smoked crack cocaine was last night, but it's not like she's going to start smoking it like the other people she sees, she said.

Before last night, she always said she never would smoke it. She had said that since she heard about it in elementary school. Now, though, she is 17.

"I just wanted to see what the big deal is all about," she said. "It was the last time, too. But you can't understand something if all you know about it is that people are always telling you don't do it."

She lives with her mother in a duplex in Curtis Park and has seen people smoke their lives on crack, she said. She also has seen somebody get shot in the arm and somebody else get beaten up so bad he needs a machine to breathe. "I seen all those guys and some girls walking around looking stupid and smelling and asking for money for crack," she said.

This summer she was either going to take dancing lessons at the Curtis Park Recreation Center or hang around with her friends. Dancing lessons were only three nights a week. Besides, they probably would have been when her friends were doing something fun. To make money, she baby-sits for the lady who lives two houses down and goes to the bar in the morning.

"I'm not going to say I didn't like it," she said. "But it's not like I'm stupid."

Her older brother also used to say he would never smoke crack, but he stole her Walkman to buy it a couple of weeks ago, she said. Her older sister has three kids and probably doesn't. Her mother, all she does is drink.

"You think I'm stupid?" she said.

The guy who had the crack didn't make her pay for it even though she didn't know him, she said. Her friends had to pay for theirs. So it's not like she had anything to lose.

"Even if I do smoke it again, I'm not going to do it enough to get hooked," she said.

She probably will start her senior year at East High School at the end of the month, she said. She would be more sure if they didn't make her take science. She isn't going to take something if it doesn't have anything to do with what she's going to be.

"Not like those people you see all the time," she said. "You think I'm stupid?"

She said this three weeks ago. On Thursday afternoon at the Pioneer Bar on Larimer Street, her mother said she hadn't see her since sometime last week. If she doesn't come home soon, her mother is going to do something. Her mother heard she was smoking crack, but her mother didn't want to start a big fight with her.

She had said she just wanted to see what the big deal is about.

"So now I know," she said.

Written in early 1996 for the *Rocky Mountain News*.
The story never ran.

26th and Arapahoe Streets

DENVER — At the pay phone on the corner of 26th and Arapahoe streets, Jeffrey Handy was telling his girlfriend in Montbello about true love, the 10th grade and which bicep he should get her name tattooed on, when a car that looked like a black Jeep came up 26th.

Handy dropped the phone and ran up Arapahoe, and the two women waiting to use the phone crouched on the sidewalk. It is the corner where two people have been shot, one stabbed, one beaten with a baseball bat and one cut next to his eye by a piece of brick chipped off by a bullet, all since the weather turned warm.

The gun is a black Raven .25-caliber automatic, and if you stand close enough it can make a hole in a fence you can stick your little finger through, and it also comes in silver, he said. He will be 14 in November, and this is his first gun, he said. A guy his older brother knows sold Raven .25-caliber automatics to him and one of his friends last summer. He lives within a block of the corner of 26th and Arapahoe streets, within a block of where four people have been shot and killed in the past three months.

"I like this thing OK, but someday I want a silver one," he said. "Black looks too much like plastic."

The Raven .25-caliber automatic is three inches long, so he can hide it in his sock or his belt with his shirt hanging over it. He had it in his belt because it was President's Day. He would have left the gun at home if school was open Monday, because he would have had gym class.

He is in the seventh grade at Cole Middle School.

"It took me almost two weeks to get $90 for this," he said. "You got to do things to get money here. Not like other places, where parents just give their kids money for things."

He will be 14 in November, old enough to realize he won't always carry around a .25-caliber automatic.

"I saw a .38 Phoenix," he said. "Silver. You pull back that thing to cock it, you know goes ca-chick.

"It sounds like a real gun."

The other kids were walking home from the bus stop Tuesday afternoon, and she pulled the curtains together and sat on the floor against the wall.

She is 13, in the sixth grade at Morey Middle School, but she hasn't gone since a girl pulled a knife and called her a snitch on the school bus. It has been two weeks. She was in here, near Arapahoe and 26th streets, the afternoon Joseph Green was shot and killed outside the window.

She has had knives pulled on her before, but nobody ever called her a snitch.

"If I was a snitch, why wouldn't I tell the police she pulled a knife on me?" she said. "Huh? I'd like to just go out there and say 'Answer me that, Miss Smartypants.' "

She lives with her mother and her brother. He is 16, and he was shot in the head and paralyzed from the chest down last year four blocks from here. Her other brother is 14, and he is in the Gilliam Detention Center because he is a suspect in the killing of Joseph Green.

"I was here when I heard the shot, but everybody knows I had the curtain closed," she said. "I didn't see anybody until they ran in here. It's not like I look out every time I hear a shot."

Ida Hernandez was walking down Arapahoe Street from the grocery store Thursday afternoon when one of the kids ran up and pointed a finger at his head and said, "Pow!"

Hernandez lives at the corner of 26th and Arapahoe streets. She had seen the police cars go past and was hoping it was just a drug bust. She shifted the groceries into her other arm.

"Dead?" she said.

"It looked like," the kid said. "It started in a snowball fight."

"A snowball fight?" she said. "How many times do I have to tell you how dangerous those are?"

Three people have been killed in the past year within a block of the corner. Also, Hernandez's grandson was stabbed, and her granddaughter's fiancé was shot and paralyzed.

A police officer was looking at the bullet hole in her window.

"I know you guys have other things on your mind, but the doormat isn't just for decoration," she said. "I just get your muddy footprints cleaned up, and here you come back again."

In a glass cabinet in the dining room, she keeps a slug she took out of a wall in the dining room after Bernadette Trujillo was shot and paralyzed May 11. She had counted 57 bullet marks in the brick outside before her landlord came and smeared concrete over them a couple of months ago. Now, there are seven bullet marks on the concrete.

The officer left.

"I hope you guys take that yellow tape down when you leave," she said. "Last time, the kids put it in the trees like they used to with toilet paper."

In the street the kids were throwing snowballs.

Rocky Mountain News
Excerpts from 1993-95 columns

Greg was a person that cared. Because of him people are able to walk around here more comfortably. He gave us a little pride in ourselves.

IDA HERNANDEZ

Chapter two

A Child's Life

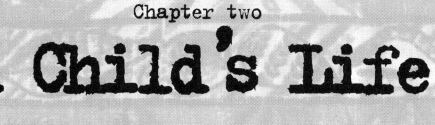

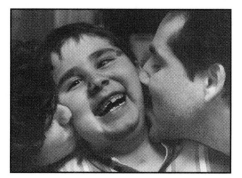

"The irony is

that no one expected Petey to live,

and no one expected Greg to die. Long after the media

frenzy surrounding the accident all but disappeared, it

was Greg who showed up three years later to let everyone know how he was doing. He treated us

like real people and not just a story he was doing — he did it from the heart. Greg told the world

our headstrong son was no longer Petey — he was Pete. **"**

JOSEPH GARCIA, PETE'S FATHER

Pete's Miracle

ALAMOSA, Colo. — The story was about a little boy running through a field, looking for he knew not what.

PETES PARENTS, TORI AND JOE GARCIA, GIVE THEIR SON A KISS.

It was reading time in the first grade in Polston Elementary School, and Pete Garcia sat in his wheelchair behind his class.

He...ran...fast...and...he...ran...far...

"I used to do that," Pete said. "Sometimes I got in trouble then, when I had muscles. Getting in trouble was fun."

Pete Garcia turns 7 on Sunday. Three years ago in the hospital in Denver, he heard one of his doctors on television saying he never would walk again and could be on a ventilator the rest of his life. This morning at home before school, he heard his mother tell him he never will hit his younger brother over the head with his Mighty Morphin Power Rangers sword or he will be in big trouble.

His father kneeled next to him.

Davey...went...up...the...tree.

"Hah," Pete said. "He lets people call him Davey. I get mad when people call me Petey. I'm Pete."

He used to get 350 letters a day from people who called him Petey. He got three official NFL footballs autographed by John Elway. Mayor Wellington Webb used to cite him as an example of what an inner-city public hospital can accomplish and say, "Petey Garcia is learning to walk again."

About 25 more letters were addressed to his parents and said things like, "They should take your children and your pets away from you."

To...see...what...he...could...see.

"Don't fall," he said. "Not like Humpty Dumpty."

He leaned forward so he could press his fist to his cheek.

He moves his arms like a puppet. He can do 21 situps in two minutes in gym class. He can take steps for 20 feet when his father holds him up.

His father hasn't been away from Pete for more than a few hours since Pete was in the hospital.

Davey...looked...and...looked...until...he...saw.

On Aug. 22, 1991, his mother put Pete in the back seat of her 1977 Grand Prix at her aunt's house to drive three blocks to her sister's house.

"I don't want this to sound like an excuse, but Pete was an awful, awful little boy sometimes," Tori Garcia said. "We'd put him in a car seat, and he'd be out of it and standing up before you could get in your seat. I just figured we were going to my sister's house, so it wasn't worth spending more time fighting with him that day."

When Pete was 13 months old, he crawled out of his crib and opened all of the presents under the Christmas tree. When he was 2 ½, his grandfather looked everywhere for him until he looked up and saw him 15 feet up a tree. When he was 3, he watched his father change a tire on his car, and when his parents woke up the next morning he had the car jacked up.

That day, Pete was standing up behind his mother when she drove away. She turned the corner. The back door swung open.

Pete fell out, and his head caught in the seat belt.

"Then I saw my grandpa again," Pete said. "He was standing there. He said, 'Go home, Pete.' I cried."

His grandfather had died a week earlier, and in the hospital Pete died. A doctor at the San Luis Valley Regional Medical Center punctured his right lung and forced oxygen into it. Pete cried.

The next thing he remembers is his father looking down at him.

"He was in jail," Pete said. "I thought I wouldn't see him anymore. I thought he wouldn't get out."

Joe and Tori lived eight blocks apart. When she got pregnant he was 18 and she was 14. He had dropped out in the ninth grade and she quit after the eighth grade to have Ryan.

He worked in the lettuce fields. Pete came two years later, and Cruz came two years after that. The police came in February of 1989 and found a pound and a half of marijuana in the refrigerator.

He was sentenced to serve four years.

"I did it," he said. "I did a lot of stupid things. I was out being a stupid kid when Ryan took his first steps, and I was in prison when Cruz took his first steps. I just happened to be around when Pete took his first steps."

He got his general equivalency diploma and was released from prison March 22, 1991. He did body work out of his garage and worked in the lettuce fields. His grandfather died Aug. 10, 1991.

As they lowered the body into the grave, he and his family each did a shot of tequila, and he drank one more, he said. On the way home, he hit a dip in the dirt road and lost his front license plate. The deputy who stopped him smelled the parole violation on his breath.

Twelve days later, the sheriff released him from the county jail to go to the hospital to say goodbye to Pete.

Pete's skull was separated from his spine by two centimeters. Doctors still don't understand why the spinal cord was not damaged when Pete's mother picked him up and her stepfather put him in the car to go to the San Luis Valley Regional Medical Center. When Dr. John Nichols, head of trauma neurosurgery at Denver General Hospital, saw the X-rays, he assumed the patient was dead.

He found reports of only 18 other similar cases of traumatic atlantooccipital dislocation in which the patients survived. He and another doctor made a steel pin in his garage. They used the pin and pieces of bone from Pete's ribs and pelvis to fuse his spine to his skull.

A halo flown in from Salt Lake City was screwed into Pete's skull to support his head. There have been 17 operations since then.

The school has a speech therapist and an occupational therapist who work with him, and he goes to a physical therapist three times a week.

His teachers say he is above average in math and reading, works and plays well with others.

Nichols, who now is at Provident Health Partners, St. Anthony Hospital Central, still thinks Pete might walk again.

"Fifty-fifty," he said. "I do think he can walk again, but even if he doesn't he can lead a productive life. Maybe whether he'll ever walk again isn't the main issue, though.

"His life and the lives of his family will never be the same, but that's not necessarily bad."

Police in Alamosa didn't charge Tori for not having Pete in a seatbelt, because they felt the injury to her son was punishment.

Joe Garcia had to report to his parole officer every day for six months for the parole violation and has a clean record since then.

He is 28 now and was hired last year to be an aide to Pete and other special-needs children, because Pete needed someone to help him get around and because Joe was there anyway. He is on the advisory board of Regalo de Tiempo, a program to give care to special-needs children so their parents can have free time. He plans to start part-time at Adams State College in January to get a degree in elementary education.

Tori Garcia is 24 now, and she also got her GED and started this semester at Adams State to get her degree in psychology. She cleans the Rialto Theater every day after classes, before she picks up the boys and her husband at school. During the summer, the whole family picks up trash every day at the Star Drive-In.

"One morning — this was after we'd gotten home three years ago, after some of the other doctors had said Pete would never use his arms again — I put Pete's arms over my shoulders so I could pull up his pants," Joe said. "I felt something on my neck. Pete said, 'Dad, I'm hugging you.'

"I promised myself right then I will be here if Pete walks again."

They live in a three-bedroom, double-wide mobile home in the Century Mobile Home Park. They took over payments last year. There are mirrors on the wall to make it feel bigger.

The mirrors are decorated with comic book characters and the Denver Broncos logo painted by prison inmates and sent to Pete in the hospital.

"Please put me on the floor," Pete said. "Let's wrestle."

Pete weighs 73 pounds and is bigger than either of his brothers. When they wrestle, he usually wins. When he is in his wheelchair and gets mad at one of them, he says their name and speaks softly so they will bend over his wheelchair where he can swing his arm to hit them.

At night, Pete sleeps next to his parents in a bed that looks like a racing car, so they can hear him when he needs to be turned over by his father.

He is too heavy for his mother to lift.

He and Ryan wrestled until he rolled over on his older brother and lay on him until their father pulled him off.

"Let's go outside," he said. "I want to make a snow angel. I make big snow angels."

People contributed $89,624 to help pay for Pete's care, and it is in a trust with Joe Garcia and Jill Mix, one of Pete's nurses at Denver General, as co-trustees. It has been used to buy a van, ramps and desktop and laptop computers. The fund now has $64,956 left.

His father picked him up out of the snow.

"Sega, please," he said.

The closets are filled with boxes of letters Pete got from people who called him Petey, and each of the boys has one of the three footballs from John Elway. The braces and the halo are in a box on the bottom. This spring, they plan to leave the braces at Sanctuaria de Chimayo in New Mexico, where Tori's aunt went and prayed all day during the surgery to fuse Pete's skull to his spinal cord.

He beat Ryan at X-Man.

"Let's draw a picture," he said.

He bent over a piece of paper with a pen in a fist and drew a picture of himself.

Some afternoons, Pete talks other kids into taking him outside to push his wheelchair over the speed bumps.

Two weeks ago, he talked his cousin into taking down and unwrapping his birthday present, the Mighty Morphin Power sword he used that morning to hit his brother on the head.

He looked at himself in the picture he had drawn. He was standing. He picked up the pen and leaned forward in his wheelchair.

He added muscles.

"I already know what I'm going to do when I can walk," he said. "I already know what I'm going to do. I'm not telling.

"I want to do it before I get in trouble."

Rocky Mountain News
November 24, 1994

PETE'S PARENTS
BELIEVE GOD SPARED
THEIR BOY.

Dennis Schroeder/Rocky Mountain News

The Rebel Way

DENVER — What football players do, Nick Williams said, is play football.

They wear helmets, too, he said. The best helmets are blue and have a silver "C" on the side. He is 16, mentally retarded, and he practices with the Columbine High School Rebels football team.

Nick is a football player.

"If you wear a Rebels football helmet, you've got to keep your mouthpiece in, too," Nick said. "So you don't talk when the coach tells you where to go."

Nick, 5-foot-4, 130 pounds, was at practice last week at Ken Caryl Junior High School, working on the scout team to get the starters ready to play against seventh-ranked Pomona on Friday night. He hasn't decided what position he wants to play. So he plays all of them except quarterback.

Before every play, the coaches tell him where to go.

"I'm working hard, keeping my chin clean," Nick said. "It's the Rebel way."

His favorite football team used to be the Green Bay Packers because he liked their helmets, and last Christmas he got a Green Bay Packers helmet. One of his teachers last year at Ken Caryl was Ryan West, who also is an assistant football coach. Nick took his helmet to school and said he wanted to play football when he went to Columbine this year.

West said maybe he could be a manager, and Nick asked why managers wear football helmets.

"Hah," Nick said.

The week before school started, Nick had a dentist's appointment, and afterward his mother let him walk home. He walked to the football field. That night, his father called West.

He got a blue helmet with a silver "C" on the side.

His first practice, he didn't know which bus to take to the field, so he walked two miles to Ken Caryl.

When Columbine scored a touchdown in the first game, against Evergreen High School, Nick ran into the stands to hug the fans.

"I've been doing an outstanding job of staying on the sidelines during the Rebels games," Nick said.

The other Rebel football players don't hit him the way they hit other Rebel football players. They make sure he gets on the right bus to practice. They call him their Forrest Gump.

"Forrest Gump is a fine football player," Nick said.

His work in his special-education classes has improved, because the coaches have told him that is part of being a football player, too. He wants to learn to read. He wants a play book.

He can't remember how many points a touchdown is worth, but he can name 27 players in the NFL who have helmets with face masks like his.

"Greg Lloyd, No. 94 for the Pittsburgh Steelers," Nick said. "Wayne Simmons, No. 59 for the Green Bay Packers, Marc Spindler, No. 93 of the Detroit Lions..."

Nick says the prayer for the team before every game.

Before Friday night's game, Nick thanked God, the coaches, the players, his parents, his friends and whoever made his football helmet. Columbine won 36-23. After the game, Nick hugged some of the Pomona players and told them to keep their chins clean, because that is what football players do.

"Winning isn't the only thing, you know," Nick said. "But we did anyway."

Rocky Mountain News
October 8, 1995

NICK WILLIAMS LOVES FOOTBALL.

Essdras M. Suarez/Rocky Mountain News

A Mother's Day

DENVER — In the morning in the intensive care unit, Casey Yarger's mother was trying to change the subject.

Diana Yarger stood next to his bed at Children's Hospital with her hand on his arm, between the tubes that feed the needles that give him what the doctors say he needs. It has been 172 days since they left the ranch 13 miles outside Circle, Mont., to come here. Casey is 18, her youngest.

He has a new heart and a new liver, and now all he wanted was a piece of crushed ice.

"So let's talk about what you want to do when you get out of here, Casey," she said.

"Drink. Water," he said.

"What do you want to do after that?"

"Drink more."

"What about going to the lake and water skiing?"

"I'll fall and drink the water."

Today is Mother's Day, and today she will do what she has done since Thanksgiving.

The heart transplant worked, but his liver failed. The liver transplant on Dec. 28 worked, but the medication and the strain caused ulcers. On Tuesday, half of his pancreas was removed.

Diana, 47, has stood next to his bed every day except two. She learned to read his lips after his tracheotomy. He had two spoonfuls of Fruit Loops for breakfast April 6 and told her he didn't feel like eating any more. Since then, he can have only small amounts of crushed ice she and his father, Floyd, give him with a spoon.

"The doctors say it's a good sign you're hungry," she said. "I know, I know. But it's a good sign."

He was a guard for the Circle High School basketball team, and his coach would pull him out of the games when his lips turned blue. He has a 1965 Chevrolet pickup he won't let anybody else drive. In school, he signed his papers "Casey the Great."

He is the third child, after Denim, 22, and Rebecca, 21, and he was born with one chamber in his heart instead of two. He had an operation when he was three months old and two more after that. He told people he got the scars in a knife fight.

In June 1993, he went on the list for a new heart.

"How about if I open your mail?" she said. "They look like graduation announcements....It's OK, I understand."

In auto-repair class last fall, he would crawl into the back seat of a car when he was tired, and his friends would raise the car on the hoist so the teacher couldn't see him.

After basketball practice Nov. 22, he asked his mother to drive him home in his pickup. He leaned against the door. He said he didn't think he would be able to play basketball anymore. The next morning, he came home from school because he didn't feel well. It was the first time he ever had done that. His mother was making food for Thanksgiving dinner the next day.

The telephone rang at 11:30 a.m.

"Floyd, that's a big ice cube you're giving him, Floyd," she said.

"I know," Floyd said.

"You're going to spoil him."

Floyd is here when he doesn't have to be home to keep the ranch running.

Neighbors and relatives do the chores. Rebecca moved down and comes to the hospital after classes at Bel-Rea Institute of Animal Technology.

They got an apartment in Aurora on the ground floor because Casey will be in a wheelchair when he is released.

"The lambs were delivered today, Casey."

"Looks like I might get out of shoveling this summer."

Casey wanted to go out for his 18th birthday, April 22. He was taken at 2 a.m. to University Medical Center with an embolism. He got a replica of a Dodge Viper, a hunting knife and money.

Diana flew to Billings to see Denim graduate May 6 from Rocky Mountain College. She was gone two days. Those are the only days she has not been at the hospital.

"Don't you dare squirt me with that squirt gun, young man," she said. "I know that look in your eyes. Don't...

"Just don't squirt it in your mouth."

She has been told he won't make it through the next operation, the next night, the next two hours.

She squirts saline solution into the tracheotomy and guides the suction tube down into his lungs to pull out the fluid that builds up. She puts drops in his eyes. She straightens his toes to keep them from curling from not being used.

She feels relaxed when he is in surgery, because she knows there is nothing she can do.

She started reading *When God Doesn't Make Sense around Christmas,* when she gets back to the apartment at night. She thinks she is reading it for the second time. She doesn't remember anything she has read, but she needs something to read until she can fall asleep at night.

Today is Mother's Day, and she will spend it with her son.

"Asleep?" she said. "Well, then I'm going to talk about the kind of son you are. You're up at 6 o'clock in the morning, yelling 'The world's on fire — wake up!' You asked your mother to go deer hunting with you even though I've never fired a gun, and we had a wonderful time. You told me things you wouldn't tell anybody else, and even when we didn't talk we were communicating with each other.

"That's the kind of son you are."

Rocky Mountain News
May 14, 1995

The Game

DENVER — The boys in the pod at the Gilliam Youth Detention Center were talking about how one of the kids who got arrested in the killing of Casson Evans also is really good at Monopoly.

It was lunch. The one they call Moot when he isn't in here was talking to the one they call Li'l Butz when he isn't in here. Lunch was spaghetti.

"Man, I'm glad I was in here already," Moot said. "Not in the middle of that with him. Wait'll I see him this time."

"Last time, he got all the hotels and Boardwalk and Park Place," Li'l Butz said. "I told myself it'd never happen again."

Gilliam had 69 kids that morning, which meant it had room for nine more, which meant it would get nine more by that night. The kids were in group discussions, classes, counseling, isolation. In the pod, they had learned in the morning about the battle of Vicksburg, and they would talk in the afternoon about the kids who are suspects in the fire bombings and the killing of Casson.

"I wished they'd invented Monopoly when I was a kid," Moot said. "It took me a while to learn you got to buy property."

Moot is 14 and has been here four weeks on drug charges. It is his third time in here since he turned 12. Li'l Butz also is 14 and has been here two other times, this time for four weeks on first-degree assault charges.

"I'm gonna teach my son, soon as he's old enough," Moot said. "You need a crib. Hotel's the good investment."

Capacity in Gilliam is 78 kids. Capacity is 120 percent of the capacity it was built for. Capacity used to be more than 200 kids, but the U.S. District Court ruled last year that 120 percent was 100 percent.

The state has allocated $6.7 million to build another juvenile facility, but the state and the city still are arguing over who will buy the property.

"The other night, I got 'Go directly to jail' three times," Moot said. "How you gonna win that way?"

Kids here are waiting for hearings on criminal charges or serving sentences of up to 45 days.

One day, a counselor brought in one of his suits so everybody could feel what it's like to wear one. Another brought in jacks to show the kids how to play. Another one taught the kids how to play "Go Fish," and they liked it better than gin rummy.

Courts decide who will stay and who will go, while the city and the state play their own game of Monopoly.

"You got to pay the consequences," Moot said. "You get 'Go directly to jail,' that's where you're gonna be. You can't pull a gun or run."

Most of the suspects in the firebombings and the killing of Casson had been in here before, and the courts had released some early because of crowding. Another kid who was in here three times just called to say he'd just been made manager at a Taco Bell. A girl released at noon called four times that afternoon to ask what was going on.

Meanwhile, capacity is capacity.

"Yeah," Moot said. "But where else you gonna get spaghetti, too?"

Rocky Mountain News
February 2, 1996

A Bus Ride for Taisha

DENVER — Bus No. 2167 left University Park Elementary School on the way to more equal educational opportunities, and Taisha Brown started to count the street signs.

The kids who live close enough to come here waved goodbye, and the kids who live far enough away to come here waved back. There are four buses. Capacity on Bus No. 2167 is 65, so there are 65 kids on it.

Every day, Taisha counts the street signs on the way home, at least until she gets to 59.

"My mom, she's never been this far," Taisha said. "I want her to come to my school sometime. So I'm trying to show her it's not too far, but I lose count."

While the 440 first- and second-graders at University Park were at recess Tuesday, a federal judge said half of them didn't need to take a bus 72 blocks from the Columbine Elementary neighborhood to learn anymore.

The way U.S. District Judge Richard Matsch put it, they have achieved "unitary status."

The way second-grader Lawrence Mason put it, "Maybe I won't get bus-sick and throw up anymore."

And that is pretty much what busing comes down to for first- and second-graders.

The bus passed the Country Club neighborhood.

"I tell my mother about the big houses we go past, and I want to live in this one with a big old dog and a red door, and you know what she said?" Chantyl Busby said. "She said, 'Dream on.' She's real funny that way."

Now that the schools are supposed to be the same, the difference is busing. About 90 percent of the kids who live in the neighborhood around University Park are white. In the neighborhood around Columbine, about 80 percent are black and 15 percent are Hispanic.

The bus passed the Botanic Gardens.

"I asked the bus driver, and she said it was big gardens or something like that, and then I told my mom, but she didn't believe me it was there," Michael Grant said. "We took the other kind of bus. The kind you have to pay on.

"Then my mom, she believed me, but she still didn't believe it, it was so cool."

Rashe Howlett fell asleep, and Rayesha Wright pulled her ponytail. Lamar Mason slid down so the driver couldn't see him in the mirror and made burping noises. Rudy

Maihs kicked the seat in front of him.

Which is to say they are the same as first- and second-graders who don't have to be bused.

"Same old, same old," second-grader Danielle Barksdale said.

The bus stopped at the corner of East 35th Avenue and Elizabeth Street, the last stop, and Taisha got off. Four kids had left their jackets. It is one of the problems with busing that never gets brought up.

Taisha had lost count after 42 blocks. She said it didn't matter. Maybe she was right.

It took 21 years to get here, and there still is more to go.

"I told my mom it's not too far, but she said why go all that way just to see a school?" Taisha said. "I said because it's my school. Anyplace it is, it's still my school."

Rocky Mountain News
September 13, 1995

A Gift of Love

WESTCLIFFE, Colo. — Supper is at 5:30 p.m.

Enos Mullett sat at the head of the table, held out his arms and bowed his head. Davey Lamorie sat in a high chair to his right and reached out. Lydia Mullett sat on the other side and reached out for her husband to begin, for it says in the Bible, 1 Corinthians 11, "The head of every man is Christ; and the head of every woman is the man."

Around the table, nine pairs of hands joined, and Enos began to say grace.

"Dear Lord, we thank you for the gifts at this table," Enos said.

The table seats 12. This night, it was only Enos, Lydia, their sons Steve and Ryan, 18 and 15, Christa Martin, 21, Dominick Pacheco, two months, Kellie Stiles, nine months, Evan Mollett, 18 months, and Davey, two years, eight months. The mothers of Davey, Dominick, Kellie and Evan are in prison, jail or halfway houses.

Before Davey and the other children came to them, the Mulletts sometimes had to reach across the table to say grace.

"Amen," Enos said.

"And then we saw them dig a big hole, Mommy," Davey said.

The Mulletts have taken in 22 babies born to women in the Colorado Women's Correctional Facility in Cañon City, because their Mennonite beliefs instruct them to serve others. They started the New Horizons ministry in April 1992, and today two other families have seven other children. Davey is the age of the ministry.

He was the first child the Mullets brought home, and they have given up trying to tell him he should call them Grandma and Grandpa.

"They used a backhoe, Mommy," Davey said. "And a big dozer."

The Mulletts' five oldest children are grown and married and have 13 children of their own. Enos works with his son, Myron, digging foundations and pouring concrete around the Wet Mountain Valley. That afternoon, Enos had taken Davey to work so Lydia would have time to sew new dresses for their granddaughters.

Mennonite women wear dresses that button up to their necks, the Bible instructing them to be modest. They don't wear lipstick or other makeup. Lydia and her daughters never have cut their hair and always wear a prayer veiling — "Every woman that prayeth or prophesieth with her head uncovered dishonoureth her head" — pinned to their hair.

"I brought you home a rock, Mommy," Davey said.

Supper is baked chicken, mashed potatoes with gravy, corn, coleslaw and homemade bread with apple butter, and dessert is apple crisp.

The house is four miles south of Westcliffe, a mile south of the asphalt. It is heated by a wood stove. In the pantry, the shelves are filled with vegetables and fruits Lydia has canned.

"It's a rock just like Davey used to slay the big giant in the story, right, Daddy?" Davey said.

Enos does not allow television, except to watch videos he brings home.

Dominick, Kellie and Evan sleep in two bedrooms with Christa and Barb Yoder, who help care for the babies through the Mennonite Volunteer Service program. Each boy has his own room. Davey sleeps in a crib in Lydia and Enos' bedroom, holding a toy John Deere tractor.

It was Tuesday, five days before Christmas, and Lydia still hadn't had time to put up decorations.

"Can you tell me that story again, Mommy?" Davey said.

Visitation rites

Door A-13 slid open at 9 a.m.

Two mothers came into the visiting room at the Colorado Women's Correctional Facility and held out their arms. The babies had been frisked. Bridget Sidner stood on her toes to look over the shoulder of the guard who was frisking her, to see Mariah Gabrielle Sidner, 5 days old, asleep in the arms of Theda Martin.

"Boo-boo boo-boo, baby," Sidner said.

The mothers wore forest-green prison uniforms over T-shirts, prison rules requiring that inmates be covered up to their necks. Somebody had put a garland

Dean Krakel/Rocky Mountain News

THE MULLETT FAMILY, ENOS AND LYDIA, SIT THROUGH SUNDAY SERVICE AT THE SANGRE DE CHRISTO MENNONITE CHURCH IN WESTCLIFFE.

around the bulletin board that shows pictures of mannequins wearing "allowable" and "unallowable" dress for visitors. The guard sat in a chair in a corner.

Bridget Sidner lowered her arms, and Martin put Mariah into them.

"Sleeping?" Sidner asked. "She do this a lot?"

Mariah was born at 11:05 a.m. the Sunday before at St. Thomas More Hospital in Cañon City.

Sidner is 23, and Mariah is her first baby. The prison allows an inmate to spend the first 24 hours with her baby. The ministry picked up Mariah on Monday afternoon, and Sidner came back here.

Mariah is cared for by Martin, who is in the Volunteer Service program.

"She's a good sleeper, huh?" she said.

Next to them, Maria Gomes sat on a chair with D.J. on her lap. D.J. is 13 months old. He is cared for by Darlene Miller, who also is part of the Volunteer Service program.

"He can say horsey," Miller said.

"Can you say horse for Mama?" Gomes said.

D.J. turned his head to watch Lydia, who had picked up Dominick. Lydia hadn't known that Dominick's mother had a court hearing this morning.

Sidner held Mariah up to the window of the control room so inmates could see her from the window on the other side of the control room.

Last year, 32 of the 350 women who came through the prison had babies. This year, five have had babies. At least three more are pregnant.

"Last time I was in here, I was one of the ones looking in at the babies and saying, 'Not me,'" Sidner said. "Of course, I also said I wasn't ever coming back here."

Miller bought D.J. a package of cheese and peanut butter crackers from the vending machine with the quarters they are allowed to bring in. They also can bring in two diapers, two bottles and wipes, but they must be in a clear plastic bag so the guards can see what's inside. When they take the babies to see their fathers in the men's prisons, they can't take in wipes, but they can use diaper bags.

A voice on a speaker started to call units to lunch.

"OK, ladies," the guard said.

"Horse?" Gomes said. "Want another cracker?"

"Open your eyes just once, baby," Sidner said. "Time for you to eat. Mommy's gonna have to go to lunch."

Sidner rubbed noses with Mariah.

The baby opened her eyes for the first time since visitation began, made a sound that could have meant anything and went back to sleep.

Door A-19, the door to the dining area, slid open.

"Ladies," the guard said.

Lunch is at 11:30.

"I wish I could sleep like that," Sidner said. "They don't even let you turn on the TV in here until 3:30."

She kissed Mariah and handed her to Martin.

Martin wiped the lipstick off Mariah's cheek and wrapped her in a blanket to go home. Door A-19 slid closed.

All in the big family

Lydia Mullett was the third of 15 children, and Enos was the oldest of seven. She lived near Washington, Ind., he lived near Akron, Ohio, and they met at the Messiah Bible Institute in Canton, Ohio. Their first child was born a year and a day after they were married.

"There was that year, and the year between the time our fifth started school and Steven was born, when I didn't have a baby to take care of," Lydia said. "Other than that, there's always been baby brothers, baby sisters, sons, daughters and now prisoners' babies. I honestly don't really remember what I did those two years."

They lived in Saratoga, Fla., and the family ran their own lawn-service business until Enos came to Westcliffe to go deer hunting. He went back, and they loaded everything into a trailer. That was three years ago, and they were the first Mennonite family in the valley.

"The girls got quite a lot of attention because of the way they dressed, and that was good," Enos said. "Some Mennonites, they like to stay to themselves. Myself, I believe that we should reach out rather than just reach inside."

Dean Krakel/Rocky Mountain News

LYDIA MULLETT, THEDA MARTIN AND DARLENE MILLER CARRY BABIES THROUGH THE GATES OF THE COLORADO WOMEN'S CORRECTIONAL INSTITUTION IN CANON CITY, ON THEIR WAY FOR A WEEKLY VISIT WITH THEIR MOTHERS.

Mennonites rose out of the Anabaptist movement in the 16th century, and today there are 850,000 in 60 countries. They believe in pacifism and in following the teachings of the Bible rather than the ways of the secular world. They believe the way to serve Christ is by serving people.

Today, there are nine Mennonite families in the valley, including those of two of their children, and services are Wednesday and Sunday mornings at the Sangre de Cristo Mennonite Church.

Enos and Myron had started Bible-study classes at prisons in Florida and Alabama, and in March 1992, they met with prison officials to ask whether there was anything they could do here. The prison officials said an inmate was expecting a baby and didn't have family who could take it. Two weeks later, the Mulletts brought Davey home.

They had to buy a crib and clothes, because they had given theirs to their children for their grandchildren.

"For a week, he jerked and cried until he turned blue," Lydia said. "We didn't know what it was. It turned out it was the drugs his mother had taken before he was born, and it turned out to be something we'd have to get used to with these babies."

The Mulletts and the other families in New Horizons are licensed by the state Department of Human Services. Medicaid covers the children's medical needs. The other costs — about $2,000 a month — are paid by the families and by donations.

The Mulletts encourage the mothers to call collect, which is the only way they can call from prison, and their phone bill is about $300 a month.

They hope to raise enough money to build another home in Westcliffe, where the mothers could live with their babies after they are released.

They have had as many as six babies, and they now have five cribs, six car seats, a trailer filled with boxes of clothes labeled by ages, and a 12-passenger van.

"The only real problem we have is that we can't spank them," Lydia said. "Some of them — Davey especially — could use a paddling sometimes. But other than that, we raise them just like they were our own babies."

The Mulletts drive 60 miles to the prison every Thursday night to lead a Bible-study class, and Lydia goes back every Friday morning for visitation.

They don't know why most of the mothers are in prison because they don't ask.

At the Bible study, an inmate told Enos he would be surprised at the things she had done.

"Let me tell you something from personal experience," Enos said. "When I was 17 years old, I didn't always listen to the things my father told me. So I had this 1949 Dodge, and I was going home one day, and when I slowed down to turn a corner, some kids jumped on the back without me seeing. When I drove past their farm, they jumped off, but I hadn't slowed down because I didn't know they were back there, and one of the boys was in the hospital for two weeks.

"I'm sure that was the Lord's way of warning me for being wayward and not listening to my father, so I know a little something about these things."

The Mulletts also have to explain to their own grandchildren why other babies sometimes get more of their attention.

"We have one who was born four days after Davey," Lydia said. "How do you explain to a child why you gave more to Davey than to your own blood? How do you tell him that Grandma and Grandpa gave more to another child because otherwise he wouldn't have gotten anything?"

Good homes hard to come by

The house where Cody's mother lives is in Northglenn, in a subdivision where for every street name there is a court, a way and a place.

Inside, Cammie Churches and her mother had miniature Christmas scenes on fake snow on every shelf and table; cookies, candy, cheese and crackers on the dining room table, and packages piled under the Christmas tree. It was Saturday morning, eight days before Christmas, and the Mulletts had brought five-month-old Cody home.

"He looks like the baby I dreamed about," Churches said.

Cody slept in a swing in the house where he will live with his mother, his grand-mother and his brother. Enos, Lydia, Churches and her mother sat around him in the living room. Davey was in the back yard, teaching Cody's brother how to dig a hole.

"I'm afraid a lot of these Christmas decorations are going to be new for Cody,"

Lydia said. "I just haven't had the time yet."

"Time is something I've had a lot of the last couple of days," Churches said.

Churches found out she was pregnant when she was in the Jefferson County jail. Her older son, Tyler, is eight and lived here with her mother. She was in Cañon City when Cody was born.

She was released from a 45-day drug treatment program in Greeley on Wednesday and will live with her mother.

"It was just luck I made it to Cañon City by the time he was born, so you could take him," she said.

"The Lord works these things out," Lydia said.

Lydia and Churches went into the kitchen so they wouldn't wake Cody and cried and hugged and promised each other it won't be long until they see each other again.

Churches had come to every Bible-study class when she was in prison, and she was waiting for the door to slide open for visitation at 9 a.m. every Friday.

In the living room, Enos lifted his glasses and wiped away a tear.

"Well, Cody," he said, "you make three. Twenty-two babies, and you're the third baby I've felt good about the home you went back to."

He went outside and put the extra car seat in the trunk. He called Lydia and Davey. Everybody cried and hugged and promised again, until Enos said they were going to be late.

He strapped Davey into his car seat to go to the Arapahoe County Regional Center.

"We're going to see your mom, Davey," Lydia said.

"We see a dozer?" Davey asked.

The Arapahoe County Regional Center is a halfway house in an old motel on South Santa Fe Drive.

Enos had just taken Davey out of his car seat when Sherri Kalber ran out with a disposable camera.

"Smile, David," she said.

She is 33, and Davey is the 10th of her 11 children. She is finishing a four-year sentence for attempted forgery. Davey's father is in prison in Los Angeles.

Davey hid behind Enos' leg, and when he peeked out Kalber took his picture.

"His father sent him a Christmas card and a picture of himself," Enos said.

"I talked to Jake," Kalber said. "He still wants to use when he gets out, so I can't have anything to do with him. Does he have a lot of gray hair?"

She knelt and reached out to Davey, who stared at the needle scars on her hands and arms.

Seven of Davey's brothers and sisters have been adopted. Two sisters live with his father's family. Two others died of what a coroner ruled was crib death.

Kalber wants to get Davey placed in a foster home in Denver so she can see him more often.

"Come to Mom, David?" Kalber said.

Davey ran from behind Enos to hide behind Lydia.

When Kalber was in prison, Lydia sometimes had to ask a guard to go and remind her it was time for visitation. The last time the Mulletts brought Davey to see her at the halfway house, they left them alone for six hours. For two weeks after that, he cried whenever one of the Mulletts left the room.

They walked into the dining area and sat around a table, Davey in Lydia's lap.

"So," Enos said, "Sherri..."

"So I'm doing good," Kalber said. "Next month it'll be a year that I've been clean. I've just got to stay away from the wrong people."

Kalber looked down at the Colorado Rockies logo on her sweatshirt.

She talked about working the swing shift as an aide in a home for mentally retarded adults. She talked about the Narcotics Anonymous meetings she goes to. She talked about the mistakes she won't make again.

Davey turned and looked at Lydia.

"Dig a hole?" Davey said.

"Yeah, David," Kalber said. "Your mom dug a big hole for herself. But I'm going to get out of it and be with you."

Kalber looked up at the clock on the wall and said she had to get to her job.

They walked to the car, Davey holding Lydia's hands. Kalber bent and picked up Davey's other hand, but he pulled it away. Enos put Davey in his car seat.

Kalber took the last picture in the disposable camera through the window.

"You didn't happen to bring that picture of Jake, did you?" Kalber asked.

Enos started the car and drove out of the parking lot, south on Santa Fe Drive.

They would be home in time for supper.

"Do all to the glory of God"

After supper, Enos would play *Building Up the Temple* and *Bringing in the Sheaves* on his harmonica, and Davey would dance.

It was five days before Christmas.

When the children were in bed, Lydia, Steve, Ryan and Christa would sit around the table. Enos would read to them from the Bible. For it says, "Whether therefore ye eat or drink, or whatsoever ye do, do all to the glory of God."

"That's why we're here," Enos said.

"I just hope I can get everything decorated in time, so it really feels like Christmas, Daddy," Lydia said.

"It already does, Mommy," Enos said.

For Christmas dinner, they expect about 50 people. Two will be mothers with babies the Mulletts cared for, the first two Enos felt good about when they got back their babies. Another will be a man who drove from Alabama, who was in one of Enos'

Bible-study classes 17 years ago in the Huntsville State Prison in Alabama.

For it says, "Wherefore, my brethren, when ye come together to eat, tarry one for another."

Davey would come out, saying he couldn't sleep, and Lydia would lift him onto her lap and read him the story of Davey and Goliath.

"You like that story, don't you?" Lydia said.

"Yes, Mommy," Davey said. "Davey slays the big giant. It's a good story."

Rocky Mountain News
December 24, 1995

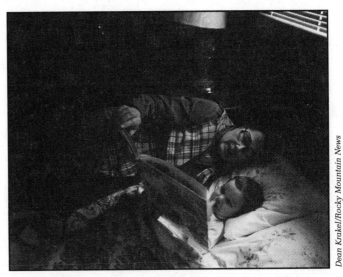

LYDIA MULLETT READS TO DAVEY FROM THE *BIBLE WORD BOOK.*

Blind Actresses Make Magic

DENVER — The wedding scene in *Fiddler on the Roof* was about to begin, and Leah Williamson and Loretta Morton were trying to remember what scared looks like.

Leah is 10 and plays Bielke, Loretta is 12 and plays Shprintze, and it was their last rehearsal for the latest production of the Physically Handicapped Amateur Musical Actors League. They are blind. The actress who plays their mother is blind, their father has a steel rod for a leg, one sister has Parkinson's disease, one is in a wheelchair and one has Ollier's disease and Maffucci's Syndrome.

They both were getting ready to act in front of an audience for the first time when the play opened Friday night, but they still weren't sure what scared looks like.

"Scared is the one where you hold your hands to your cheeks and make your mouth in a circle," Leah whispered.

"Sad is difficult," Loretta said. "Even though I'm an actress now, I don't like to act sad."

Fiddler on the Roof is the fifth production by PHAMALy, and it is a play that could have been written for PHAMALy. The group was started by physically handicapped actors who couldn't get parts in other productions. They have received positive reviews when they have been able to get reviewed.

This isn't about people acting like they don't have handicaps, it is about people acting.

Leah and Loretta are the first children to act in a PHAMALy production, and after they both acted scared, their sister in the wheelchair led them offstage. They sat on a couch — one black, one white — and waited to go back on stage and be sisters. While they waited, they each tried to guess what the other looked like.

"You have hazel eyes, and your nose scrunches up when you laugh," Leah said.

Loretta was born four months premature, with retinopathy that caused blindness. She lives with her grandparents. Her grandmother has looked out the window and seen Loretta riding a bicycle, and she also has had to track down Loretta's cane after she traded it for a Garfield book.

"You have a lovely smile and blue eyes," Loretta said. "I'm not sure what a beautiful smile looks like, but I'm absolutely positive you have one."

Leah has craniopharyngioma, a benign brain tumor that presses on her optic nerves, and she had sight until she went into a coma two years ago. When she came out of the coma, she was blind. She went back to her school the next week, learned Braille and finished the school year with straight As.

They got their cue. They each had been wrong about the other's eyes and right about the smiles. They started toward the stage. This time, they were supposed to act happy.

"Back into the spotlight," Leah said.

"Yes," Loretta said. "It's time to make magic."

Rocky Mountain News
July 24, 1994

Michael's Favorite Things

DENVER — Sunday after church, Michael Crisler went to Elitch's, which is his favorite thing to do, he said.

Michael is seven, and last week he finished first grade at University Park Elementary School and started summer. He had seven days. This morning at Denver Children's Hospital he will have his fifth operation on his face.

"Why Elitch's is my favorite thing to do is because if you aren't scared to go on the rides, nothing will scare you," he said. "Now I know nothing will scare me."

Monday morning, Michael played baseball in his grandparents' back yard, which is his favorite thing to do, he said.

He put off the operation a month to raise money for people in Oklahoma City who need it because a bomb exploded there. He needs the operation because he has Treacher Collins Syndrome, which keeps the bones in his face from forming. He had a bowl-a-thon and knocked on doors, and by Wednesday he had raised $28,797.

Dennis Schroeder/Rocky Mountain News

MICHAEL CRISLER, 7, TALKS ABOUT HIS FAVORITE THINGS TO DO.

"Baseball I like best because you can play it all day," he said. "Unless you have to go to the doctor or something."

Monday afternoon, Michael went swimming, which is almost his favorite thing to do, he said.

The doctors said he will be in the hospital for up to two weeks, then will have to stay inside for another month. He plans to be home next week. He will miss soccer camp because he pushed back the operation, but he thinks he might be ready when karate starts.

"Actually, my favorite thing to do is bowling, but swimming comes next," he said. "Under water, it's your own private world. Everybody looks different, too."

Tuesday morning, Michael went to his doctor and spent the day having X-rays and examinations for the operation, which isn't his favorite thing to do, he said.

Doctors will cut a piece of bone from his skull and use it to build up his cheekbones, take skin and muscle from his upper eyelids and graft it to his lower eyelids, and put in a chin implant. He wanted to start on his ears this summer, but the doctors will wait until the rest of him grows. He will have at least 10 more operations.

"But the good thing about going to the doctor is it gets me closer to not having to go," he said.

Wednesday, Michael went to the Colorado Rockies game, which is his favorite thing to do, he said.

This year, before the bomb exploded in Oklahoma City, he raised more than $400 for the Muscular Dystrophy Association, $3,500 for the Children's Miracle Network and gave all of his stuffed animals except two to children in Englewood after their apartment building burned down. He has been on television and in the newspaper. People have recognized him everywhere he has gone this summer.

That isn't one of his favorite things.

"Everybody recognizes me at the Rockies games or whatever I'm doing," he said. "I like meeting people, but if I have enough operations I won't look different. Then I'll be just like other kids."

Rocky Mountain News
June 5, 1995

The Dropout

DENVER — When he was supposed to be in American government at West High School listening to a teacher talking about people who are mostly dead anyway, he was lying on the couch at home watching a movie that had something to do with girls in bikinis on the beach.

He is 14 years old — 15 next week — and he hasn't gone back to school since the Christmas vacation. A woman from the school has called three times. He acted like he didn't know who she was talking about.

If some state legislators have their way and get rid of compulsory education for kids under 16, the woman at the school won't be bothering him all the time.

"People in history are dead, mostly," he said. "People on television are alive, mostly.... Yeah, TV gets boring all the time, too, but you get used to it."

When he was supposed to be in geometry, he got up and called his girlfriend, but she still goes to school a lot. He has two other friends who didn't go back to school after the Christmas vacation. Kids under 16 quit going to school all around the state. Enough that the schools can't track all of them, even though the compulsory-education law requires them to.

"I figured out something," he said. "Multiplication, instead of memorizing all those times, you just take one number and add it together with itself how many times the other number is. It doesn't work so good with big numbers, but when do you got to worry about them?"

When he was supposed to be in physical education, he got up and made himself a bowl of Cheerios.

His brother waited until he was 16 to quit school. His mother quit when she was 16 or 17. Now, his mother cleans hotel rooms, and his older brother is 18 and in the Denver County Jail because the police say he broke into somebody's house.

His mother says he's got to find a job or someplace else to hang around all day.

"It didn't do my brother any good to stay in school that long," he said. "I just don't want nobody telling me what to do. I got a mom for that."

When he was supposed to be in English literature, he went to see a friend of his who is 17 and quit school last year.

They drink beer and go out at night and spray-paint their tags on buildings and fences. He has been in the Gilliam Youth Center twice, once for breaking car windows downtown and once for a fight in a 7-Eleven parking lot. He already figured out that it's better to do things on a school night because there aren't as many police around, and now he is trying to figure out how to tag one of the signs over the highway.

He's 14 — 15 next week — and he's still learning.

"What's it supposed to do for me, reading all these books about people who don't know what it's like?" he said. "Me, I'm in the real world now."

Rocky Mountain News
January 14, 1996

The Youngest Suspect

DENVER — Anthony Nadeau was in the street in front of his house, seeing how high he could bounce a golf ball, when he saw him.

Anthony is seven years old and one of the victims of the youngest suspect. The youngest suspect is seven years old, 3-foot-6 and 75 pounds. He has threatened other children around his home in north Denver with a knife, a belt, a broken bottle, a base-ball bat and a pipe, and he threatened to kill the police officers who came to his house.

Anthony was on the porch before the golf ball hit the ground.

"Thanks for the ball, slob," the youngest suspect said, and he put it in his pocket.

The youngest suspect has been reported to police at least four times, according to police reports, although no more information could be released because he's so young.

He started assaulting other children as soon as he moved into the neighborhood two years ago with his parents.

"It wasn't so bad until he learned how to ride a bike," said Natasha Carder, nine, who lives two blocks away. "He's tried to come out and make me get off my bike or he'd kill me."

Two families with children said they moved because of the boy. One family said he whipped their pit bull with a belt. Two fathers of victims said they tried to talk to the boy's father, who refused to listen.

"At least I think he did," said Carlton Gordon, who moved to another neighborhood so his three children could play outside. "Before he could say anything (the boy) comes running around the house with his belt, whipping it at me, so I had to run and hop over the fence to get away."

Anthony is afraid to go out unless he is with his older brother or sister, who also have been attacked by the boy.

He stood on the porch and watched the youngest suspect walk up the street with his toy.

The toy now was a weapon.

"Golf balls hurt," Anthony said.

Rocky Mountain News
December 19, 1993

She's Here Because Her Mother Loved Her

DENVER — The baby was in the bassinet, doing what babies do, and the father was trying to figure out what fathers do.

Elizabeth is six weeks old, and Tuesday morning she was acting her age. Maybe seven weeks. John Eger picked up the stuffed Miss Piggy with the sales tag still on it and made the noises Miss Piggys do.

It worked.

"I wonder sometimes, are you wondering why your mother isn't here?" he said. "I know you're a baby. But I'm 41 years old, and I wonder why, too."

Elizabeth was born Aug. 31, five weeks premature. Melissa Smart died of breast cancer 18 days later. The mother had decided the baby would live.

It meant the mother wouldn't.

"I look at Elizabeth and see her mother," he said. "I think about what I'll tell her about her mother. I'm afraid she'll feel she's why her mother isn't here, and I'll tell her she's here because her mother loved her.

"It works both ways — when she's quiet I think maybe she's feeling sorry for me.

"And when she cries, I have to remind myself that babies are supposed to cry sometimes."

They found out Melissa was pregnant in March.

In June, she told her obstetrician about the lumps on her neck. The doctor was telling her she could abort the baby and have radiation, chemotherapy, Taxol....She said, "Well, I'm having the baby, and then we'll worry about that."

Elizabeth was born five weeks premature, 2 pounds, 13 ounces, in Presbyterian / St. Luke's Medical Center. Melissa went back to the oncology unit. The mother couldn't leave her unit, and the baby couldn't be away from the maternity ward more than an hour a day.

"Melissa always called her Elizabeth," he said. "Maybe they didn't have enough time together to start calling her Liz or Beth, or maybe she wanted her to always be called Elizabeth. Either way, she'll be Elizabeth.

"There's so many things I never asked."

Elizabeth came home from the hospital a week ago today. A spiral notebook is a log of every time she has been fed or cried or had her diapers changed, because it seems like something that should be written down. He is on page 173 of *Your Premature Baby*.

"When Melissa and I talked about having our first child, I never said anything, but I couldn't imagine changing diapers," he said. "She would have laughed, and now it's all right. It means she had a movement.

"Of course, I never thought I'd call it a 'movement,' either."

She weighs 5 pounds, 6 ounces and is healthy. She goes to day care while her father goes to sell used cars at Lakewood Fordland. On Tuesday morning, he would be late for work, spill Enfamil formula on his pants and forget his tie.

He is getting used to being a father.

"They grow up too fast," he said. "I don't know that for a fact, of course, but I look at her and think it. Not yet, but give me a couple of years."

Rocky Mountain News
October 18, 1995

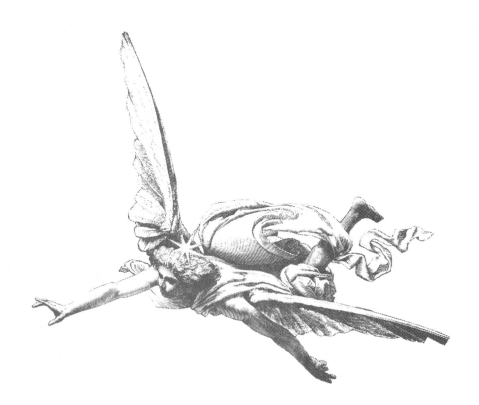

The Civil War

NEW IBERIA, La. — At 4 o'clock on Tuesday afternoon, he is the only one on the school playground.

He lives two blocks from here, and he comes here every afternoon since his family moved here from Baltimore. He is in the fifth grade, where they have just finished the Revolutionary War and are about to start on the Civil War, he says. He already knows all about those wars and what started them.

I don't even have to ask.

"You know what started the Civil War?" he says. "We haven't started it in school yet, but I already learned it in Tacoma. Slavery. Did you know slavery is what started it all?

"I already learned it in Tacoma, so now all I got to do is learn it all over again here."

Tacoma, Wash., was where he was before his father was transferred here. Since he started the first grade his father has been transferred from Little Rock to Tacoma to Baltimore to here. They have been here since last August. They probably won't be here very much longer, he says, because his father is considering a job with another company back in Baltimore.

Anyway, since he started the first grade he has learned cursive writing and how the human body works twice, and he has missed division and which continents are in which hemispheres. In Tacoma and Baltimore he was in the fast reading group, but down here he's just in the normal group. Down here they read the same, except most of the kids in his class do it faster. He's not sure why.

He lived in Tacoma last year until they were about to begin World War I. The beginning of World War I is probably as good a time as any to move, but by the time he started school in Baltimore they were already up to John F. Kennedy. He isn't sure what happened from the beginning of World War I to John F. Kennedy.

"I know there was World War I and II, but I'm not sure what started them or how many people got killed," he says. "I don't know, it's probably going to be something that's hard to learn. I know it's not slavery or anything like that. They got rid of slavery after the Civil War."

I start to tell him to wait until he got to high school, when they teach you that it wasn't anything as simple as slavery that caused the Civil War, that what really caused it was economic factors. And if you go to college they teach you it wasn't anything as simple as economic factors that caused the Civil War, that what really started it was a lot of factors that are so complex I forget what they are. I started to tell him, but I decided not to. It wouldn't be fair.

Instead, I say, "Is it better learning it the second time?"

"Last test, I only missed one answer," he says. "My teacher said it was the best grade in the class. And she said that she was very impressed with how well I absorbed things."

"She doesn't know you already absorbed it in Tacoma?"

"No way."

He has two best friends, Chris in Little Rock and Daniel in Tacoma. In Baltimore, they were only there for four months before his dad got transferred again, so he didn't have time to make many best friends. He hasn't made a best friend here yet, although he did make friends with a different Chris. They both used to come here after school, until Chris got mad at him after the test on the Revolutionary War, when he got the best grade in the class and Chris got one of the worst.

It is one of the problems with absorbing things that way.

"They just get mad because I know more than they do," he says. "My parents tell me to not pay any attention whatsoever to them, they're just jealous. My parents say they just haven't had a chance to learn as much as me."

"It sounds like you've absorbed everything on the Civil War so far," I say. "But what are you going to do from the time they start World War I until they get to John F. Kennedy?"

He thinks about that a second. From Little Rock to Tacoma to Baltimore to here he has somehow managed to miss that part, and he knows it is coming. World War I is inevitable.

He thinks about it a second, and then he sees the solution.

"By that time," he says, "we'll probably be back in Baltimore."

The Daily Iberian
October 15, 1986

The Light Talker

NEW IBERIA, La. — Kevin Viator is trying to say what he likes to do.

He can like "the zoo," or "to ride," or "to fish" or "to walk." He is limited in what he can say he likes, but he is also choosy. He picks No. 20 on his Light Talker.

He moves his head to the left, tapping a microswitch. A red light flashes. What he likes to do appears on a screen, and a synthesized voice pronounces it.

"To eat."

Kevin nods and laughs.

He is seven years old and has cerebral palsy. He is strapped into a wheelchair. He has very few motor skills, and his speech is severely impaired.

He understands what is said to him. "Sometimes I think he even understands when we talk in French," his mother says, but he cannot answer.

He has bangs cut straight across and glasses that are strapped on, and he nods and laughs when he wants to say something.

The light talker is a small box attached to his wheelchair, directly in front of him, with 128 red lights that flash under words or phrases written above them. It is operated by a microswitch attached behind the left side of his wheelchair. The movement he has the most control over is the movement of his head to the left.

He is working on his primer in the class for the orthopedically handicapped at Dodson Elementary School, according to his teacher, Joyce Joseph. If he shows enough progress, he will be mainstreamed into the classrooms with the other students. When someone asks him if he wants to graduate from high school, he laughs and nods so hard he almost knocks off his glasses.

When he was born doctors told Curtis and Lorie Viator not to get attached to him, because he probably wouldn't live two weeks. When he survived the doctors said he almost certainly had suffered brain damage. When he was three years old he was enrolled in the Iberia Special Services Center and was put in the Augmentative Communication Program.

Speech therapy couldn't improve his speech to make him understandable. He learned sign language but doesn't have the motor skills to make definite, understandable signs. He was given a communication board with words and symbols on it and a pointer that strapped onto his head, but he couldn't control his movements well enough to point at what he wanted to say.

Fourteen months ago he was taken to Children's Hospital in New Orleans to be evaluated, according to Nannette Kibbe, a speech therapist at ISSC. He was given a microswitch and tested on a computer. They had him match colors and sounds and be a frog trying to zap flies.

He got perfect scores on every test.

He got the Light Talker last spring, and last fall he was mainstreamed into Dodson.

Terry Magar, a speech and language pathologist for Iberia Parish Schools, had never worked with a Light Talker. When she made mistakes setting it up, he would shake his head and use his eyes to tell her what to do.

He can't take the Light Talker home at night, because it might get damaged on the bus. When Kevin wants to say something to his parents, they guess, and he nods when they get close. They keep guessing, getting closer each time he nods, until he nods and laughs.

When he isn't in his wheelchair he gets around by lying on his back and pushing himself with his feet. He likes to watch other children color in coloring books. When the "Raise your hands if you re sure" deodorant commercial is shown on television, he raises his hands.

He can dress himself. He lies on the sofa and struggles like a person trying to get out of a straitjacket. It takes him an hour, sometimes an hour and a half.

Their telephone has a speed caller, which dials a phone number by pushing one button. About two weeks ago Kevin pulled the phone cord until the phone fell to the floor and pushed the number three button. It dialed his grandmother, Louise Viator.

She answered. When nobody answered she was about to hang up when Kevin laughed. She talked and he laughed.

Curtis, an unemployed roofer, and Lorie are trying to get a Light Talker — everything costs just under $4,000 — so Kevin can talk to them at home.

Kevin has learned parts of four overlays, about 350 different words and phrases. The Light Talker has lights for 128 words or phrases listed on each overlay, and the capacity for 99 different overlays. That gives him 12,672 choices.

After he says he likes to eat, Dennis Duhon, the paraprofessional who is working with him, asks him if he likes to eat vegetables.

Kevin goes straight to No. 54.

Yuck!

The Daily Iberian
May 1, 1987

Chapter three

Spice of Life

"**He was** rumpled. He was sweet. He was innocent. And nobody listened like Greg. He became a friend from the first day I met him. I just wanted to take him home and adopt him."

EDIE MARKS

Queen Bee

DENVER — Edie Marks just missed her turn.

She is driving her new Jaguar down Belleview Avenue to show a client a home in Cherry Hills, talking on the car phone, writing down the message on her pager and trying to eat a McChicken sandwich. She bought the Jaguar for $46,000 on her 25th wedding anniversary, so it is silver. It has a speaker phone.

"It's not 200K," she says. "It's Zook, Z-O-O-K, the name of the builder. It's $795,000."

She looks in the rearview mirror at the turn she just missed, dials the telephone without looking and accelerates. The license plate says EDIE 1. The phone bill for the car is $750 a month.

A fire truck passes in the other direction, which reminds her that, as chairman of the Castlewood Fire Department, she has to sign some papers.

"I know a faster way. Not you, Ralph," she says to the lender she is talking to. "We're going to have to go through the whole process."

She hangs up and reaches into the back seat for the leather-bound desk book she uses to keep track of her appointments.

Edie Marks, 48, has been one of the most successful real estate agents in the Denver area for 14 years. She and her husband, Mort, have become two of the most powerful people politically and socially in Arapahoe County. She has gone from teaching third graders with behavioral problems in the Bedford-Stuyvesant section of Brooklyn to never being able to turn on the stereo in her Jaguar.

Which brings up the question: What do you buy 300 people for Christmas?

"Desk books," she says. "What do you think about getting some people leather-bound desk books for Christmas?"

She gets 40 to 50 messages on her pager a day, electronic voices that tell her what she has to do, so driving around with her is like being inside a Nintendo game. She has dislocated her shoulder three times reaching into the back seat for her desk book. The car phone has call waiting.

"The view, it's magnificent," she says two calls after Ralph. "It's just priceless."

Four-point-two percent of priceless won't make a down payment on a Jaguar, but she sees Mort in the next lane in his Olds Cutlass.

They roll down their windows.

"The market's up 100 points," he shouts.

"Pick up the sign on Kearney," she shouts.

He turns, and three calls later she pulls up in front of the house. She takes her first bite of the McChicken sandwich. She is three minutes early.

She points at the two gold and diamond bees she always wears pinned on her dress.

"Because of its size and shape, aerodynamically a bee shouldn't be able to fly," she says. "But it doesn't know any better, so it does."

Of course, most people who don't know any better can't afford Rosenthal bees with 23 diamonds each, but right now the phone is ringing.

Jane and Steve Flechner of Harrison, N.Y., bought the house with the priceless view. It is in Cherry Hills Farm. Marks also was the seller's agent.

"Our neighbor in Harrison told us about Edie, so we called her and she told us she had a wonderful house we had to see," Jane Flechner says. "After I got here, I was riding in a taxi, and when I mentioned to the cab driver we were moving he says, 'I know the best real estate agent in town. Edie Marks.'

"So then I'm in the gift shop at the Westin (Hotel), and the person who worked there asked me what I was doing in Denver. When I told her we were moving here, she says, 'Everybody knows the best real estate agent in town is Edie Marks.'

"Then I was buying something in a clothing store in Writer Square, and somebody saw that I was from New York. When I said we were moving here, they said, 'If you want the best real estate salesman in town, call Edie Marks.'"

The Flechners bought the first house she showed them.

Marks has sold real estate for 14 years, and every year she has been in at least the top five in sales in the Denver area. She sold a house in Cherry Hills Farm for $1.76 million and now has Lucy Dikeou's Polo Club house on the market for $2.4 million.

She makes more than $300,000 and sells an average of 60 houses a year for Dawson & Co.

Most real estate agents cannot handle more than 40 houses a year over a long period of time, says Carl Otto, a real estate analyst in New York.

"The pressure and the amount of time almost always take their toll," he says. "For someone to maintain a pace like she has for as long as she has, it takes a very unusual person."

Marks can be "overbearing," "pushy" and a "publicity hound," according to several realtors who asked to remain anonymous.

"Of course," she says.

John Nelson of Perry & Butler Realty and a member of the South Suburban Board of Realtors, sometimes goes with her on showings to watch because she is the best he ever has seen at that.

"I was at an open house in Piney Creek that backed onto a really busy street, and I was watching to see how she handled it," he says. "She said it was a real plus, because it didn't back onto any nosy neighbors. She had me believing that since it backed onto a busy street they were better off.

"The thing that made it work is that she really did believe that."

She grew up in Brooklyn, the daughter of a truck driver, graduated from Brooklyn College with a degree in psychology and got a job as a teacher for third-grade students with behavioral problems in Bedford-Stuyvesant. It was the last step before they were expelled from the system. Her first day, a boy broke a bottle and chased another student with it.

She made all of the students be silent during lunch. She stood on a table in the lunchroom with a megaphone. She would praise the ones who stood quietly in line or ate all of their food.

"At first, they would look up at you, and their eyes would be like razor-blade slits," she says. "They already knew they were bad, so it meant so much to them to hear when they were good. It has been 25 years, and I have never had a feeling like I had when I would see them soften and open up."

She and Mort were married in 1965. He had a degree in economics and another in engineering from Columbia. He and a partner renovated and rented low-income housing. They had two daughters, Lori and Elise, and made a comfortable living.

In 1969, some of his buildings were burned out in riots.

They decided to move to Denver to raise their daughters. Edie was a part-time interior designer and part-time lobbyist for the conservative suburban women's group Common Sense. Mort invested in commodities.

In 1972, when the Soviet Union bought one-fourth of the wheat grown in the United States, Mort was short on wheat. Over 17 days, they lost almost everything but their house and car.

"That's a feeling that never leaves you," he says. "You look at things differently after something like that."

They decided Edie should get a full-time job.

The only thing she knew about real estate was that they had trouble paying their mortgage, but she took classes and got a license to sell real estate. Dawson and Co. hired her. Right off, she decided to have an open house.

"The problem was, she didn't realize they were having a Super Bowl that day, too," says John Dawson of Dawson and Co. "We told her nobody looks at houses when there's a Super Bowl. She said she'd turn on a television, and if anybody was really interested in buying, they'd be there.

"Well, she sold that house that day."

She got into politics in 1973 when she became the Arapahoe County chairwoman in the campaign to approve the Poundstone Amendment, which halted Denver's expansion. Since then, she has served on committees for just about every major disease and Republican cause. She is chairwoman of the Castlewood Fire Department, a Republican committeewoman, a member of the board of directors at the Metropolitan Club and chairwoman of the corporate fund-raising committee for the Cancer League of Colorado.

When she heard this story would appear in *Sunday Magazine,* she got Stevinson Jaguar to donate $500 to the Cancer League of Colorado.

After he got out of the commodities business, Mort started a paint contracting business and became more active in politics.

He ran for chairman of the Arapahoe County Republican Party in 1983, losing by 25 votes to former Littleton mayor Charlie Emley. When asked to congratulate Emley,

EDIE MARKS SHOWS STEVE FLECHNER
A CHERRY HILLS FARM HOME.

to show party unity, he walked up to Emley and said, "(Bleep) you."

He sold the painting business in 1984 to help Edie and to be field director of the Colorado campaign to re-elect Ronald Reagan. He was a delegate for the 1988 Republican Convention and currently is a board member of 11 county and state Republican organizations. Mort writes a weekly column in the *Greenwood Villager* on politics and anything else that needs to be addressed. Both have been leaders in the fight to keep commercial flights out of Centennial Airport.

He bought Edie's first bee. She lost it. He bought her two, in case she lost one.

He has lost everything, and he has given it all up.

"It's a complete role reversal, our marriage," he says. "It works."

The last vacation they took was 14 years ago, a Caribbean cruise she won in a drawing at a Republican fund-raiser.

She has heard all the questions about whether she is afraid of burnout, if she is afraid she is missing something and why she doesn't start her own real estate business.

"I could make more money," she says. "But there's no way I could have more fun. The trick is, everything I do now is part of my work.

"No, I guess the trick is that none of it seems like work."

When she gets home, Mort is waiting.

They live in a 4,700-square-foot home with a walkout basement in the Hills at Cherry Creek. They both are Jewish, but the second Saturday in December they always have a Christmas party at their house for 400 people. Edie is president of the homeowner's association.

The house is decorated an afterthought at a time, with paintings from charity art shows, a restored Wurlitzer jukebox, statues of clowns, an electronic player piano, a flag that flew over the U.S. Capitol on George Bush's inauguration day, an Elvis Presley decanter. There are photographs of each of them with Bush and Ronald Reagan. It says something about both of them that somehow it all fits.

Mort always waits. He cooks breakfast every morning, and they go out to eat every night. In between, they meet two or three times at the Metropolitan Club and page each other 10 or 15 times.

Sometimes, she doesn't get home until 10.

"Edie's hungry, too," he says. "I just don't understand what takes her so long. I mean, the way I put up the (for sale) signs, it's easy."

Razor-blade eyes.

They get in the Jaguar. Mort drives. They talk about Lori, 24, who sells travel packages to corporations, and Elise, 22, a senior in political science at Colorado State University who got the most votes in the student senate election.

They end up at Panda Chinese Restaurant in Aurora.

After they order, they synchronize their calendars, writing down the plays and other events they will attend between now and March. They talk about the U.S. Senate race, about the house she just sold for the bartender at their Christmas party and about their daughters. The pagers are at home.

"Do we really want two senators from the United Soviet Socialist Republic of Boulder?" she says.

"We're going to have to find somebody good to check the coats at the Christmas party," he says.

"I wish we could get this Centennial Airport thing taken care of," he says.

"I wonder how many plays we'll miss this year?" she says.

Dinner always takes two hours.

They get into the car and start home. He has to make some calls about Centennial Airport. She has to address letters to corporations for the Cancer League fund-raiser.

Right now, though, it is silent. There is no telephone ringing, no pager beeping. It is for moments like these they put stereos in Jaguars.

And then it is over.

"Potpourri," Edie says. "I've got to get out and get a wonderful potpourri for Christmas."

Rocky Mountain News
September 16, 1990

Just a Lucky Guy

DENVER — And so here he was, Brian "Kato" Kaelin, who is famous.

Being there is what made him famous, and Friday he was here being famous. He was at Denim Works at Villa Italia Mall. He was signing autographs for $10 each.

A portion of the proceeds went to the Cystic Fibrosis Foundation, and he went to Aspen.

"To my friend, T-R-A-C-I?" he said.

"No, just E-Y," Tracey Evans said. "That's so sweet. 'My friend.'"

He signed his name for people who stood in a line 100 yards long, holding red roses and signs that said things like "Kato 4 President."

His publicist stood behind him, making sure he didn't say anything about what made him famous. He was admonished by Judge Lance Ito. He cannot discuss the trial of his friend, O.J. Simpson, in the killing of his other friends, Ron Goldman and Nicole Brown Simpson.

For example, on a KBPI-FM show Friday morning, a man had asked Kaelin, "Does Marcia Clark wear undies?" Kaelin

Ellen Jaskol/Rocky Mountain News

KATO KAELIN, FORMER HOUSE GUEST OF O.J. SIMPSON, MAKES A DENVER APPEARANCE.

looked at his publicist. His publicist shook his head, so Kaelin did not answer.

And, when a man asked who was the most famous woman he ever had sex with, he had his publicist call the woman in Los Angeles to see if he could tell. She said no. So Kato didn't answer that question, either.

He signed his name for "My buddy" David Mullen. "Did you ever think this would happen to you?" Mullen asked.

"I always knew I'd be in entertainment, but it's all up to the guy up there," he said.

He signed his name for "A real nice gal," Carrie Suello. "Your hair in real life looks just like on television," she said.

"Thank you," Kato said. "Thank you very much."

On Thursday, he filmed an episode of *Roseanne*, but somebody told him he couldn't talk about that, either. The night before that, he had been at the premiere of the new Pauly Shore movie, *Jury Duty,* which is loosely based on comedy. The night before that, he was a murder victim on *The Watcher,* which he could talk about but nobody seemed to want to.

He signed his name for "A real sweetee," Denise Schear.

"I don't think you're a moron," she said. "Really."

He came around the table and hugged her.

He was living in O.J. Simpson's guest house the night Nicole Simpson and Goldman were killed, so now he can afford his own apartment.

Now, he can drive to McDonald's in his own red Jaguar. Now, he gets $10 an autograph and won't say how much he will get by signing the back of the check from KBPI.

He signed his name for "A true friend," Susie Goldie.

"If things don't work out, you always can come and stay with me," she said.

"Thank you," Kato said. "I'm just a very lucky guy."

Rocky Mountain News
April 15, 1995

Braintown, U.S.A.

LAUGHING COYOTE MOUNTAIN, Colo. — T.D. Lingo is picking the last wildflowers of the season when all of a sudden he straightens up and says, "Click."

He is standing outside the Dormant Brain Research and Development Laboratory, 10,000 feet above sea level and, he claims, several hundred IQ points above mankind, looking down at Central City and Black Hawk.

He sticks the last wildflowers of the season into his hatband. He has spent 34 years up here trying to prove that people use only 10 percent of their brains, and says he has discovered how to click into 100 percent so he can communicate with other species, experience extrasensory perception and have multiple orgasms.

He closes his eyes and the idea comes out punctuated.

"Gambling causes individuals to click backward into his or her devolution comma reptile-brain comma killer-ape greed comma rather than clicking forward into his or her 100 percent creative intelligence comma galloping galaxies and licking the cosmic lollipop period," he says.

He opens his eyes and puts his hat on his head. "See?"

The Dormant Brain Laboratory is seven cabins arranged, one afterthought at a time, on 250 acres. Lingo lives on vegetables and vodka. He goes down to Black Hawk once a month to pick up groceries and his mail, after he clicks down to using 10 percent of his brain.

T.D. LINGO OPERATES THE DORMANT BRAIN RESEARCH CENTER ON LAUGHING COYOTE MOUNTAIN.

Dennis Schroeder/Rocky Mountain News

He has just finished the book that will sum everything up in chapters with titles like "Quick/Easy Neurology" and "Quick-Fix Nirvana."

"It's going to be a national bestseller," he says. "Even my mind has trouble comprehending it. Black Hawk is going to be known as Braintown, U.S.A."

Lingo grew up in Chicago, fought in World War II and killed a German old enough to be his grandfather, he says. After the war ended, he went to the University of Chicago and three other universities he will not name. At all of them, he asked, "Why must I kill my brother?"

A professor at the University of Chicago told him the answer was inside the brain, not the classroom. He gave himself the names Theocharis Docha Anthropotis Lingo, which he says means "The love of God and the spirit of mankind." He became Lingo the Drifter, a folk singer with three chords and nine songs.

He got on *You Bet Your Life* with Groucho Marx in 1957, wearing buckskins and the hat he still wears, and won $16,000. He cashed his check into small bills that filled two shopping bags and gave one to the Internal Revenue Service. He hitchhiked back to Colorado and bought Laughing Coyote Mountain.

Of course, most of his theories are contradicted by the accepted theories of science.

Of course, this only proves his point, he says. He mails out thousands of letters a year trying to get attention for his ideas. He has designed an entire program of brain calisthenics for anybody who writes back.

"Where did I leave my brain?" he says.

He goes inside one of the cabins. He moves boxes of books stacked on the floors. The walls are covered with writing, thoughts like "The ecstasy of daily suchness" and "Chop. Thumb. Rock. Eyes. Yapple."

"Damn if I know what I was thinking when I wrote that," he says. "Must have been drunk..."

Finally, he opens a metal box and takes out a specimen jar. The object inside is dry and white because somebody spilled the formaldehyde. He takes the object out.

It is the brain of the professor at the University of Chicago who told him the answer was in the brain, he says. "Right there. That's exactly where that idea was that's going to change the world. Brilliant...

"For a professor, I mean."

He puts the brain back in the specimen jar, back in the box, back behind the other boxes.

He walks outside and closes his eyes.

"Click," he says. "One-hundred percent brain evolution is ultimate life-meaning comma clicking out of brain chow mein comma spontaneously playing ping-pong with the life force period."

He opens his eyes and smiles.

"It's beautiful," he says. "It's like wildflowers."

Rocky Mountain News
September 26, 1991

Hell Hello Hellow again, Greg! Your excellently acerbic profile of this

wild mountain man triggered mail response avalanche: "Kiss those freedom mountains

for me Mister Natural Animal!" Soh soh Brother Gregorie, shall we re-start ethical

healing of crashing America the Beautiful? Unto thee in gleee.

— T D

Jailbird Bruce Not Crying in His Milk

DENVER — Going into the 19th hour of his jail house fast Friday morning, Douglas Bruce wanted everybody to know he still is drinking his milk.

He was in the visiting room at the Denver City Jail, serving 15 days for contempt of court. He has spent the past 10 years fighting government. Now, he is its guest.

"It's not really a hunger strike," he said. "I just don't trust what they might put in my food. But just because I'm in jail, don't think I'm going to stop drinking my milk."

In a cell between inmates facing charges of cocaine possession and wife-beating, Bruce added by one to the problem of jail overcrowding.

Of course, he always has had contempt for anybody who doesn't agree with him, but this time it was a judge. Fifteen days flat time. He was sentenced by Judge Celeste C de Baca, and he says it was because he is Doug Bruce.

Because he is Doug Bruce, he can't see it any other way.

"The guys I've met in here so far don't know who I am," he said. "They say they're in for beating their wives or drunken driving, and I say I'm a political prisoner. They just get a quizzical look on their faces."

He wrote and got voters to pass Amendment 1, which says they get to decide whether they will pay more taxes, and he is working on more tax-limitation proposals.

He was convicted July 19 on charges that he had not repaired a roof damaged by a fire in a rental duplex he owns in Five Points. He represented himself. At one point, the judge sustained 50 consecutive objections by the city attorney.

He got a 30-day deferred sentence on the original charge.

Rick Giase/Rocky Mountain News

DOUGLAS BRUCE SITS IN A VISITOR'S CUBICLE IN DENVER CITY JAIL.

Then C de Baca called him "continuously offensive" and sent him to jail for contempt.

"I'll learn a lesson," Bruce said. "But not the lesson they want me to learn."

He was handcuffed and brought to jail. His belt, watch, wallet and 64 cents were taken. He got a cell to himself and tried to sleep in the clothes he wore to court.

He was allowed to have a copy of the New Testament.

"I read Matthew, that part about the righteous who get persecuted," he said. "That helped a little, me being in that situation."

Since he's Doug Bruce, a judge had to postpone a hearing in federal court to appeal another conviction on charges of maintaining a dilapidated and unsafe building. He has a hearing on the 16th with the secretary of state's office on a petition proposal for another tax-limitation amendment. And he has a hearing on the 17th on a charge that he has a cracked sidewalk in front of a house he says he doesn't own.

He doesn't know how he will deal with those hearings from jail.

"There's not much to do except think about what they're doing to me, unless I can find somebody who plays chess," he said. "I could do push-ups or sit-ups. But then I'd get stinky, and, of course, I don't want to take a shower....

"At lunch, I did trade my apple to another prisoner for an extra milk, so I'm learning something."

Rocky Mountain News
August 5, 1995

He saw the person

behind the story,

not just the chance to

pounce on something.

Douglas Bruce

Tutu James Waskosky

DENVER — James Waskosky performed a pirouette in his tutu on his roller skates Thursday afternoon on East Colfax Avenue, and East Colfax Avenue performed for him.

Daya Winger dropped a forkful of Caesar salad in her lap in York Street Cafe when she realized what she had just seen. By that time, he was doing a split while Stan Meinenger stopped his car in the left lane in front of Walgreen's to get his camera out of the glove compartment. By that time, he was gliding backward with his arms arched over his head in front of The Upper Cut while Dan Kassenbaum walked into a parking meter.

"I like people watching," Waskosky said later. "I really like people watching people watching me. I'm not sure that makes sense, but who cares?"

Glenn Asakawa/Rocky Mountain News

JAMES WASKOSKY CATCHES THE EYE OF PASSERSBY AS HE SKATES DOWN COLFAX AVENUE.

Waskosky goes out most days around noon down the north side of East Colfax, because that's where the sun shines, and skates for two or three hours around Capitol Hill and downtown.

Besides a different tutu every day, he wears mirrored sunglasses that reflect the mirrored windows of the office buildings that reflect him. He wears radio headphones tuned to country, rock or classical. He wears silver lipstick that matches the chrome on the bumper of the 1964 Impala that just honked at him.

He is unemployed, trying to decide what he wants to do with the rest of his time. He used to sew upholstery and clothing.

He decided he needed a change that involves more than different clothing.

"I don't want to be a girl, I don't want to be a drag queen," he said. "I want to be me. Whoever that is."

He grew up in Billings, Mont., and started to skate 12 years ago when he rented a pair while he was visiting his son in Spokane, Wash. He skated around Billings in shorts and a headband. Sometimes, he would get up at 4 a.m and skate for the mannequins.

In 1988, he left Montana for Santa Barbara, Calif., and left sweat bands and shorts for everything else.

"A girlfriend got me started into leg-warmers and bandannas, and from there it just kept going," he said. "By now, I probably have enough that I could wear a different outfit every day for three months. I've got to get more."

Waskosky came to Denver for his 40th birthday in February and decided to stay. He started skating in sweats so he could get used to Denver and Denver could get used to him. It probably is more than a coincidence that he was staying near Colfax.

He buys his outfits in thrift stores and modifies them.

The only problem he has had was when a police officer stopped him and said he would be responsible if anybody driving past got in an accident because they were watching him.

"I said, 'I drive a car, and if I see a woman with big breasts it's my responsibility to pay attention to my driving,'" Waskosky said. "So anybody driving should worry about driving first. That's what everybody should do.

"No, what they really should do is pull over and watch me."

Rocky Mountain News
May 15, 1992

The Coffee Lady

DENVER — The No. 48 bus came down Brighton Boulevard to downtown Denver, and Donna Gunnison sat in her seat saying, "Mr. Biggley, der wienerschnitzel tomorrow?"

She changed the phrasing of "der wienerschnitzel." She frowned, she shook her head, she smiled. She acted.

She had an audience.

"People look at me, and I say, 'I'm the Coffee Lady,'" she said. "Some still don't understand. So then I tell them she was created specially for me."

She is one of the 25 people in the Physically Handicapped Amateur Musical Actors League who rehearsed five nights a week for two months to perform *How To Succeed in Business Without Really Trying* at the Space Theatre. She is one of the 360 people in Colorado who have been diagnosed with Prader-Willi syndrome, a genetic disorder that causes compulsive eating and affects the nervous system. She is the Coffee Lady.

"I'm a very intelligent person who cares a lot and really wants to reach out to people," she said. "I'm just the Coffee Lady, but I know everything that's going on in the World Wide Wicket Co. If people would take the time to get to know me, they'd see I'm a very special person, but most of the other characters just look at me as the Coffee Lady."

She just got off work at Rossi's Catering. She also works Friday mornings at Target as a receiving clerk's assistant, getting shoes ready for display. She is 40 and has lived alone for nine years, five blocks from her parents.

"My other lines are 'Early in the week?' 'Hey, guess what? There's no coffee,' 'Look like yesterday's goulash,' and 'Coffee, tea or me?'" she said. "The 'coffee, tea or me' one I came up with myself."

This is her fourth PHAMALy production. She has taken acting lessons. Her performance has been singled out in reviews each year, and for this production *Rocky Mountain News* critic Jackie Campbell called her "PHAMALy's secret weapon."

There wasn't a Coffee Lady in the original script, so she was created for Gunnison.

"You want to know what's funny?" she said. "I'll tell you what's funny. The first time people laughed, I wondered why everybody was laughing at me.

"Then I realized it was because I'd said something funny."

She would get off the No. 48 bus at 16th and Champa streets and walk to the theater. She would sit on a bench and read her script for an hour until the theater opened. She would change from her white skirt, white blouse and pink socks into the white skirt, white blouse and pink socks of the Coffee Lady.

She would go on stage, and everybody would laugh because she'd said something funny, because she is the Coffee Lady.

"Sometimes, when I'm going down there, I think about how she got to be the Coffee Lady," she said. "I think about how special she is. I just hope I'm a good enough actor to show people who the Coffee Lady is."

Rocky Mountain News
July 30, 1995

The Opportunity of a Lifetime

DENVER — John Bobbitt was standing at the urinal Thursday morning, and all of sudden he realized the implications of what he was doing and stopped.

"You don't have a camera or a tape recorder, do you?" he said. "Promise? Janet wouldn't like that."

Bobbitt was in Denver on his national tour of FM radio stations to discuss his penis. It was cut off by his estranged wife and reattached by doctors, making him more famous than anything he could have done himself. Janet Fallon is his publicist and she controls just about everything in his life these days.

Still, now we know Bobbitt can control at least one thing.

"Thanks for not filming this," he said. "Janet will be relieved."

Bobbitt, 26, and Fallon arrived at 7 a.m. at KRFX 103.5-FM, where the deal called for three hours with Rick Lewis and Michael Floorwax, who would have been making jokes about somebody's penis, anyway.

Over three hours, he revealed on the air that he never wears underwear, that he immediately called his mother the first time he got an erection after the operation, and that he tried to have sex since then but couldn't.

Off the air, Fallon revealed something he sometimes forgets.

"Johnny doesn't do newspaper or television reporters," she said.

Fallon has worked for Bobbitt since December, and Denver was the ninth city on a tour scheduled to include 25 to 30 FM stations. She is behind the "John Wayne Bobbitt's Severed Part — Love Hurts" t-shirts. She is talking about book and movie deals.

She wouldn't say how much Bobbitt gets paid for this, but Bobbitt forgot he doesn't do newspaper or television reporters and said he might be able to pay off the $250,000 legal fees and about $340,000 in medical bills he owes.

"I'll probably come out OK," he said. "All I want to do is get attached to Mrs. Right. Get it?"

A caller to the radio show asked if he had any advice for other men since Lorena was found not guilty by reason of insanity last week in Manassas, Va.

He said Lorena is "evil" and will hurt another person until Fallon handed him a note. The note said, "Advice: sleep on stomach." He said, "Yeah, I sleep on my stomach."

His own lawyer regularly says in interviews that Bobbitt "is not very bright," which might help to explain the $250,000 in legal fees.

After the radio show, he went to Soapy Smith's Eagle Bar as part of the deal with KRFX and autographed cans of Vienna sausages, Twinkies, steak knives and a banana for men and women.

He forgot again and told a newspaper reporter he hopes to move to Colorado from Niagara Falls, N.Y., that he has a girlfriend in Colorado Springs, and that he wants to learn to fly helicopters. He said every man should read the book *How to Satisfy a*

Woman Every Time... and Have Her Beg for More! by Naura Hayden because it works for him. He said most John Bobbitt jokes are funny, although he can't remember them.

"I never was very good at remembering jokes."

He and Fallon left in the afternoon for Kansas City.

He wasn't sure where he would go from there.

"To tell you the truth, it doesn't really matter," he said. "I mean, how many people get an opportunity like this?"

Rocky Mountain News
January 28, 1994

JOHN BOBBITT DOES DENVER.

Linda McConnell/Rocky Mountain News

The Black Avenger

DENVER — Listen to Ken Hamblin:

"I chose the music to lead into me," he says to the board operator. "It's Handel. It's me."

It is two minutes to 7 Tuesday morning at KNUS-710, the first show since Hamblin was suspended. He goes on the air at 7. He just walked in.

"What you've got to understand is that my obligation is to be fully aware that I am an American hero," he says to the producer of the crew filming the show for *Eye to Eye With Connie Chung.* Seven U.S. Postal Service tubs of mail are waiting for him, mostly letters from people who want his "Certificate of Absolution from White Guilt."

"I got a minute and 15 seconds?" he says to the programming manager. "That ought to be long enough for a colored guy to tinkle."

One minute and 10 seconds later, he is walking back from the restroom to the studio to do his first show since he was suspended after a co-worker accused him of harassment.

He hears Handel.

"There's my cue," he says to nobody in particular. "The Messiah."

Listen to Ken Hamblin:

"I've got seven tubs of mail here, but you won't hear about this in *The Denver Post* or the *Rocky Mountain News,*" he says to the audience of "The Ken Hamblin Show." "You don't hear about any of the good things that are happening, because I'm persona non grata in the Denver media."

He has been featured this month on C-Span and *Today,* and he is scheduled to appear on *Good Morning America, Montel Williams,* National Public Radio and *Eye to Eye with Connie Chung.* He just signed with the Fox Network to do a commentary on *The Front Page* Saturday nights. He agreed last week to write a column for *The New York Times* syndicate in addition to the two he writes every week for *The Denver Post.* He is considering offers from publishers to write a book, although he isn't sure what it would be about.

All this has happened since — and probably because of — an unsuccessful attempt last month by the National Black Caucus of State Legislators to get the Federal Communications Commission to take him off his 7-to-10 a.m. show on 5,000-watt KNUS.

Now, at 53, he is "a player in the national game," a "darky in the spotlight" and "the new voice in the crusade for truth, justice and the American way," and those are only some of the ways he describes himself.

Listen to Ken Hamblin:

"I can't remember the last time I did something that was wrong," he says. "The last time I did something stupid was Dec. 31."

He has been charged with harassing Karen Kennedy, a KNUS news anchor, on New Year's Eve in the reception area of the KNUS offices. She told police he held her down for two to five minutes, simulated a sex act and said, "Oh, baby!" He says he grabbed and kissed her but did not hold her down.

He is charged with misdemeanor harassment.

KNUS suspended him for four days for naming Kennedy as the alleged victim on the air before police released the report. *The Denver Post* suspended him for four columns.

At least four women who know Hamblin say he regularly makes remarks that could be called offensive, but they consider it to be more Hamblin than harassment.

"That's just Kenny," says his producer, Cecily Baker. "If somebody else did some of the things he does, I might think he was a wise guy or even be offended, but that's just Kenny."

Listen to Ken Hamblin:

"I've marched and sung *We Shall Overcome*," he says. "I've worked to register black voters. I've fought the power, and I'm the proudest black man you'll ever see. Make that the proudest colored man — we were nicer when we were colored."

Hamblin grew up in the Bedford-Stuyvesant section of Brooklyn, raised by his mother after his father left. He graduated from high school and went into the Army. He had spent all his life in a predominantly black neighborhood, so it wasn't until he was in the Army that he first recognized racism.

He was in a diner in Clarksville, Tenn., when a waitress said, "We don't serve niggers." He said, "I don't eat niggers, but can I have some service?"

After the Army, he worked as a clerk, a typist and a freelance photographer in New York. He got married, had a son and a daughter and divorced. He became the first black photographer for the *Detroit Free Press*.

He married the consumer columnist at the *Detroit News*, who is white, and they moved to Summit County.

He started at KOA in 1982. Since then, he has worked, in order, at KOA, KNUS, KUVO, KNUS, KUVO and now KNUS for the third time. He has been fired twice and quit three times, always for "philosophical differences."

In that time, he has moved politically from the left to the right, skipping the middle.

"Maybe what I've done is panicked," he said. "Because, instead of listening to me, these poverty pimps, these quota blacks, these liberal egg-sucking dogs have decided to do nothing."

Listen to Ken Hamblin:

In three hours on the air, he uses the phrase "quota blacks" nine times and says "egg-sucking liberals" seven times, not including the time he uses it in a commercial for Qualite Pistol & Revolver. He attacks the media 17 times and calls himself an "American hero" four times. He refers to himself as "colored" six times and as "black" 13 times, not including the seven times he calls himself "the Black Avenger."

In between, he talks to 12 callers. The main subject of seven of the calls is race. Five of the callers identify themselves as black, with three supporting him and two disagreeing with him.

A monologue that lasts four minutes and 47 seconds and touches on black leaders and liberals "making unlubricated love" to the United States, elephants eating overripe fruit, "the weenie roast in Waco," and "what cats do best in a litter box" is prompted by a caller's saying, "Yeah, but..."

While most people speak in words and phrases that might lead to complete sentences, Hamblin speaks in chapters. He goes to a break in the middle of a monologue about Jesse Jackson because he forgets to breathe and feels lightheaded. Nothing he says is planned.

For him, there is no difference between doing a talk show and doing lunch.

"I am my work," he says. "My work is me. I don't have to think about what I'm saying, because I just say what I'm thinking."

At 9:15 a.m., a photographer from the *Rocky Mountain News* comes into the studio to take the picture of Hamblin and his seven tubs of mail that appears on this page.

You won't hear about this on *The Ken Hamblin Show.*

Listen to Ken Hamblin:

"I hear these black leaders talking about how Darktown, America, is beautiful," he says. "Well, beautiful is a river in the mountains and a rainbow trout in the sun."

He and his wife have a town home on Capitol Hill, a house in Frisco, two Quizno's Classic Subs restaurants, two Saabs and a pickup truck. He has Japanese and southwestern paintings on the walls, coffee he started the day before in the kitchen and 5,240 newspaper articles clipped and cataloged on his computer. He has two of his columns, "Ronald Reagan's Legacy to America," from *The Denver Post,* and "Please, Don't Feed the Blacks," from the *Baltimore Sun* framed and hanging on the bathroom wall above the commode.

He has taken up scuba diving, flying and riding his quarterhorse and his motorcycle.

He has given up sugar, smoking and meat, and he is trying to think of a way to give up vegetables.

Listen to Ken Hamblin:

"I've got no place to go but up," he says. "My enemies have cut the rung of the ladder below me every step up I have made. I am now in the arena where the only words to say before the last flutter of my eyelids are 'Et tu, Brute?' "

On his first day back after the suspension, four women who work at KNUS hug him.

He walks up a dark hallway, and programming director Mason Lewis says, "Good thing you're still smiling, so I can see you."

He says, "What's not to smile about?"

On the way out of the building, he meets the mail carrier. Normally, he would hug her and kiss her. This time, though, he can't because she is carrying another tub of mail for him.

Since he was accused of harassment, if he is alone in an elevator when a woman gets on, he steps off, he says.

He has received death threats for his political views.

He will not say whether he carries a gun.

"Ken Hamblin will not be a victim," is what he does say.

Once, he sang *We Shall Overcome*.

Now, most black leaders believe he is something to overcome.

Blacks criticize him for what he says.

He says things he can say only because he is black.

Either way, people listen to Ken Hamblin.

Rocky Mountain News
January 16, 1994

Reading The Vance

DENVER — Vance Johnson had just signed a copy of *The Vance: The Beginning & The End* for a woman who said she used to dream about him, then hated him and wants to read the book to decide what she will think about him now.

He sat behind stacks of autobiographies in the art history section of the Barnes & Noble on South Colorado Boulevard and waited. He asked to sit with his back to a wall in case one of the husbands of one of the women he used to know came in. He would sign 37 books for people in one hour.

He watched a man look through a book about Greek art and explained why the man didn't come over to get his autobiography.

"A lot of people, they're embarrassed to come up to me when my mugshot from the Arapahoe County Jail is right there on the cover," he said. "I don't mind. But they don't know that, so they buy the book later and don't get it signed."

Johnson, 31, has lived in Fort Collins with his third wife, Holly, and their daughter, Paris, two, since he and his $2.4-million, two-year contract were cut last month by the San Diego Chargers.

He does a sports report at 7:40 a.m. on KGLL (FM-96.1) and at 4:35 p.m. on KTRR (FM-102.5). He also sells advertising. His first paycheck was for $473.

He plans to go to court to reduce his child-support payments to the other six children he has had with five other women.

"You know, this is a new bookstore," he said. "A lot of people probably can't find it."

The other children are Nicole, 10, and Vance Jr., 8, who live with their mothers in Tucson; Vaughn, 6, and Vincent, 5, who live with their mother in Westminster; and two daughters whose names he can't remember.

"Also, people forget about books when the weather's nice like now," he said. "Except for people interested in things like art."

The Vance, co-written with Reggie Rivers, has sold about 3,500 copies, he says.

It tells about the night he got 22 or 23 phone numbers from women to win a contest with his teammate, Mark Jackson, and about the night he lost $50,000 gambling and the morning after when he had to borrow $8 to get married. It tells about the times he beat his first wife until she was unconscious and rammed his second wife's car. The appendix gives his statistics for nine seasons as a wide receiver for the Denver Broncos and a list of the 40 cars, six motorcycles and three boats he has owned.

He can remember each of those.

"I've got to cut back on these signings," he said. "I've done, like, five already. People think they can just wait until the next one."

The book also tells about how he goes to counseling, and how men have told him his story inspired them to find help. He says he has found the shy and lonely person inside. He says he has learned to stop making excuses for the things he did.

"You know why a lot of people don't come?" he said. "People haven't read the book yet. If they'd read the book, they'd know I've changed.

"If they'd read the book, they'd see that I've learned to take responsibility.

"They'd see who I am now."

Rocky Mountain News
September 28, 1994

Under the Big Top

DENVER — Erin Presley pressed a fist against the blue dot on her chin, and with her other hand she scratched her yellow yak hair.

She was on clown alley, waiting to go back out and jump out of an exploding turkey at the Ringling Bros. and Barnum & Bailey Circus. The last time out, she had shaken the hand of another clown, done a flip and landed on her back.

She is making her last appearances in Denver, through next Sunday at the Coliseum, before she retires to be a clown around Longmont.

Still, there are things clowns just don't talk about.

"Well, a lot of things happen when there's 13 clowns in a little car," she said. "But it's a matter of honor among clowns that we don't really talk about it. You don't want to ruin the illusion."

She turned 24 on Saturday, and this is her fourth year with the circus. She is four-foot-four. Her sister and parents also are dwarfs.

"I've heard people talk about that crying inside stuff with clowns," she said. "I never was that way. To me, being a dwarf just means I don't have as far to fall."

She grew up in Lewis in southwestern Colorado and moved before her senior year in high school to Longmont, where her father is a USDA turkey inspector. She wanted to be an aerialist. She worked as a magician at Elitch's, and somehow it all led to Clown College.

She became an Auguste clown, the kind with a red face and white circles around her mouth and eyes, because it fit her face and her personality.

ERIN PRESLEY AND GREG

Her wigs are made of yak hair for reasons that are obvious to anybody who has seen a yak. Her shoes are size 5EEE. Her noses are made by sticking her real nose in rubber cement to make a mold, then using a plastic compound to make a red ball.

"The thing with noses is how often they get smashed with pies," she said. "You'd be surprised what those pies can do to a nose."

For 11 months a year, she lives in a 3-foot-by-6-foot room on a train. She performs up to 16 times a week. In between, she is not allowed to go anyplace she might be recognized without her wig and her clown nose.

"That's no problem, because sometimes I put on my makeup and dress up when I'm all alone," she said. "The problem might come when I don't have any excuse to be running around like a clown."

After the last performance of the season Dec. 11 in Rosemont, Ill., she will fly home to Longmont.

She had surgery to correct bowed legs, and one knee has been bothering her. She will marry Andy Weller, who was an elephant trainer and plans to become a veterinarian.

"When he finally came up to me, he said he thought I was a showgirl because of my long blond hair," she said. "I probably shouldn't say I have long blond hair, but that's why he thought I was a showgirl. This might sound funny, but when you've been a clown for as long as I have, it's kind of neat to be mistaken for somebody else."

Rocky Mountain News
October 9, 1994

This Bud's for You, Dow Blake

BLACKHAWK, Colo. — Dow Blake walked into Crook's Palace the other night and stood at the corner of the bar where he always stands, where a Budweiser is always waiting.

Once again, he had met all of the requirements for a Budweiser. Crook's Palace, which calls itself Colorado's oldest saloon, was sold last week with the agreement that Blake gets free Budweiser whenever he comes in. The agreement is good for the rest of his life.

So far, both have kept their part of the agreement.

"I'm here, so I must be alive," he said. "So set 'em up."

Blake, 64, a retired electrician, has been coming into Crook's Palace for as long as he can remember. It is the last bar in Black Hawk and Central City where you don't have to be afraid if you go to the bathroom they'll put a slot machine in your spot. He comes in every afternoon about 4 or 5 and stands at the corner until he or the Budweiser decides it is time to go home.

"You've got to watch yourself with free beer," he said. "You start thinking the more you drink, the more you save. Pretty soon, you start thinking you're rich."

And pretty soon, his Budweiser is empty.

Steve Stone, who has been on one side of the bar or the other for the past 20 years, sets another Budweiser in front of him.

"I think I've seen Dow actually sit down a couple times, and sometimes he has to wait for a tourist to finish his beer before he gets his corner," Stone says. "Other than that, it's been pretty much the same with Dow until this happened. It's only right, since he's probably paid for the place a couple of times anyway."

Blake's house, where he has lived for 38 years, is a block and a half away. It is next door to the house where he was born. His grandfather came here in the 1870s, and his family has left enough of a mark that some people call it Blake Hawk.

He started coming to Crook's in elementary school, when draft beer was 10 cents and Billy Lannigan would forget he was blind and leave without his seeing-eye dog.

He has seen people ride their horse into the bar. He has watched Dick Hicks weave genitalia and grape vines into the paintings on the walls. He has looked out the window of his house and seen employees of Crook's shoveling his driveway so he can come down here.

"So one time, I'm standing here, of course, talking to a fella standing there," he says. "He's a fine fella, and I ask him his name. He says, 'It's Blake Dow.'

"I say, 'Blake Dow? I'm Dow Blake. We sat down and had four or five beers before we got it all squared away. What other place would you run into a fella who's got your name, only backward?'"

Rocky Mountain News
February 5, 1992

A Faint Is as Good as a Standing Ovation

DENVER — Jim Rose can eat razor blades, stick a screwdriver up his nose and let people stand on the back of his head with his face in broken glass, but he still has bad days.

He was charged with drunken driving this summer in Holland while he was on tour with The Jim Rose Circus Sideshow, although his lawyers said the Breathalyzer test was inaccurate because of the lighter fluid he uses in his fire eating. Then he collapsed with stomach cramps and internal bleeding.

"Too many light bulbs," he said this week from Seattle. "You eat too many, you feel like an inverted porcupine. You'd think I'd learn."

Rose will bring the Sideshow, a group of people who do things that would be disasters if they weren't on purpose, to the Ogden Theatre at 8 p.m. Saturday.

It is the kind of show where a person fainting is as good as a standing ovation.

"We're like the Three Stooges," Rose said. "Except the eyes really get poked."

Rose grew up the son of college professors in Phoenix, and during the summers his father once worked as a clown who insulted people while they threw balls at a target to dunk him in a tub of water.

As a boy, he would lie down and pour milk in his mouth, then let his dog lick it out. He moved to Europe 11 years ago to learn how to lie on a bed of nails, swallow razor blades and catch a bullet with his teeth. He was The Rubber Man of Venice Beach, Calif., then got off the streets by teaming up with a belly dancer in a Middle Eastern restaurant in Seattle.

Three years ago, he met Mr. Lifto, who lifts household appliances hooked to rings through 11 body parts that have been pierced, and got the idea to start "The Circus of the Scars." It has been featured on MTV and toured with Lollapalooza '92. Earlier this year, it received what might be the highest compliment for a freak show in the United States, an invitation to appear on *Sally Jesse Raphael.*

Success also has meant that Rose has had to turn down hundreds of people who wanted to join the circus, either because they can do only one trick or they bleed.

"Like, I'd be interested in having the Human Marionette, who sticks hooks through his body and lets himself be lifted and controlled by ropes, but he bleeds all over," he said. "I can't reward people for being stupid. I hope he's doing what's best for him, which is not doing what he was doing."

He did hire Matt "The Tube" Crowley, a pharmacist who got his start in bars sticking seven feet of plastic tubing up his nose into his stomach, then pouring two quarts of beer in it.

For the Sideshow, Crowley has added ketchup, chocolate syrup and Maalox, then sucks it back out.

"The audience is welcome to drink it, but I don't push it on them," Rose said. "I have an obligation to be responsible about things."

Superglue, for example. The Torture King attaches household items to his body and lets people from the audience tear them off. They dropped the part where he is glued to a board and raised to the ceiling after the time in Norway he fell 9 feet and landed on his chin.

They also had to drop the part of the act where The Enigma ate maggots that were injected with steroids to make them four times the size of normal maggots.

The Enigma can put out a blow torch with his tongue. He can start an industrial grinder and clamp a piece of metal on it so it throws off a shower of sparks, then stick his face in it until his cigarette is lit. He can lie on a bed of razor-sharp swords with a concrete block on his chest while it is pounded with a sledgehammer — something that resulted in three deaths recently in South America, Rose said.

The maggots were too risky, though.

"He was having these mood swings," Rose said. "I guess they inject them — the maggots — with steroids for (bait for) fishermen, but they're not good to eat. We don't know for a fact that it was the maggots that were causing the Enigma to get surly, but we don't like to take any chances."

Rocky Mountain News
October 15, 1993

Manley's Moderately Marvelous Martinis

NEW IBERIA, La. — When Conrad Manley retired a year ago, he wanted to do some of the things he's always wanted to do.

One of those things was to see Rome, and he just got back from a month over there with his brother, Rufus, and his sister-in-law, Dorothy. They went to see the area and take some courses on "Culture, Art and Architecture of Ancient Rome," "The Renaissance in Italy" and "Modern Italian History."

When he signed up, Conrad, who is 72, found out he wouldn't be allowed to smoke in the dining hall or on the bus. A month before he left he took a course to quit. After 57 years and about 1,185,600 cigarettes, he took that class and quit smoking.

That is the way Conrad is.

So he gets over to Rome thinking everything's going to be all right and he'd take tours and hear lectures on things like Roman architecture and the development of the modern state, and he finds out they don't know how to make a proper martini.

Losing one vice a trip is enough. Over there, they think you're supposed to pour sweet or dry vermouth in a glass. "They're very positive there wasn't supposed to be gin in it, much less as a main ingredient," Conrad says. Sometimes he'd send it back, but usually he'd drink it and try again.

That also is the way Conrad is.

"I've had trouble with martinis most of my adult life," he says. "Especially where the British have been. They leave a heritage of drinking things warm. Even beer.

"When I was stationed in Khartoum one of the first Arabic phrases I learned was *wiski bitalj*—scotch with ice. And even that doesn't always work."

By now you probably have guessed that there are all kinds of stories about martinis and Conrad.

There was the young lady who used to make casseroles for him, and when he was finished he washed the dish, filled it with martini and returned it.

And there is the story about Jim Webb, a public affairs officer in Montevideo, Uraguay, who got Conrad started with martinis 30 years ago. Webb mixed martinis by the pitcher, then filled everybody's glass so full the surface of the drink was convex above the rim of the glass. No matter how many people he served, every glass was full and there wasn't a drop left in the pitcher, Conrad says.

You get the idea.

After a few more failures in Rome, Conrad drew a diagram. The diagram showed an old fashioned glass with a line slightly below the rim of the glass to indicate the surface of the drink, and another line slightly below that to indicate the bottom of the vermouth. Beside it, he wrote, "Vermouth 10 percent." Under that he wrote, "Gin (or vodka) 90 percent." He drew an oval with something stuck through it and labeled it "Olive," and two cubes and labeled those "Ghiaccio (ice)."

That isn't the ratio for "Manley's Moderately Marvelous Martinis," the drinks Conrad mixed at home. Those are five-to-one, with a few drops of olive juice. In the right light, a Manley's Moderately Marvelous Martini has a rainbow.

But in a foreign country you have to make do. Sometimes he supervised while they mixed, sometimes they let him behind the bar to mix it himself. One bartender — the only one Conrad saw actually try the drink — had him sign the diagram to prove it was authentic, then stuck it up on the wall behind the bar.

The diagram solved most of the problems with martinis.

When they didn't feel like trying to explain martinis, he and Rufus rounded up the ingredients and made their own. In Italy it's easy to get gin and vermouth, and it became Rufus' job to get the liquor.

Because he knows a little bit of Italian, it was Conrad's job to get the ice. When he saw the Romans were having trouble understanding his Italian, he started speaking Spanish and they seemed to understand a little more.

Besides that, Conrad did a lot of things he had always wanted to do. He learned a lot about "Culture, Art and Architecture of Ancient Rome," "The Renaissance in Italy" and "Modern Italian History." He drove 200 miles to eat lunch in Budapest, and saw Pompeii and Mount Vesuvius, Spoleto, the Tivoli Gardens, the Abbey at Monte Cassino that was bombed during the Italian campaign of World War II, the Lipizzan horses and the Danube River.

It turned out the Danube is brown, not blue, and there still are times when he wants a cigarette. But other than that, everything turned out fine, Conrad says.

The Daily Iberian
June 21, 1985

GREG AND CONRAD MANLEY.

Governor Edwards — No Reservations

NEW ORLEANS — He comes out of the U.S. Court Building smiling, and they are waiting on the steps.

He is surrounded by his family and his bodyguards, and he bounces down the steps past the people who have been waiting for him. The people on the steps shout questions and aim cameras at him, needing something for the afternoon deadline. He doesn't stop.

He will only repeat. "All I can say is that everything this morning went very, very well. As you know, I'm not allowed to talk about the case, per se."

His name has been mentioned only in passing during the proceedings inside the building this morning, but he is the one they are waiting for on the steps. He is facing 50 counts of racketeering and fraud. He is the governor.

I am walking next to the bodyguard on his right, just watching.

He reaches out and shakes the hand of a baby held out by her mother. He seems to recognize a friend across the street, smiles and waves. There's nobody across the street.

The newspapers will call his mood "buoyant."

He turns right and starts down Poydras Street. The people with the notebooks, microphones and cameras run ahead of him so they can walk backward in front of him. He tells them when they are about to back into a bench or a trash can.

"Tomorrow, we'll reverse it," he says. "Tomorrow, I'll walk backward."

The group reaches Mother's Restaurant. His daughter, who sits and does crossword puzzles with her mother during the trial, goes inside and comes right back out. It's too crowded, she says. Part of the reason it is crowded, of course, is because it is full of people who are on the lunch break in his trial.

I had planned to just watch what is going on, but I don't understand this. I say "You don't have somebody call ahead and make reservations?"

He turns and looks at me. It is the first question he has been asked that he can comment on. He doesn't stop moving.

"I never make reservations," he says. "I just go."

"Do you know a good place around here? Are you from around here? What are you doing here?"

I tell him where I'm from and why I'm here. I say I spent six hours Tuesday riding the St. Charles Avenue Trolley, asking people what they think about him, and now I want to find out what he thinks. I ask him if it always like this, with people asking questions he's not allowed to answer and sticking cameras in his face.

"I've got four kids," he says, "so they aren't always around."

He stops and grabs a cameraman who is about to back in front of a car that has sped up to beat the light. I say, "Would you feel bad if somebody got injured trying to cover you?"

"Which one?" he asks.

The other reporters are getting annoyed because I'm not asking per se questions. He seems to enjoy talking about something different. He seems to enjoy asking the questions.

"What are they saying about me on the trolley?" he asks.

"To tell you the truth, governor," I say, "all but two of them said they think you're guilty as hell."

He stops and looks at me. His family, his bodyguards and the people who are walking backwards stop too. They are in front of the Royale Crown Plaza, where he has decided to eat lunch.

As a rule, this is where everybody except his family and his bodyguards rush away to meet the afternoon deadlines.

He says, "Care to join us for lunch? This is a pretty good place. We never talk about the trial during lunch."

He bounces up three flights of stairs — "He always runs up stairs," a bodyguard will say later. "You know how hard it is to keep all those reporters from falling down in front of him when he's running up the stairs?" — and enters the restaurant.

It is a buffet and he takes his place at the end of the line. When it is his turn, he puts a few pieces of lettuce on a plate, covers it with Italian dressing and hands it to a bodyguard who takes it away. He picks up another plate and looks over the entrees.

He takes two spoonfuls of something that looks like fried shrimp covered with cheese sauce and two more of something that looks like chicken covered with tomato sauce.

"To tell you the truth," he says, "I've got more worries running the state than I've got with this thing. What they did this morning was very boring, very technical. To me, it didn't really have anything to do with the guilt or innocence of the parties involved.

"How's that Brown & Root thing coming along over there?"

He walked to the back of the restaurant, looking for his family. A bodyguard chases him down and guides him to the table his family has picked out. It is near the front, next to a window.

At the table are his brother, who also has been indicted, his daughter, his wife, his sister-in-law and his niece.

They talk about his oldest grandson, who was in an accident and broke his pelvis, and about his youngest grandson, who has been put on a heart monitor. His daughter has been offered a role in another movie. Like he said, they don't talk about the trial.

All of a sudden, he tosses his napkin on the table, stands up and says, "Let's go."

On the walk back, he tells Sid Moreland IV, his executive assistant, to call Pat Norton, his secretary of the Department of Environmental Quality, and ask her to expedite something. A bodyguard appears in his Lincoln, in case he decides to ride back. He walks, stopping to shake hands with a parking lot attendant and a woman who is pushing a shopping cart full of aluminum cans.

"I'm sorry, but I don't think it's going to be any more interesting this afternoon," he says.

When he reaches the U.S. Court Building, he tells the people waiting for him that he can't comment on the trial, expect that everything's going very, very well. He bounces up the steps. A bodyguard opens the door and he disappears inside.

The Daily Iberian
October 3, 1985

Chapter four

Small Town Life

One of the first things *that impressed me about Greg Lopez,*

one of the best staff writers to walk through the doors at The Daily Iberian, *was that he wasn't*

impressed with himself.

Fresh out of college, Greg could rub shoulders with the most influential people or the

most downtrodden unfortunates and write copy doing justice to both. He never hesitated to try

something different, a new angle.

Greg was my friend, more than a drinking buddy. We went bass fishing in the nation's last

great overflow swamp here numerous times, despite the fact he wasn't a fisherman.

It was a slice of life he hadn't tried. He wanted to experience it and write about it and he

did, opening my eyes to another way of looking at the sport I love.

He touched many lives. I'm thankful he touched mine.

DON SHOOPMAN, *THE DAILY IBERIAN*

George and Annie

CYPREMORT POINT, La. — Late autumn. The last alligator of the season will be killed this morning. George Ewing, 85, has killed and skinned 12 alligators this season. The 13th will make his limit.

The boardwalk is in back, a quarter mile of warped 2-by-12s, 250 yards through palmettos, then left for another 200 yards through triangle grass. George found the boards washed up on the beach 35 years ago, so they are beginning to rot. The boardwalk leads to the marsh near Cypremort Point, where George and Annie keep the pirogues.

When it is hot, snakes basking in the sun slide off into the water, when they feel footsteps coming. This morning, it is cool, so there are no snakes. Maybe there will be no alligators in the marsh, either. Reptiles are funny that way.

The old man paddles the pirogue through the stench of stagnant water and the water lilies. Water lilies are taking over the marsh — it will take the winter freeze to kill them.

The power behind the old man's strokes is hidden. Instead, each stroke adds to make it seem you are 85 and you are still doing what you have done since you were a young man, that is how life must seem, too.

Annie is back at the house, cooking dinner. Then she will feed the chickens, cats, dog and the sow. In another month, when the cold comes, they will butcher the sow.

After Annie finishes her chores, she'll go into town to run errands and to visit with Miss Olander. She is a short, round woman with a man's haircut. She giggles a lot, and she wears bright clothes George's daughter-in-law sews for her. When she leaves, she'll leave their sign in the front door:

"Miss Annie is going to town. If you come, come on in. Papa is fishing. See you later."

The wife of George's grandson wrote that for them. It has been three years since George went to town. He doesn't remember what he went for, but it had to be pretty important.

George parks the pirogue near where he had set he first hook. You never get to know the marsh well enough to not misstep and sink to your waist in mud and stagnant water. The old man carries the .410 above his head, so it won't get wet, no matter how deep he sinks.

When he sinks to his waist, he grabs a clump of grass and pulls himself up. They are wonderful hands for an old man to have, huge and knotted. This winter while he is working his traps, the hands will freeze. They'll turn blue and he'll lose a nail, but it will almost be grown back by spring. The same will happen to his toes.

He finds the first hook. The line leads from the branch down into the water.

"Got one," George says.

He pulls on the line, and the line pulls back. He pulls until the alligator surfaces. The old man aims the .410 and shoots. The water is white with thrashing, and he aims and fires again. The water calms.

"Don't know what happened," he says, and he shakes his head. "Never took me two shots before."

Eight feet of alligator are pulled to land, and George cuts through the flesh near the end of the tail. He sticks one of the hands through the cut like a handle, and drags the alligator back to the pirogue.

He paddles back to the end of the boardwalk. From there, Annie helps drag it home to be skinned.

"Got a bird, too?" she says. "I heard two shots."

"Missed," he says. "Don't know what happened."

That afternoon, the alligator will be skinned, and the hide will be stored in salt. The skins are stored like that, a layer of salt, a skin, a layer of salt.

This year a skin will bring only $10 a foot. This will be the last year he hunts alligators, the old man says.

Annie was sitting next to George on the sofa 22 years ago. Annie's husband had died, and George's wife had died.

"Miss Annie, are you thinking of getting married again?" George asked.

"Well," Annie said, "I don't know."

"Well, George said, "if you decide to, I'm looking."

George has lived here all his life. He built this house after he got married the first time, and it probably still has the same paint. It used to be gray, maybe even white. Maybe it still has the same dented tin pans, rubber boots, brooms and mop hanging beside the kitchen door.

The Daily Iberian

GEORGE EWING, 85, MAKES HIS LIVING KILLING ALLIGATORS.

He and his first wife had 10 children. For awhile, he and his oldest son were shrimpers together, and George always said that when he retired he'd give his son the boat. When he retired, his son got the boat. Later that season, while working on a sail, his son had been electrocuted.

The rest of his children, George says, never were very interested in this life.

"But my two wives, it turned out they're exactly the same," George says. "When I married her, it was just like there was no change."

"I like a woman who wants to work in the garden, raise chickens, raise pigs, stuff like that. A country woman is what we call that."

Annie is 66 and grew up in Plaquemines Parish near Bayou Pigeon. She says she does most of the bossing around here, but he's stubborn. When they got married, they never sat down and figured out who would do what, but everything gets done. Things just worked out.

The Daily Iberian

"He'd work, I'd work," Annie says. "That's the way things go."

"You don't get nothing out of fussing at one another," George says.

You don't get nothing out of lying in bed, either.

ANNIE GOES TO TOWN.

"Sometimes when the rooster crows, I don't get up," Annie says. "I just lie awake until I figure it's time to get up."

She gets up and starts making the coffee and cooking dinner. Every day they eat two good meals, dinner and supper. They never eat breakfast.

When she makes enough noise to wake him, George gets up. He watches *Passe Patout*, waiting for the sun to come up.

"That's life for you, huh?" he says.

Now he only sets about 150 traps, where he used to set 600. Partly because when you're 85 you can't run as many traps, partly because there aren't as many muskrat, nutria and mink.

Now the animals are gone, and George's children and grandchildren, the ones in the graduation pictures on the mantel, are scattered.

"Whenever they want to find me, they know where I'm at," George says.

Every other Thursday for eight years now, Annie drives up to Lafayette for treatment — "Chemotherapy, the bad kind." She tries to catch up on whatever she has to do before she goes, because after she gets back, sometimes she feels too sick to work for a few days. A while back she asked the doctor how much longer she'd have to keep going.

"He says, 'Are you glad to be living?'" Annie says. "I say, 'Well, yeah.' He said, 'Well, then, you better keep coming.'"

Early spring. Annie is raking leaves and George is plowing when he sees the hen. The chicken is in the garden, working its way down a row of Irish potatoes.

"Damn chicken," George yells. "Grab it."

She grabs it and throws it in the pen for chickens who don't know enough not to cross Annie. Now there are two hens in the pen. Two chicken stews.

It is three weeks until Holy Week, when they will do most of their planting. On their Ibert's Mortuary calendar they circle in red the dates when they've planted, and the dates when Annie has to go to the doctor.

George will have five rows of Irish potatoes, six beds of cantaloupe, four rows of tomatoes, three rows of cucumbers, six rows of field peas, two rows of butter beans, two rows of snap beans. Annie will have a row of eggplant, a row of tomatoes, two rows each of bush and butter beans, a row of green onions, three rows of garlic. She wants to plant two more rows of bush beans, but she hasn't asked George to plow them.

"If you ask for too much, he gets grouchy," she says.

The chickens, all but two, are roaming around the yard, and the piglet is in the pen. Dinner is cooking, and Annie is finished feeding the chickens, cats, dog and the piglet. Then she hoes the garlic and checks what the hen did to the Irish potatoes. She scrapes away the dirt and there are her Irish potatoes in the dirt, pink. They will go nice French-fried with the chicken stew.

The Daily Iberian

ANNIE BRINGS HOME AN ALLIGATOR.

George keeps plowing. He moves like a man who is 85 years old, slow and deliberate. At the end of each new row, he stops, looks up at the sky, says "Phew!" and starts on the next row. Sometimes he stops in the middle of a row and takes a flat brown bottle out of his back pocket, unscrews the cap, takes a sip and screws the cap back on.

"Coffee," he says. "That's what's keeping me alive, I think.

"Every couple of hours now I have to sit down five, 10, 15 minutes before I get up and go again. Been old for about 10 years now. I don't know what happened.

"My daddy worked until he was 89 years old. I don't think I'm gonna last that long. Four years is a long time. A long time."

It takes a long time to plow another row, then he's finished for the morning. When he goes in to rest, he watches the game shows, especially the one with Bob Barker. This morning on a show called *Press Your Luck,* a woman moans after she loses $5,000 on a spin, whatever that means.

"All that money," he says, and he shakes his head. "I wonder if it's true."

They eat dinner, corn, French-fried potatoes, and fried pork, then he's out in the field.

You get some work done, but you never get it all done. The plants you want to grow, you have to water and sweat over. The grass and the weeds you have to keep plowing under. Plants are funny that way.

He stops and a drop of sweat hangs off his nose. Annie finishes spreading the leaves on the rows of garlic, to keep the weeds down.

"Time to stop, old man," she says.

"How do you know it's time to stop?" he says. "If I don't plant the tomatoes now, I'll have to plant them by headlight."

Still, he stops and scrubs the tools clean with Spanish moss and rests in the shade of the yard. On summer days when the wind gauges are still, they will sit in the shade out here on homemade wooden yard chairs, weathered, and drink iced tea with visitors.

And next fall the water lilies will be back, and George will hunt alligators again.

"Well," he says. "It's like a habit, you know."

The Daily Iberian
April 1, 1984

A Heavenly Calling

STERLING, Colo. — It is white, and the first angel appears. The angel blows her trumpet. White becomes shades of white. The other angels appear, holding their trumpets, rising 11 feet from the floor.

Bradford Rhea appears with the grinder, wearing navy blue overalls, his first name stitched on the pocket.

"Wings," he says. "Wings are funny things. You start on them, and then you just see where they take you."

Three years ago, the white was a 21,000-pound block of marble in the back room of an old dance hall in Merino, 15 miles southwest of Sterling. The studio is on Main Street between Mom's Coffee Shop and a bar that doesn't have a sign. In the front room, there are plastic molds for carousel horses, a roller-coaster car that looks like a tiger and busts of Julius Caesar.

In the back room, seven angels have appeared. He has not made a sketch or a model. He has a Bible.

It is open to Revelation 8:6, And the seven angels which had the seven trumpets prepared themselves to sound.

"I just started up there on the corner," he said. "There was the first angel, blowing the trumpet. I pictured them all together, sounding their trumpets at the same time, and then I just started."

Rhea, 40, grew up in Bear Valley and went to the University of Northern Colorado to study fine arts. He took drawing and went that summer to Florence, Italy, to study the marble sculptures of Michelangelo. He admired the works so much he changed his major to nuclear medicine.

He graduated in 1978 and became a diagnostic technician at Logan County Hospital in Sterling.

"I had an MG convertible and a good job and everything except something I couldn't figure out," he says. "I'd look at my life and try to see the shape it was taking. I didn't want to be 40 years old and still trying to figure out what I wanted to do."

In 1980, he quit his job, sold the MG and rode his bicycle to the Wisdom Manufacturing office in Sterling, where they make carnival rides. He was hired to design carousel horses, roller coaster cars and other things that are shiny and fiberglass. He had just started when he heard someone talking about having someone take out the dead cottonwood tree in front of the office.

After work, in light from the office windows, he carved the cottonwood. It became a mermaid with wings and a gremlin on its tail. He called it Mermoid.

He carved 15 more trees that now are around Sterling. He carved a tree into five life-sized giraffes, another into five women whose hair and gowns flow together, and another into a lamb, a lion, an eagle and an old man. He did some on commission —

a king in a milkshake for the Burger King — and the rest he gave to the city.

The city put up signs that say "City of Living Trees."

"People were calling me, asking me to carve their trees," he said. "There were a few that were still living. The idea was to create something from trees that weren't living and creating their own beauty."

The sculptures weathered. Bugs ate them. A woodpecker pecked out the right eye and the navel of the Mermoid.

In 1993, he read that the marble quarry in Marble had reopened. He drove — he had bought a 1952 Chevrolet pickup for $425 — to the quarry. He saw a block 5 feet wide, 4 feet deep and 11 feet tall.

He isn't sure why his work became angels. He doesn't believe in organized religion. He did get married and adopted his wife's 11-year-old daughter, and he thinks that might have something to do with it.

"There's this big movement about angels now, and people say, 'This is a good time to be making angels,'" he said. "I don't want to get carried away with that, to forget what this is all about. The angels are just messengers."

He borrowed money from his father to help pay $4,000 for the marble and $1,000 to haul it here.

The marble fit in the studio by a quarter of an inch.

"After the first angel, they weren't sounding their trumpets," he says. "If you read further in Revelations, they blow them one at a time, bringing down fire mingled with blood, then a great mountain burning and so on. Sometimes, you just have to wait for things to reveal themselves."

Cyrus McCrimmon/Rocky Mountain News

BRADFORD RHEA, A SCULPTOR IN MERINO, COLO., WORKS ON HIS SCULPTURE OF ANGELS.

Early in August 1993, he got a call from a woman who said she was a protocol officer for the U.S. State Department and wanted to know if he could carve a walking stick. He said he didn't carve walking sticks. She asked him how fast he could carve one.

He said, "Is this a gift?"

He figured she had forgotten somebody's birthday.

She said, "Well, I'm not really supposed to tell you this, but it's for the president to give to the pope next week."

He told her it probably would be angels. He went out behind his studio and found the trunk of a locust. The roots would be wings.

He started to carve a face and saw two faces. The faces became Jesus on the cross and Jesus rising. They reach out to each other, becoming the other.

He finished the staff the night before the president and the pope arrived. He drove to Denver. He gave it to a protocol officer and went home.

He works four 10-hour days for Wisdom and the other three days on the marble. He has most of the rough work done, hair flowing into gowns into wings. He has gone through three grinders.

He isn't sure how he will afford the diamond grinding pads he needs to polish the marble, but he did come up with the idea to sell chips off the marble as "Angel Tears" to raise money for the battered women's shelter in Sterling.

"Our purpose on Earth is to glorify the Lord," he says. "Every move is irrevocable, working on this or in life. I like that."

A year ago, he thought he would be finished in a year.

Now, he doesn't know when he will be finished. He isn't sure how he will know when he is finished. When he is, he will find out where the angels will go.

"When I get finished I'll think about what I'll do with it," he said. "It'll probably have to be someplace big, like a cathedral. Where it's quiet.

"Where you hear your footsteps echo."

Rocky Mountain News
April 16, 1995

With Greg's passing,

I feel a connection with him

through the angels.

He was a talented, caring man

and will truly be missed.

Brad Rhea

Kerrudy Lewis Is Alive and Whole

NEW IBERIA, La. — The guy in the convenience store was having trouble believing what he'd heard.

"It was bad, I'm tellin' you," he says. "From what I hear, there was blood everywhere and she was just laughin', laughin', laughin'. I heard he had it coming to him, the way he'd treated her. But that still don't give her no cause to go and do something like that..."

He is talking about Wilson "Kerrudy" Lewis and his wife, Evelyn. She cut off his male parts. Everybody in this area of Jeanerette knows about it.

The family has received flowers and sympathy cards. A relative from Alexandria called to ask when the funeral would be.

The problem is, Kerrudy Lewis is alive and whole and working offshore. He moved to Baytown, Texas, and is staying with his mother-in-law's sister. If the job works out, his wife and his four-year-old daughter will move there, too.

The rumor started about three weeks ago, after Lewis left for the job. His wife and her family say they don't know how it started, but they have tracked it as far back as a barber shop.

"When I first heard it, I started laughing," Evelyn says. "We had our fights, just like everybody else. But why would I go and do something like that?

"Then it just kept up. Women look at me funny, guys take two steps back. People started saying I made what I cut off into a trophy, and I was walking around carrying it around my neck."

Her father, who commutes to Houma, heard it where he works, and it got so bad he skipped a day. Her younger brother got in fights at his high school. Her younger sister's elementary school wanted to know what happened.

The guy in the convenience store knows all about it.

"Now it's not something a person wants to go poking his nose into," he says. "But it's common knowledge. Of course that family's gonna try and deny it, but what do you expect them to do?"

The family went to New Iberia attorney Don Fuselier when the rumor stopped being funny. He confirmed Lewis is all in one piece. He doesn't plan any legal action, because the best thing to do is to just let the rumor die.

It is dying very slowly, Evelyn Lewis says. She avoid going places. When she does go, she takes side streets.

"I tell them, 'No, I didn't do it. Do I look like the kind of person who'd do that?'" Evelyn Lewis says. "They say, 'Yeah, you did too do it.' So what's the use?"

An acquaintance said, yes, she'd read all about it in the newspaper.

A woman approached Mrs. Lewis in the supermarket and said, "It's all right what you did, honey. You got a right to do that."

People started driving down the street where she lives with her mother, stopping in front of the house. When they walk down streets in Jeanerette, people stare at her until she stares back. Men driving by shout obscenities.

"Yep," the man in the convenience store says. "It's a bad thing. But these things happen."

"I'm tellin' you," says a man who came in for a loaf of bread and three packages of lunch meat. "She didn't do it. I know for a fact she didn't."

"It was her mother..."

Kerrudy Lewis will be back in Baytown later this week. When he finds out what people have been saying, his wife knows exactly what he'll do.

"He's gonna come back and take all his clothes off to show everybody," she says. "I just know he will. That'll shut some people up."

The Daily Iberian
January 28, 1985

Yellow Jackets, Forever

NEW IBERIA, La. — Because she is so young and pretty, and because it means so much to her right now, it's a shame to see the Yellow Jackets losing. The Yellow Jackets are her team, and she is a senior, so this might be the last game.

"Omigod! Omigod!" she says after the Yellow Jackets are scored on the first time. "Oh my God! It's my last game as a senior. Oh, I'll cry my eyes out if they lose."

"How long will I feel terrible? Forever."

The student section of the Lloyd G. Porter Stadium is full of all sorts of pretty young girls and boys who for some reason or another aren't down on the field playing football. Some don't pay attention to what the Yellow Jackets do on the field, they just come to cheer.

Two rows up, a pair is cuddling.

"What's the score?" she asks.

He looks at the scoreboard. "Fourteen to zero," he says.

"Who's winning?"

"They are."

"How much time is left?"

He looks at the scoreboard. "Four minutes and 10 seconds."

"Who's got the ball?"

He looks down the field. "We do."

"Go, go, go!"

Sometimes you see a group of them pass a Coke from one to the other. They take a sip, scrunch up their faces, shiver and say, "Whooo-eeee!" Then they pass it back down.

For some, it will never be this good again. Some will try, of course — you see them come back and sit in the student section — but it won't ever be the same. You are only a high school senior once.

She has it all figured out what she'll do after she graduates. She knows where she'll go and what she'll study and what kind of job she'll get when she gets her degree. First, she'll get her own car, so she doesn't have to keep borrowing her parents' or calling friends every time she wants to go somewhere. It sounds too simple.

She has a friend who has a friend who works in a convenience store and will sell her a six pack. Three beers apiece. I have to swear to God not to tell anybody.

"My mom would kill me, and I would kill you — Oh, I'd just die!" she says, then she stops and looks down on the field at the Yellow Jackets. "Number 17, he's sooooo fine."

Three rows down a romance has just broken up, and one up and to the right, one might be beginning.

"Well..." he says.

"Yes?" she asks.

"Um...." he says.

"What?" she asks.

"Well..." he says.

Down on the field, the Yellow Jackets are scored on again. The score is 21-0 late in the first half. It's beginning to look like this might be the last game.

"Omigod! Omigod!" she says. "Oh my God!"

I ask what's so great about the Yellow Jackets.

"Are you seeer-ious?" she says.

"Well, sort of," I say.

"They're my high school," she says. "It's something to really get excited about. We're seniors, and they're the best."

"What's so great about being a senior?"

"Are you seeer-ious?"

"Yes."

"After waiting forever to be a senior, it's great to know that we're the Class of '85. We're the best class they have. Why? Because I know."

Then the Yellow Jackets are scored on again. The score is 28-0 in the third quarter and everybody knows it's all over.

"Omigod! Omigod!" she says. "Oh my God! What'll we do?"

There's a party after the game. Somebody's parents — again I have to swear to God I wouldn't tell who — are out of town. Tomorrow, a lot of the Class of '85 probably will forget about the Yellow Jackets' loss.

This spring they'll be graduated. After graduation, everything changes. Next year they'll be working or they'll be freshmen again.

And next year the football coaches will have a new group, and there will be the Class of '86.

After the game, when the scoreboard says it was 42-0, those who are left swarm the field, the ground littered with confetti and Coke cups. A senior Yellow Jacket runs off the field carrying a chunk of sod. She stands with two friends in the middle of it all, crying.

"Omigod! Omigod! Oh my God!" she says. "I told you I'd cry my eyes out. I feel terrible."

Forever, she'd said.

The Daily Iberian
November 26, 1984

Smoking Dope

NEW IBERIA, La. — Sitting at the kitchen table with a two-by-four between them, squinting at each other through a cloud of marijuana smoke, nothing happened.

After all these years wondering what some kids think is so great about marijuana and then finally trying it themselves, Louis and Harold still don't know. Louis and Harold aren't their real names. They say their kids would never speak to them again if they found out their fathers had smoked pot.

"I think Harold's second oldest daughter does it," Louis says. "Just the way she acts."

"Nah," Harold says. "She always was just a little bit crazy. But nothin' like that."

They share a house in New Iberia, since Louis' wife divorced him and Harold's wife died. Louis has two more years working construction until he's 60 and gets his pension. Harold is 58, retired with a bad leg, and he spends most of his time fishing. When they have money — generally at the beginning of the month — they have beer.

"We see all them kids running around smoking that stuff with their eyes all crazy," Louis says. "And we got to wondering what was so great about it. If there's that many kids smoking that dope, we figure there must be something to it."

"You never know," Harold says. "We figured maybe we'd get to liking that dope more than beer."

It all started when Louis brought home a marijuana plant from the Atchafalaya Basin.

He had been fishing when he came across four plants somebody had been raising, the earth around them was freshly turned. Other times when he found marijuana plants in the basin — "even if you've never seen it, you know what it is when you do see it" — he pulled them out and threw them in the water. But when he found these four plants, he pulled one and hid it in his boat under some life jackets.

For the drive home he hid it in the trunk of his car under some blankets, and when he got home he hid it in the garage behind some old cardboard boxes and the bag of empty aluminum cans. He told Harold about it and they decided to try it some day. After it was dry, they still didn't do anything with it for almost a week.

"Something like that, you don't rush into it," Harold says.

"Something like that, you're kind of afraid," Louis says.

One afternoon at the end of last month they were sitting around doing nothing, and they decided they might as well try it. Louis went out and pulled off two leaves. Harold got his pipe. They sat down at the kitchen table.

They crumpled the leaves, put them in the pipe bowl and were about to light it when Louis stopped. He went out to the garage and found a two-by-four. He brought it inside and set it across the kitchen table.

"I said if either of us starts actin' crazy, the other was supposed to hit him over the head with it," Louis says.

And they lit up.

Harold took the first puff and while he was still holding it in he whispered that it didn't taste very good. It was too harsh. Louis took a puff and agreed.

They passed it back and forth until it was gone. Then they sat there, squinting at each other through the cloud hanging over the kitchen table, waiting for something to happen.

Nothing happened.

"Right then I say to Louis, 'Let's just give this up, we're too old,'" Harold says.

"And I say, 'We've already gone this far and broken the law, we might as well go all the way,'" Louis says.

Louis got two more leaves, crumpled them up and put them in the pipe. They smoked that, and nothing happened again. For 45 minutes, they sat there squinting at each other.

They smoked a third pipeful.

The rest of the afternoon they sat there in the kitchen filled with marijuana smoke and with a two-by-four across the table, waiting for something to happen.

"I'd say, 'Do you feel anything?'" Louis says. "And he'd say, 'Nope. Do you?'"

After an hour of asking each other, they opened the door to the garage and the door to the backyard to let in some fresh air. Louis took the two-by-four back to the garage and put the stalk of the plant in the trash under some old newspapers.

"That stuff didn't do one thing, as far as we could tell," Harold says. "I don't see what all those kids see in it."

"I'll stick with beer," Louis says.

The next time he's out in the basin, he says he's going to pull out the last three plants and throw them in the water.

The Daily Iberian
May 31, 1985

A Beautiful Day

BELLEVUE, Colo. — The sun, it finally comes up and touches Bob Bland on his right cheek.

He is going to feed the turkeys. He had fed and watered the steers, sheep and chickens. He stops, sets down the bucket of feed and turns his face to the morning.

"See how it comes up over Buffalo Cliff over there about a mile to the east?" he says. "All these years, there's still nothing like a sunrise. Looks like it's going to be a beautiful day, doesn't it?"

He has been blind since 1959. He is 67, and he and his wife, Helen, have lived on these eight acres since 1961. He picks up the bucket and uses his cane to follow the wire that is seven feet off the ground, until he feels the electrical tape wrapped around it.

He opens the gate.

"That black walnut over there, 50 feet to the south?" he says. "I'm cutting weeds, smell something, and I say to myself, 'That smells like black walnut.' So I feel around until I find what I figure it is, dig it up real careful to get the roots and move it over there.

"Now look at it."

He was born with congenital cataracts and was blind until

Dean Krakel/Rocky Mountain News

BOB BLAND MOVES WITH A WALKING STICK AND GUIDE WIRES ON HIS BELLVUE, COLO. FARM.

he was three, when doctors operated on them. He grew up on a farm in Fort Collins that now is a subdivision. He could see, but he knew the way doctors performed the surgeries at that time made it likely his retinas could become permanently detached.

When he was old enough, he went to work as a clerk in a lumberyard, filling orders, making deliveries, keeping books.

He came with his church group to sing Christmas carols to the woman who lived here then, but couldn't see it because it was dark. He married Helen 45 years ago.

They had a daughter and two sons. He was taking his daughter to her music lesson on their horse, and the horse bucked.

"I hit the ground, and it was all gone," he says. "We went to doctors, even clear out to San Francisco, but there was nothing they could do back then. It's scary, going out into someplace you don't know, but now that I've got everything connected with these wires it's a easier knowing there's nothing I can do to change the way things are."

He thinks about this.

"Then again, you never get used to bumping your shins."

When the woman who lived here decided to sell the property, Helen described it to him. She described how the sun rises over Buffalo Cliff a mile to the east, how the Highline Ditch runs through it, how the 1872 homestead cabin the woman lived in needed repairs. It was the kind of place he had pictured in his mind when he could see.

He follows the wire down to the east edge of his property, and a plant brushes against his pants.

"Darned Canadian thistle," he says, and he pulls up the weed.

He built the fences, workshop and pens, laid the irrigation pipe and added to the cabin to make it a house. He set posts and ran No. 14 wire to where he had to go. No. 16 wire is cheaper, but when it breaks he has to wander around until he bumps into something he recognizes.

A hen cackles back at the chicken coop.

"Another egg," he says.

He turns right at the fence, walks a plank over a ditch, climbs over a barbed-wire fence, finds the irrigation gate and pushes down on it.

It doesn't move.

"Got to go back to the shop and get a sledge hammer," he says, and he turns to the sun. "Getting on to be about 8:30."

He built the workshop, working on the roof after the sun went down. He just got a new 10-inch table saw. He just finished eight picnic tables for his church.

"See these drawers?" he said. "How they're all tilted? But at least they're all tilted at the same angle.

"It kind of bothered me, but Helen said she likes them like that, for some reason."

After he lost his sight, Helen went to school and became a registered nurse at Poudre Valley Hospital. They took in foster children. She described their children as they grew, and then their eight grandchildren, but he still sees her the way she looked in 1959.

It doesn't even bother her anymore when she sees he has moved the pickup.

"When we first moved here, I'd stand at the window and see him doing something and wonder what in the world he was trying this time," she said. "But now he knows where everything is, because it's where he put it. Oh, there's things he can't do, but I don't want to mention them because it'll just make him try."

Still, he doesn't keep a ram with the sheep, because he can't trust one. He called an electrician to hook up the pumps for the sprinkler system he is putting in. He can't find his new sod turner.

In the afternoon, he would stand in a field until the sprinkler soaked him, to make sure the water hit where he wanted it. He would work on an irrigation pump. He would collect the eggs the hens had laid, and he will go everywhere the wires go.

He will do all of this because he can see everything is connected by more than No. 14 wire.

"My daughter, the one I was taking to the music lesson that day?" he said. "Now she teaches music to kids in Fort Collins."

When he says this, he is standing on the edge of a platform five feet off the ground, holding a rope. The other end is attached to a branch of a cottonwood over the Highline Ditch. He jumps.

He swings over the ditch and back, out into someplace he doesn't know and back.

"Remember what I said back when the sun came up?" he said. "About how it was going to be a beautiful day? I was right, now, wasn't I?"

Rocky Mountain News
July 23, 1995

Eddie's Girl

NEW IBERIA, La. — About two months ago, Eddie started acting strange.

He started coming in late at night and he seemed distracted, his mother says. She would ask him where he'd been, and he'd just mumble some excuse. She'd ask him what was wrong, and he'd just say it was nothing.

She didn't know what to do, because Eddie is 42 years old.

"All I did was worry to myself," she says. "It was sort of like what you see is what happens to a young person when he's on drugs, except Eddie says just a sip of alcohol and he gets sick to his stomach. I never had to worry about Eddie about anything, thank God, until this time."

This time, all she could do was worry.

Eddie is a foreman for a construction company. He has worked there for the past 17 years, and the bad habits of the other workers never rubbed off on him, his mother says. He always just did his work and came home.

At home, he'd work on his car, a 1981 Buick Skylark that hasn't run right since he bought it, or he'd work in his mother's garden or they'd watch television together. Except when he went to visit his friend, Alton, he generally stayed home. Since his father died 11 years ago, it has been Eddie and his mother.

She used to wonder out loud why her son couldn't find himself a "nice girl." About 10 years ago he came home after work one day and told her about this girl named Cecilia. His mother asked him to invite her over to dinner, and Eddie said Cecilia was an airline stewardess and she was almost always flying somewhere.

Finally, he said she'd died in a plane crash.

Since then, Eddie had never mentioned anything about any girl. His mother eventually stopped bringing up the subject, except sometimes when they were watching certain television shows. She had almost given up.

And all of a sudden he started acting strange.

Almost every night after dinner he'd leave, saying he was going over to see Alton. She worried about the way he was acting, but she managed to keep it to herself for almost two months. Then one night she called Alton's house to see if he could pick up her medicine on the way home.

Alton said he hadn't seen Eddie for three weeks.

She didn't say anything to Eddie that night, or the next night, or the night after that. The fourth night, she decided to confront him. When Eddie came home at 10 o'clock she said there was something they had to talk about.

Eddie asked if it were her arthritis again.

She said, "No, Eddie, dear. My arthritis is fine, except some days it does seem like it's getting worse. But what I'm worried about right now is you. I know you aren't going over to Alton's at night, and you've been so cross with me lately..."

Eddie was silent a few seconds. She says she almost told him to forget it and go on doing whatever his was he was doing until 10 o'clock every night as long as he'd promise her it wasn't anything bad. The silence almost broke her heart.

Finally, Eddie said, "Mother, I met a girl."

Her name is Rebecca. She is a secretary for an oil company. She is three years younger than Eddie and her husband died seven years ago.

Eddie had been working on an addition to the house next door to Rebecca's, and one day when she was working in her yard, he went over and pointed to a pile of branches about eight feet high and said, "You wouldn't want any help with that, would you?"

It turned out she did, and after that things got going faster than Eddie ever imagined they could. He started going over there, watching television and just talking. Sometimes Rebecca would ask about Eddie's mother, and Eddie would mumble something about how she wasn't feeling well.

Sometimes especially when they watched the same television shows he watched with his mother, he felt guilty.

When his mother found out about Rebecca, she wanted him to invite her over for dinner as soon as possible. She didn't want Rebecca to "turn out just like that Cecilia girl." Eddie called Rebecca right then, and she is coming over to meet Eddie's mother tomorrow night.

Eddie says in his 42 years he has never been so nervous.

The Daily Iberian
September 30, 1985

Playing Hooky

NEW IBERIA, La. — The kid didn't look lost, but then again he didn't look like he should be in City Park Thursday afternoon. Maybe that's why I sat down next to him.

For about 10 minutes we just sat there, both of us not saying anything at one on a Thursday afternoon. He was swinging his feet in the air, I was tapping my foot to a song I'd heard on the car radio.

We could have sat there like that for the rest of the afternoon, but I finally gave in.

"Nice day," I said.

"Yeah," he said.

Another five minutes went by.

"What's your name?" I asked.

"John," he decided. "What's yours?"

I thought awhile too.

"Fred," I said.

That put us on equal terms. Then we sat there like that for awhile, neither of us wanting to break the balance. It was too nice a day to worry about things like that.

It wasn't fair to ask him how old he was, but he looked like he was the same age I was when I became actively interested in not going to school.

"You go to school?" I asked, finally.

"Yes," he said.

"Does your teacher now you're in City Park and instead of in school?"

"Yep. You gotta job?"

"Yes."

"Does your boss know you're in the park instead of at work?"

"Yep."

I figured that if it was OK with his teacher, it was OK with my boss.

"Want to walk around?" I offered.

He shrugged and got up and we started walking around the park, clockwise. I have been in City Park enough to know that the older people had already taken their walks and the executives had already taken their jogs. It was too early for the rest of the executives to be out for their afternoon jogs or a game of tennis.

This afternoon workers were trimming the shrubs and working on the softball field. Spring is only a few weeks away.

Three guys, who were about as many years younger than me as they were older than him, were leaning against a tree drinking beer in the sun.

I wondered who wasn't supposed to know they were here.

A squirrel looked down at us, scolding us both. Or maybe it was just our consciences. We kept walking.

"Did you go to school?" he asked.

"Sort of," I said. He obviously knew about sort of going to school, too.

"What's your job?" he asked.

"I write."

"What do you ride? Horses?"

"No. W-r-i-t-e. Like your teacher makes you do."

"Oh" He sounded disappointed. "How did you get a job like that?"

"By sort of going to school," I said.

By this time we were back to where we started and we had run out of things we felt like talking about. Anyway, we turned around and started walking around the park counter-clockwise. That way you get to see the other side of everything.

We walked all the way around again, past the three guys and the workers and the squirrel, without saying a word.

Finally, he asked, "What time is it?"

"Almost three," I said.

"I'm supposed to be getting home from school now," he said. "I gotta get going."

It was time for me to get back to the office, so I asked him if he wanted a ride somewhere.

"No thanks," he said. "My mother told me never to take a ride from a stranger."

The Daily Iberian
March 19, 1984

Queen Sugar

NEW IBERIA, La. — Theresa Mary Gascon is beautiful, otherwise she wouldn't be sitting here on this bus. She is wearing black lace on an August afternoon, and her shoes are kicked off. The crown is on the overhead rack.

Queen Sugar XLII is relaxing.

"When they crown you, nobody thinks about the rest of the year," she says. "All they think about is the initial excitement of when they put the crown on your head. Then there's the whole year when you never have any free time.

"But at the same time, I have to remember that when I put on the crown, I'm putting on the pride, dignity, the Louisiana Sugar Cane Festival."

Last week we were both on the Sugar Cane Festival Good Will Tour, so I asked her if she'd mind if I kept track of her for a while, to see what it was all about.

All sorts of beautiful girls were on the bus, each one the Miss of her parish. They are the cream of the girls who grew up to participate in pageants. But there is only one Queen Sugar XLII, and all the other girls surrounded her the way electrons whirl around a nucleus.

At each stop on the tour they all put on their crowns and sashes and spread good will. They'd get off first, and when I followed, the bus driver would shake his head and say, "Man, you got it made back there."

Anyway, Theresa lives in Brusly in West Baton Rouge Parish and she has a boy-friend who is very proud of her, she says. During the week she processes applications for the Louisiana State University Law School. She is 20 and she says people seem to be nicer when they see the crown.

"Like one time on the way to New Iberia, I got stopped by a state trooper," she says. "I had the crown in the back seat, so I grabbed it and set it on the front seat. Then I didn't go to meet him, I made him come to my car.

"I gave him my license and he said, 'Miss Gascon do you realize you were traveling such-and-such speed in a 55-mile-an-hour zone?'

"I said, 'Well...'

"Then he said, 'What's that crown for?' I told him and said, 'I'm on my way to New Iberia and I'm late and I'm very sorry."

"He said, 'I'm very sorry, Miss Gascon, go right ahead.'"

Louisiana Attorney General William Guste Jr. gave her a certificate stating that she "has been designated, constituted and appointed Honorary Deputy Attorney general and Ambassador of Good Will for the State of Louisiana," and she has traveled to Washington, D.C., to spread good will.

"In Washington we went to a really fancy restaurant and all they had at the tables was Sweet-n-Low. So I had to ask the waiter to go get some sugar, and he brought back big goblets and set them on all the tables. So I guess I accomplished something there."

This weekend she will be at the Shrimp Festival in Delcambre. Queens are expected to appear just about anywhere they are invited, and they are invited somewhere almost every weekend. The more queens the better.

After a year the queens get to know each other pretty well.

"Every Sunday afternoon they'll be crying, kissing each other and saying goodbye," says Ralph St. Amant, who has been chairman of the Miss St. Charles Parish Pageant for 21 years and who has worked closely with Queen Sugars. "Then on Thursday, they see each other again at the next festival. The saddest part is when they have to watch while one of the queens they've made such good friends with, like the Swine and the Pecan queens, loses her crown."

Sept. 30 at the Sugar Cane Festival, Theresa will abdicate. One of the Misses on this bus probably will be crowned Queen Sugar XLIII. Miss Iberia, Leslie Ann LeBlanc, is asking about the pageant. She wants to know how well Theresa can curtsy.

It turns out that queens never curtsy. Somebody told Theresa after she was crowned. Probably some queen made that rule.

I have never curtsied, but it sounds like never having to do it no matter what happens must be one of the best things about being a queen.

"Definitely," Theresa says. "That's one thing I've always been self-conscious of, whether I was going to be able to come up or not. So it was really kind of a relief to find out I never had to curtsy."

The Daily Iberian
August 13, 1984

Wilbert Visits Miss Ruby

NEW IBERIA, La. — At quarter past seven on a Thursday morning, the side door opens and a man enters the kitchen.

"How are you feeling Miss Ruby?" he says.

"What?" she says, because his speech is slurred. She has been sitting at the kitchen table, playing solitaire, waiting, He repeats the question.

"Fine," she says. "How are you Wilbert?"

"What?" he says, and he shakes his head. He was born with an affliction that causes him to walk like he is stumbling and to slur his speech. "Nerves," his how he explains it, and nobody else knows any more.

She repeats her question.

"I'm doing good, Miss Ruby," he says. "Same as always."

He takes a glass from the shelf and sets it on the table, crosses the kitchen to the refrigerator and takes out the pitcher of ice water and comes back to the table. The table is set with prescription bottles, a deck of cards, the arrangement of silk flowers he gave her for her birthday in September. He pours himself a glass, puts the pitcher back in the refrigerator and sits down where she has buttered a biscuit.

All of this has taken more effort than you can imagine.

"Remember, Wilbert," she says. "You've got to go to the doctor's tomorrow, and three weeks from today is Thanksgiving, so don't forget about church."

"I won't forget, Miss Ruby," he says.

"You never do, Wilbert," she says. "You're a good boy. You always were."

Wilbert Fuzee is 64 years old and calls Ruby Rentrop "my white mama." She is 89 years old and calls him "my black grandson." It has been like this every morning for 51 years.

Miss Ruby and her husband used to have The Yellow Jackets' Nest across from the old high school, where they sold ham and bologna sandwiches for a nickel apiece. Sometime around 1934 Wilbert started coming around. She gave him sandwiches, he took care of her yard.

Her husband built a little table against the kitchen wall for Wilbert — "In those days, you just didn't eat together like Wilbert and me do now," Miss Ruby says — but now it is for the coffee maker and the toaster. Wilbert took care of yards for a living, but now his doctor won't let him do that. He works for Paul's Flowers & Plants, unpacking flowers, running errands and sweeping up.

Every morning he leaves his cousin's mobile home on Ann Street, walks here, goes to work, eats lunch at Provost's, walks home and watches television.

"Every morning when I open my eyes, the first thing I do is thank the Lord that nothing harmed me or scared me, and then I go unlock the door," Miss Ruby says. "One time I wasn't here when he came, so he went to my brother's, then to the drugstore and finally he found me at my sister's. I never go any place without telling him, because he worries so much."

"Some mornings I get here and all of a sudden I remember," Wilbert says. "I say, 'Miss Ruby, I was in so much of a hurry I didn't say my prayers.' So I get right down right here and do them."

She had to hire somebody else to take care of her yard, but he sweeps up after they leave. Monday mornings he puts her garbage out, and when she needs something he walks to Paul Theriot's Grocery Store and gets it for her. Sometimes — "Not often," Miss Ruby says, "but now and then" — he brings her a half-gallon of ice cream.

After Wilbert leaves, she will get ready for the blue bus that takes her to the senior citizens' lunch every day, and after she gets back she will watch television and sit here and play solitaire.

"Who's dead, Miss Ruby?" Wilbert says.

"What?" Miss Ruby says, and he repeats himself.

"Nobody you know," she says.

"What?" he says, and he shakes his head. "Nerves, Miss Ruby."

She repeats herself.

He shakes his head again. He looks up at the clock and stands up. He takes his glass to the sink and starts toward the door.

"Miss Ruby, you got nothing to worry about," Wilbert says. "The Good Lord knows."

"Remember, Wilbert," she says. "You've got to go to the doctor's tomorrow, and three weeks from today is Thanksgiving, so don't forget about church."

"I never forget, Miss Ruby," he says.

"I know you won't, Wilbert," she says. "You're a good boy. You always were."

The Daily Iberian
November 8, 1985

Fish Cakes

NEW IBERIA, La. — You just never know what kinds of things you're going to learn about people just from the bags of garbage they throw out on the side of the road.

For example, somebody went through four one-hundred pound tubs of various brands of whipped margarine in the time it took to fill one Glad Bag. Somebody else threw out seven Matchbox cars, a box of crayons, a coloring book and a full box of disposable diapers with elastic legs. And somebody else went through seven fifths of Old Grand Dad Kentucky Whiskey, at eight dollars a bottle.

All you read about these days is how the politicians are messing around with our garbage and how much it's going to cost us, and just when you think the politicians have won you find all these people who aren't putting up with all that. You just have to stop the next time you see a bag of trash on the side of the road and poke through it with a stick, and you'd be surprised at the things you find out about them. You just never know.

There is the couple who drinks gallons of chocolate milk and dumped their trash in the area near Admiral Doyle and Jefferson Terrace. They went through three half-gallons of Borden's regular milk, four quarts of Borden's chocolate milk and three cans of Nestle's Quick. They threw out one huge work boot, a box for a 24-piece socket set and all sorts of papers torn out of a spiral notebook.

The papers say things like: "Paint: green, gold, silver, black, yellow, orange (deep)." And "Appositives: is a noun or noun substitute. Subject Complement: renames or modifies the subject." And "Bills: Norwest $128, Liberty, $162, car $215.90, elec. $100, cable $25, total $1,014.80." And "Dear Sandy: How are you? We are fine. Well yesterday...(then it is stained with something)...Hope he can every week!

There is a letter from Indiana, signed "Love Mom and Dad." Everything was fine at home. Mom advised Glenda to see if they could find her a job typing or something — "You don't know until you've tried." It said, "Don't worry about the money. If we couldn't afford it, we would not have sent it."

Their names were on the envelope from Indiana, so I called to tell them they also don't need to worry so much about the money, because when they added up their bills they accidentally added on $100.

A man answered the phone, and the conversation went like this:
Me: "Hello, is this the man with the huge feet?"
Man: "What?"
Me: "I mean, do you drink a lot of chocolate milk?"
Man: "Huh?"
Me: "Well, I was going through a bag of trash somebody dumped on the side of the road off of Admiral Doyle and Jefferson Terrace, and..."
There was a click and the line went dead.

They went through seven boxes of fish cakes — Top Frost, six to a box. There also was 17 cans of Del Monte Blue Lake Green Beans.

They went though a can of Comet, a box of SOS pads, a bottle of Eckerd's window cleaner, a bottle of 409, and a can of Lysol. Their home must be spotless.

Their phone bill says they called somebody in Butte, Montana, seven times during September.

An unfinished letter from Judy starts off: "Dear Susan, Well, Roy's at it again. Yesterday he went and got drunk and didn't get home til three o'clock in the morning. Can you believe that? I don't know what to do. Then this afternoon he comes home from work with a big bunch of flowers. Can you believe that? That's just the way Roy is, though. You just never know..."

She's right, of course. You never know, but I called anyway. It was Roy.

Roy: "Who the hell do you think you are, going through that stuff? I don't think what I throw away is anybody's business."

Me: "I don't know, I just thought once it was dumped on the side of the road it became public record, sort of like the things at the Clerk of Court's office."

Roy: "All you newspapermen are the same, digging up stuff."

Me: "I didn't dig, and anyway, really, I just wanted to see..."

Roy: "I don't give a damn what you wanted. I'm eating dinner."

Me: "Not fish cakes and green beans agin, I hope..."

And Roy hung up.

Now I see what Judy says. That's just the way Roy is. You just never know.

The Daily Iberian
February 14, 1985

Anna, the Swedish Sex Kitten

NEW IBERIA, La. — We'll call her Anna, the name she used when she took off her clothes for a living.

She is 47 now and her measurements are still the same as they were when they earned her tips, she says. She lives in a home in one of the nicest sections of town. It has been 24 years.

It is a rags-to-riches story, without the rags.

Her husband, who we'll call James, once ran for school board in this area and lost by less than 100 votes. He is an executive with an oil-related company. They have been married for 24 years and they have two sons and a daughter, all of them in their teens.

Two of her best friends and none of James' friends know what she did before they got married. Her best friend is the next-door neighbor of somebody I wrote a column about two years ago, and she set this up. Anna said she isn't ashamed of her past, "But you know how people are."

She grew up in New Orleans and after her parents were killed in an automobile crash she was raised by her grandparents. When she was 17, a friend who was stripping in a club on the west side of New Orleans asked her if she wanted an easy job that paid well. Anna had been answering phones for an insurance salesman, wondering what she was going to do with her life. When her friend's bosses saw her, they offered her a job immediately.

She was a natural.

"I was a natural blonde, so they called me Anna, the Swedish sex kitten," she says. "I wasn't really like that offstage. I know nobody will believe me, but I wasn't.

"I got into it, but I never did anything I thought was wrong. Some girls did, some didn't. I didn't, but of course none of the guys believed me. You know how people are.

"A lot of guys come in and put down a dollar, which was a lot of money then, and you know what they're really looking for. Most of them are drunk, and they don't appreciate what you're doing up there. They're just staring at you like you're some kind of machine up there.

"James, though, he was different. When he'd look up at me, he would look up into my eyes. When he put down a dollar for a tip, you could tell he really meant it."

For the late show that night, he was in the same seat, and he handed her a cocktail napkin. She usually just pretended to read the cocktail napkins men handed her — most of them said something obscene and made her blush all over — but she read the cocktail napkin James handed her. It was an invitation to dinner after the show.

She didn't get off work until 3 a.m., so they went to breakfast.

James was in New Orleans on business nearly every week. Because they were going out, James never went to see the show. He didn't think it was proper.

One morning during breakfast, eight months after they started going out, he asked her to marry him. She said no. She had said no to the men who asked her to marry them almost every night since she started working, but this time it was different.

This time, she just didn't think James knew what he was getting into. He was rising in the business world and was considering a career in politics. "You know how people are," she said.

James kept coming back. When she agreed, she also agreed to quit her job. They told his parents she worked in a clothing store in New Orleans. They still laugh about that, she says.

About eight years ago, when they moved is not the house they live in now, James' mother was helping them pack the things in their bedroom closet when a pasty fell on the floor. She thought she had thrown them both away, but James had saved one. She told her mother-in-law it was the tassle off an old pillow.

She has a black-and-white photograph of Anna, the Swedish sex kitten, wrapped in a feather boa. It is the only thing she and James have saved to remember how they met. She keeps it hidden, because her children would still recognize her.

The cheekbones are still there.

"You know, I hardly ever even think about those times anymore," she says. "It only comes back to me when a woman is wearing too much perfume — you always wear a lot of perfume when you're performing — or when a room gets really smoky. It's not like I'm ashamed or anything, but it's just something you don't talk about.

"You know how people are."

The Daily Iberian
October 18, 1985

The New Bike

NEW IBERIA, La. — The old man sits on his front porch all day and watches the kids riding bikes past his house.

One day Timmy and Gilbert were running around and, being 8 and 10 years old, one of them accidentally stepped in his yard. The old man started yelling and waving his arms and told them to get the hell off his property and stay off or he'd call the police and have them arrested.

After that, Timmy and Gilbert avoided the old man. When they rode past his house, they sped up. The old man just sat on his porch and watched.

When Gilbert and Timmy and their mother moved into their house, the bikes were in the backyard. Their mother figures the people who lived there before didn't think they were worth taking. Some days Gilbert and Timmy ride all day. They like to do other things, but mostly they ride their bikes up and down the street.

At the end of the day they almost always remembered to put their bikes behind the house, like their mother told them to.

Their mother is divorced and works nights in a convenience store. She makes enough to pay her bills, but not much more. When one of the bikes got a flat tire, she couldn't afford to get a new one for two weeks. In the meantime, the boys shared the bike that worked.

The day after they moved into their house, she had gone around to meet the new neighbors. When she started up the old man's sidewalk, he started yelling and waving his arms and told her to get the hell off his property and stay off or he'd call the police and have her arrested.

The other neighbors just smiled and said that's the way the man is.

The new bike is shiny blue with hand brakes and padded handlebars. The mother won it in a grocery store drawing. She wrote her name and phone number, put the slip in the box, and forgot about it. When they called and said she had won, she didn't know how to tell her boys. She kept it hidden in her bedroom for a week.

"Finally I sat them down and said, 'Now boys, I have a little surprise for both of you. But we're going to have to work out a deal. You're going to have to share like brothers are supposed to.'

"They'd always gotten along, but I didn't know how they'd react with a brand-new bike."

Timmy is taller than Gilbert, even though he is nearly two years younger. Sometimes Timmy won arguments, sometimes Gilbert won. Usually they shared, but not always.

"One time I heard them arguing about the bike, so I hollered out to them and said that if they were going to argue nobody was going to ride," she says. "But they kept it up, so I hollered at them and told them to put away the bikes and come inside. When they got inside, I asked them what they were arguing about, and Timmy said it was Gilbert's turn to ride the new bike and Gilbert said it was Timmy's turn. I didn't know what to say, so I just said to go out back and play a while."

One morning the mother went out the front door and the new bike was on the front porch. She went back inside and asked why they hadn't put away their new bike. But Timmy said they'd put it away behind the house the night before, and Gilbert said, yeah, they had.

They went to the backyard, and the new bike was where it was supposed to be. They went to the front porch and the new bike was there. They were standing on the front porch, wondering, when a neighbor came over and said he'd seen the old man put the new shiny-blue bike on the front porch the night before.

She asked the neighbor why the old man would give them a new bike, and the neighbor just smiled and said that's the way the man is.

"I don't know why he did it, but he doesn't know how much it means to those boys and to me," the mother says. "Now I feel terrible because I can't think of any way to thank him."

After they learned what the old man had done, they went to thank him. Timmy and Gilbert rode their new bikes, beside their mother. When they stepped into the yard he started yelling and waving his arms and told them to get the hell off his property and stay off or he'd call the police and have them arrested.

The Daily Iberian
August 16, 1984

Once a Dog Starts Chasing Cars...

NEW IBERIA, La. — The man watched the dog coming. It came from behind the mobile home and ran across the yard toward the road. It was a yellowish color, and it looked like it had some golden retriever and some collie in its history.

When it got to the edge of the yard it jumped the ditch and ran along the side of the road. Then it ran in front of the car. There was nothing the man could do.

The kid came out from behind the mobile home and yelled to the dog to get back in the yard right now. The dog was lying on its side, and blood was coming out of its mouth, forming a pool on the asphalt. The man was already kneeling next to it.

It was still breathing hard, but he knew it would die.

The kid ran across the yard, jumped the ditch and stood looking down at the dog. He was maybe 12 years old. He kneeled and started stroking its jaw.

The man said, "I was just driving along, and it came out from behind your house over there, and when it got to the road it ran right in front of my car," but the kid wasn't listening.

Then the spasms began.

It is what happens when a dog dies that way.

The kid thought it meant the dog was trying to get up. He tried to help it up, but there was nothing there. He went back to stroking its jaw.

The front door of the mobile home opened and a man came out. He walked to the road, taking the driveway. When he got to where the man and boy were kneeling, he looked down at the dog and said, "Dammit to hell, Lee. I told you that was gonna happen. A dog starts with chasing cars, there's nothing you can do with it. Right, mister?"

The man looked up at the boy's father and nodded.

When he was 10 years old he had a dog that was part golden retriever, part something nobody could ever figure out. Whatever that other part nobody could figure out was, he always figured it was what made the dog chase birds. All day, it chased birds in the trees.

Then it discovered the neighbor's chickens. Every few days after that, it would trot home to him with a dead chicken in its mouth. He would slap the dog on the nose until it let go, and he'd take the chicken and bury it in the field behind the house.

This went on for almost two weeks.

The neighbor's dog weighed maybe three pounds — when it saw another dog it jumped straight up in the air and spun around three or four times one way and three or four times the other way and ran and hid behind the chairs people weren't allowed to sit on — and every afternoon they let it out to "tee-tee." One afternoon it came home dragging a chicken carcass. The neighbor came over that night with three dead chickens.

His father had said, "A dog kills chickens, there's nothing you can do except get rid of it."

The spasms continued for two or three minutes.

The boy's father walked over to the car, 20 feet up the road, and looked at the front bumper. He came back and said, "Looks like it didn't do anything to your car, mister. Those plastic bumpers they put on cars these days, it takes more than a dog to hurt 'em. You know what I mean?"

He walked back to where the boy and the man were kneeling next to the dog and said, "Lee, look at that, you're getting blood all over your pants. You're mother's gonna have to scrub all that out."

The man looked at his own pants. There was blood on them, too.

The boy's father noticed it and said, "Mister, you've got blood all over your pants, too. You're gonna have to scrub that out. Damn dog."

The spasms finally stopped.

The boy saw it and without saying anything he picked up the dog and carried it toward the mobile home. He carried it across his chest, getting blood on his shirt, too. The boy was no bigger than the dog.

The boy's father watched this and turned to the man and said, "When I was his age, I had a dog I cared for like that. One day it got in a fight with a dog they thought might of been carrying rabies. My oldest brother had to take it out back and shoot it.

"I don't know, I guess it's just part of growing up."

The man nodded. He looked at the blood on his pants. It was going to have to be scrubbed out.

He walked back to his car, 20 feet up the road, and drove away.

The Daily Iberian
September 13, 1985

Chapter five

My Life

Greg was born January 12, 1961, *in Rose Hospital.*

After two girls, it never occurred to us he would be a boy, so we had no names ready. We settled on Gregory Alan, only to discover that our next door neighbors' son also was Gregory Alan. As soon as the two Gregs could walk they became bosom buddies.

On weekends our family went to visit my parents, who lived on a farm east of Golden. The kids roamed the fields and played with cats, dogs and horses. When Greg was older, he visited his aunt and uncle and their 12 children in Maxwell, N.M. Together, they harvested and shucked corn and rode in the back of the pickup, singing and teasing each other.

Greg never worked on school newspapers or showed any particular interest in journalism. In December of his senior year of high school he asked me if he could stay out of school for a week. He took long walks and spent a lot of time by himself. At the end of the week he told me he wanted to go into journalism.

Greg spent four years at the University of Missouri and although we and his grandmother proudly watched him go through the graduation ceremony, he never got a diploma — one of those mysteries parents never solve!

He was so excited about his first job in New Iberia, La. He called home and said, "Mom, you should see it here, it's beautiful with the trees arching over the street."

His career was launched. He never lost his love for Louisiana and its people.

BETTIE LOPEZ, GREG'S MOTHER

A Rose for a Daughter Who Won't Grow Up

DENVER — In the baby section of Foley's in the Cherry Creek mall, there are four racks of white dresses for baby girls.

We had been to all of the other stores with baby sections in the mall that Sunday afternoon and looked at all of the other racks of white dresses for baby girls. We were looking for a white dress for ours. At 9:27 the night before in St. Joseph Hospital, she had been stillborn.

I pulled a white dress with a tiny pink rose stitched on the collar out of the middle of a rack, and when I turned around my wife was standing three racks over and holding up the same dress.

"We found it," my wife said.

The baby was due Oct. 27.

The doctor who delivered her after 16 hours of induced labor said the umbilical cord was around her neck.

We named her Mary.

The week before, I had promised to move the record albums to the basement that weekend. The curtains were supposed to be hung that Wednesday, but we had been told there was a problem with the fabric and they wouldn't be ready until next week. We looked at cribs Thursday night.

When we got home that Sunday afternoon, the book was on the bed where my wife had left it Friday morning, open to the section "I can't detect any movement. Is something wrong?"

She was 4 pounds, 11 ounces and 21 inches long. She had her mother's mouth. Even the nurse said she had huge hands and feet. "I would have had to make her practice piano," my wife said.

When we picked out a silver frame for the footprints, the saleswoman asked, "Your first?"

"Yes," I said.

"I could tell," the saleswoman said. "By the second or third, most people just stick the footprints away in a drawer."

The morning of the funeral, I pruned the roses we planted in the spring. It was something to do. It was the only thing I could think of to do, because the lawn had been mowed twice in the same day while we were in the hospital, once by a friend and once by my father.

I cut off a pink rose that had bloomed and faded, and a rosebud that almost was ready to bloom fell to the ground.

All week, friends and family had flown in, called, come over, sent a stack of cards and flowers that covered every flat surface. Almost all of them said there was nothing they could say. Some had gone on to say there must be a reason these things happen.

You can choose to believe that or not, but you can't choose when you will believe it and when you won't.

I picked up the pink rosebud and took it inside the house.

"It's perfect," my wife said.

It was in the casket when Mary was buried in the white dress with the pink rose stitched on the collar.

Rocky Mountain News
September 15, 1994

Father's Day

NEW IBERIA, La. — The father had everything he had ever wanted.

He had a wife, three daughters, two sons-in-law, his first grandchild on the way and a son who was trying to find something to mail to him for Father's Day.

"We have some nice cuff links, or maybe a nice tie clasp," a salesman was telling the son.

The father always had been difficult to buy anything for. For his children, he would do anything this side of rock 'n' roll, but for himself there was very little he wanted. The past several Father's Days, the son had settled for cards that had words that rhyme with "wonderful" or "friend" or "guy."

This year, the son wanted to do something special.

He told the salesman holding up a pair of cuff links that he didn't want to get his father anything shiny.

"Or we have some nice colognes or some nice shaving accessories."

The father had grown up in a town of about 400, and had spent of most of his time in boarding schools in a town 30 miles away. He didn't say much about those times. He went on and worked to put himself through college and medical school.

He became a good doctor. He had a successful practice, and farmers who had a bad season or people who had bad insurance often didn't get a bill. It happened often enough that it was no accident.

The man behind the counter was holding up a bronze-colored bottle with a little spray pump aimed at the son. The salesman had his hair purposefully styled like an ocean wave. The son shook his head.

From past Father's Days, the father had cologne that was supposed to make him smell like he just got back from sailing on the high seas, hiking in the Rocky Mountains, playing polo, riding bucking broncos and other things he would never do. They sat there, full, lined up in a row on the bathroom counter.

The salesman said he was sorry but that was all he had at his counter, and he called over a woman who had worked in the clothing department. She was wearing a red dress with yellow parrots on it, and her lipstick matched the part that wasn't the parrots. She led the way past the shoes — somehow she knew shoes weren't the answer — to the shirts.

She held up one printed with birds flying south and said, "How about a nice shirt?"

The father was able to give his family everything they wanted, and that was everything he wanted. There were three daughters and a son. When the son came, all hell broke loose.

The father couldn't understand some of the things his son did, because he had never had himself for a father. At first, the father thought it was a phase the son was going through. When the son thought about it — it wasn't very often — he thought it might be a phase too. But it went on for years.

For example, the son always waited until the morning of December 24 to do his Christmas shopping. Every Christmas Eve at about five in the evening, his family went to his grandmother's for dinner. Every Christmas Eve, he and his friend Ray would finish their shopping at about six, and he would come home all full of Christmas cheer, and everybody but his father had gone ahead. They would make the long drive out to his grandmother's in silence.

The saleswoman saw a shirt wasn't the answer. The father had a shirt to go with each of his colognes. They hung next to each other at the end of the closet.

"May I suggest a hardware store?" the saleswoman said.

When he was a young man, the father was a gardener in the neighborhood where he now lives. Now he works in his own yard as often as possible, and when the son was growing up he spent Saturday mornings working next to him.

The son's friend Pete used to come by and see them working in the yard, not saying anything. After a few years of this, one day Pete said, "Too bad about you and your father." The son said, "What do you mean?"

"About how you and him don't speak to each other..."

He went to one and turned down a nice digital tape measure, a nice bronze key fob and a nice air compressor.

The salesman at the hardware store suggested he just get a nice card.

The son bought a card that had a picture of a young man and an older man sitting on a log in the woods, and a six-line poem. He scratched out the poem with his pen. Below it, he wrote:

To Dad
Thanks
Love
Your son

He knew his father would understand.

The Daily Iberian
June 14, 1985

1963 FAMILY PORTRAIT—
BETTIE, LOU, LYNNE,
SUSAN AND GREG.

When I first read the article Greg wrote for Father's Day, I was so proud.
The thing that moved me was not so much the flattering things he said but that he
would write the story before I had some catastrophe. It was written while I was mostly
in my prime. Yet I can't say I was completely surprised. He was one of the most caring,
unselfish, compassionate people I ever knew, even though he was my son.

LOU LOPEZ

The Car

DENVER — The car is a 1985 Honda with 154,396 miles on it, and the first person to answer the ad was Joshua Peters. Joshua said he was 18, studying political science at Metro State College and looking for a "practical" car.

"I need something just to go back and forth to school in," he said. "Can it do that?"

"I have no idea," I said.

The car took me from *The Daily Iberian* in New Iberia, La., to *The Detroit News* and back here. It has gone to Cape Cod, Mass., to Key West, Fla., to Waterton, Canada, and to Laredo, Mexico. The car never just went back and forth.

In the glove compartment, I found a 1987 Dale Murphy baseball card in mint condition, two parking tickets I thought I had lost and directions the most beautiful girl I ever had seen wrote eight years ago for me to get to her apartment.

One Saturday night driving with her on Lakeshore Drive in Detroit, I stopped the car in the middle of the road and said, "Kathleen, I'm going to kiss you."

The next thing I remember was everything flashing.

Kathleen said, "You'd better get out." I got out, and a police officer was walking toward the car. The police officer said, "What are you doing?"

"Well," I said.

"Well, I know what you're doing," he said. "But you can't do it there."

I should have known then the car wouldn't last as long as the marriage.

It gave Leon Spinks, the former heavyweight champion of the world, a ride home after his AMC Matador had broken down, and a couple of days later he called and asked if I'd seen his front teeth.

Another night, I was doing a story about three Elvis Presley impersonators, and somewhere along the way we picked up a fourth who was drunk. They were singing, and I was driving the car. This time, I knew what it meant when I saw lights flashing. The police officer checked my license and registration and shined his flashlight in the passenger window. He shined the light in the rear right window. He walked around and shined it in the rear left window, then around the inside of the car at the four Elvises squinting in the light.

"Get back in the car," the officer said. "And go straight to the Heartbreak Hotel."

When I decided to get rid of this car, I drove a car that was low and black and shiny like an oil slick. I looked at sport-utility vehicles that felt like I was sitting in somebody else's living room. I heard at least 25 car salesmen say "Let me just ask you this..."

Joshua asked what I wanted for this car.

"You're looking for a practical car, right?" I said.

"Just to get me to school and back," he said.

"I'm sorry," I said. "This isn't the car."

Rocky Mountain News
April 27, 1994

The Mechanical Bull

NEW IBERIA, La. — Two weeks ago I got on a mechanical bull. I still don't know why.

Some things you think about, some things you just do. I got thrown off, again I don't know why. Somehow my left hand got in the way of the fall, and something bent wrong. My friend looked at it, squeezed it, and said everything would turn out all right.

The next morning it turned purple and green. It was swollen so the knobs at the base of the fingers were dimples, and it was stiff in the way you bend to scratch the back of your neck. There were everyday things, like pulling on cowboy boots and opening a new jar of mayonnaise, that it wouldn't do.

Here at work, I found entire words like "dead," "exact," and "avert," — words you try to avoid anyway — made up of letters you type with the left hand. This went on for a week and a half — there's another story about that for after Lent — so I called Dr. Castro.

He called the hospital and said it was okay for me to get it X-rayed. That's right, hospitals make you get permission and then charge you $35 plus $13 to get something

GREG TRIES TO STAY ON A BULL AT A MEDIA EVENT. HE ENDED UP BREAKING SEVERAL RIBS IN A FALL.

X-rayed. They have to pay for the magazines with articles like, "HMOs Cool on PROs," "10 Reasons Hospital Marketing Programs Fail" and "X-Ray Film Prices Fall."

That afternoon the doctor called me and said he'd found something. He asked me if I'd ever done anything like that before. I said one time in the Rocky Mountains, drunk, I fell out of a Jeep.

He said we'd do something about it in the morning. In the meantime, he said, don't do anything stupid.

The way he talked, he was the one who had to take the hand home that night.

In the meantime, I went home and went for a ride on my new bicycle. A light rain started to fall, and I sped up, again I don't know why. Maybe it was trying to prove my theory that the faster you ride the fewer raindrops will fall on you, maybe it was something else. Whatever it was, a pedal on my new bike broke, and somehow I fell off the bike exactly the same way I fell off the mechanical bull.

There is falling off a mechanical bull and there is falling off a bicycle, and anybody who tries to find any similarities is wrong.

Still, the next morning the doctor made me go back and get it X-rayed. I paid the $35 plus $13 and lied and told them they were shots for the family album.

That afternoon, waiting to hear from the doctor, I decided I didn't want to be stuck with $96 worth of pictures in my left hand, so I called the insurance people. They give you a card with a phone number on it to carry around in your wallet, and I borrowed a wallet and called the number.

Arlene, the woman who answered the phone, said I was insured and covered by the policy at the time of the accident if it occurred while engaged in work and all medical and related charges were reasonable and customary for the area in which they were rendered. Without a comma.

She asked if I was working when it happened. I said I wasn't sure — yes, there are some people in this world who get paid for falling off a mechanical bull — but I might write something about it.

Here at the Teche Publishing Co. they draw a fine line between falling off things for fun and falling off them for work, and when you cross it they let you know.

"Hooo, boy," Arlene said. "In other words, you might have been doing some type of work...we've got a real new one here. Tell me, did you get on the bull with the specific intent of writing about it?"

I said I try to never have specific intents, they get in the way. But looking back on it now, it might be something. I might even be able to work her into it, I said.

She said she'd have to check into it and call me back. Five minutes later, she called back.

"I talked to some people, and they don't think the accident would be work-related," she said. "Now, if you smashed your fingers in the typewriter that would be a different story..."

I said I hated to disappoint her, she said she understood. She said she didn't know, but it might change things if I actually wrote something about it and sent the insurance company a copy.

I said I'd see what I could do.

The Daily Iberian
March 29, 1985

An Even-Handed Punch

NEW IBERIA, La. — I don't know how long it had been since I punched somebody.

It's not something you decide — I mean, do you decide to give up punching and not give up falling off mechanical bulls? — it just happens. You wake up some morning and realize it has been a long time, and then you go on with the day like nothing happened. Until recently, I didn't know how long it had been since I punched somebody, but I do know it had been exactly as long as it had been since somebody punched me.

(Right here you also should know that this happened several weeks ago, but for Lent I promised not to write any stories where I get thrown out in the end, and that is what happens in the end of this one.)

Anyway, one night after working late I stopped somewhere to get a drink. The place gets enough bad publicity on its own, so there's no use mentioning it by name. It was crowded, there was one stool open at the end of the bar, so I sat on it.

It turned out that the woman sitting on the stool next to me was someone I had met a long time ago, I don't remember where. It might have been the last place I punched somebody. Before anything was said, a guy appeared behind me.

"Is this guy buggin' you, Debbie?" he said. And before Debbie could answer, he said to me, "You essss-ooooh-beeee, you're sittin' in my seat." Then, "Is this guy buggin' you?"

Debbie got up and left, saying, "Jamie, you gotta take care of your own problems," and he sat down next to me. And before I could do or say anything foolish, he yelled "Son of a bitch!" and swung.

He connected with my jaw, and before I could do anything then, the bartender was around the bar and pulling him away. That ended it for the night.

It was the type of punch where the next morning you stop shaving when you get to the spot on your jaw where it is stiff and puffy, and you rub it and admit to yourself in the mirror that it was a nice right cross.

So that is what happened, and a few days later I was thrown off a mechanical bull and broke my left hand. As far as I know, the two incidents didn't have anything to do with each other. Here at work there were certain words — words like "asset," "faster," "greatest" and "teetotaler," — that had to be wiped out of my vocabulary, because they are made up of letters typed with the left hand. It took an emergency, something like falling off a bicycle, to use it.

None of which explains why I went back to the same place two weeks later. I walked in and there were plenty of open stools. I sat down and ordered, and on my right — that's important here — Jamie sat down. He'd changed his shirt, so he'd left since the last time.

He sat there, thinking, and all of a sudden he apologized again.

"Lissen," he said. "I'm really sorry for the other night. I never like to punch a guy when he's not lookin'. She complains that some guy's buggin' her, then she gets up and leaves, and if I don't get mad and punch him, she gets all over me. Here, lemme buy the next round."

"Buy it for yourself," I said. "She's your girlfriend."

"No," he said. "I really want to make it up to you."

And he closed his eyes and stretched his neck so his jaw was sticking out and said, "Punch me."

I said I wouldn't punch him, not even if he was looking.

He opened his eyes and looked disappointed. I told him offering it made it even.

He closed his eyes and stretched his neck and said, "C'mon."

I told him he could buy the next round, and he opened his eyes and shrugged. "All right," he said. "But I still wish you'd of hit me."

The drinks came and we sat there a few minutes, thinking our own thoughts, and I don't know which thought was the one that changed my mind. I looked at my left hand, all purple and green and puffy and curled halfway into a fist, and I made up my mind: A teetotaler's greatest asset is faster. I stood up, "Son of a bitch!" and swung.

He sat there, rubbing his jaw and smiling at the same time. I sat there looking at the hand. Violent pain shot

GREG, AGE 3, ON A PONY AT HIS GRANDMOTHER'S FARM IN GOLDEN.

from the base of the finger, where it was broken down to places where it wasn't.

"You can buy me that drink now," I said.

He nodded and called to the bartender.

The bartender came down and saw us sitting together — him rubbing his jaw, me looking at my hand — and got a disgusted look on his face.

"Lissen," he said. "If you guys can't get along you can just get the hell out of here..."

The Daily Iberian
April 9, 1985

"what's going on?"
Photos of Life

Greg and his sisters, Lynne and Susan

Greg and friends at a birthday party

Greg clowns around with Erin Presley of the Ringling Bros. and Barnum & Bailey Circus

Greg practices with the
National Guard for a story
in The Daily Iberian

Greg rides a bull

Greg at Mardi Gras 1996

Greg with Mike Green on a road trip

Greg and mom, Bettie

Greg and sister, Lynne

Greg with Dan Oberg

Greg with Ray Lego

Greg shares a laugh with his mom, Bettie

Greg and Phil Evans

Greg's family: Lynne, Kent, Nancy, Lou, Kathleen, Greg, Bettie, Bill, Caleigh Brooke, Brian and Susan

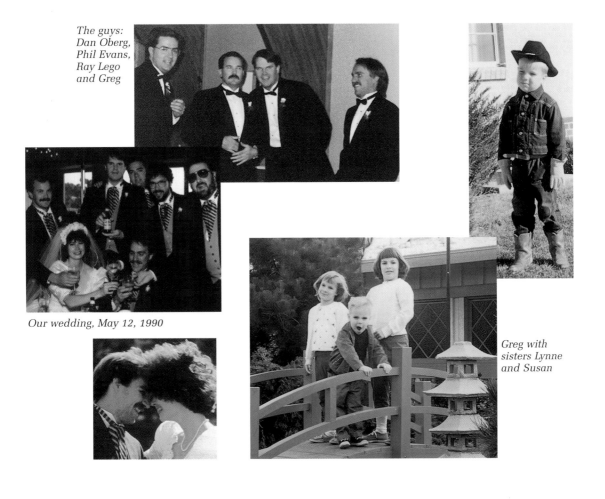

The guys:
Dan Oberg,
Phil Evans,
Ray Lego
and Greg

Our wedding, May 12, 1990

Greg with
sisters Lynne
and Susan

At the photomat
with Kathleen

Greg hanging out with Kathleen

A Day at the Opera

CENTRAL CITY, Colo. — Halfway through Act I of *La Boheme* was when everything became clear, which also was when I realized they were singing in English.

La Boheme is an opera that is four acts long. Two young men fall in love with two young women, break up and make up, and somebody dies. So I don't give away the story, I won't say who dies.

By the middle of Act II, though, it already was obvious that things weren't working out.

"Their problem is they don't talk," I whispered to my wife.

My wife is the one, by the way, who had decided to order tickets to the opera. I am the one who decided to get parking in Opera Lot A. That's how it is — one day you are young and carefree, and the next day you wake up and realize you are older than Hank Williams ever was.

"It's about fate," my wife said. "You could learn something about fate."

GREG AND KATHLEEN, CHRISTMAS 1995

Sometime during Act III, I noticed I could hear every breath the older woman next to me took and exactly where it was at any particular moment. For a while, I was worried I was using her oxygen. Then I was worried she was using mine. By that time, it also was clear that one of the women characters on the stage was developing a bad cough, and I leaned over to my wife.

"She's the one, right?" I said.

All I can figure is that this must have been what made Dick Kreck think I was nodding off. I hadn't realized Kreck would be sitting behind me. I hadn't even stopped to think that this was the kind of place where people spell their names in boldface, but he poked me anyway.

"No cheating," he said.

So I don't give away the story, I won't say anything about Act IV, but it was a wonderful production of *La Boheme* that deserves all of the outstanding reviews it has received.

My wife and I walked out into a beautiful evening in Central City, and all of a sudden I had an overpowering urge to play Texas Hold 'Em.

Five minutes later, I was sitting with a beer at a table upstairs in the Lady Luck, and my wife — this ought to tell you a little something about who learned what when it comes to fate — was downstairs standing at a slot machine. I picked up my cards. A queen and a 10, and then the dealer turned over the jack of hearts.

It was the kind of sign you sometimes receive in life, the kind you know is a sign but aren't sure what to do with it.

The face on the jack of hearts was the face of the young man whose lover had just died.

So I gave away the story.

I raised the table to $5 and ordered another beer, and the dealer turned over a five, a nine, a six and a card I don't remember.

"I was just at the opera," I said to nobody in particular.

The man next to me, who had two pair and was stacking my chips in front of him, turned and looked at me for the first time since I sat down.

"Who died?" he said.

"No," I said. "You have to go and see it for yourself."

Rocky Mountain News
July 31, 1994

The Lesson

DENVER — It was the sort of afternoon that led to the sort of place where everything sort of didn't matter.

I walked over the ridge where Pope John Paul II said Mass to 300,000 people in August at Cherry Creek State Park and saw two people, and if you don't believe I was working, just check the job description under the name under the picture.

More specifically, I saw two boys. One was aiming a BB gun at something, and the other was throwing dirt clods at it. I walked closer, until the kids and what they were aiming at saw me and stopped.

You will be happy to know at least one prairie dog is back.

"I'm shooting at him," one said.

"I'm trying to nail him with dirt clods," the other one said.

GREG'S HIGH SCHOOL GRADUATION.

It probably was not the best thing to be doing, but I figured it was better than throwing dirt clods and shooting at other kids.

"What's your names?" I said.

"Jim," the first one said.

The other one looked at him and said, "Me, too."

"I'm almost 13, and he's just 12, though," the first Jim said.

The two Jims and I stood there, each knowing what the other was thinking.

As a general rule, I don't believe there is anything wrong with skipping school for the right reasons. The prairie dog watched.

"I hope you didn't hurt him."

"Nah," the first Jim said. "It's his brother's gun. We couldn't kill him if we tried."

I used to kill things. A friend of mine named Brad Brockmeier and I made $500 one winter killing coyotes before school. My appetite for killing things ended one night after Brad killed an antelope, and we were sitting around a campfire drinking beer, when he said, "Well, since we killed it, I guess we ought to eat the brains."

Until that moment, I had never realized the responsibility that comes with killing something.

I thought about explaining this to the two Jims. There are things kids should know. There also are things kids should know even though you never explain them.

Before I said anything, the first Jim said, "What are you doing?"

"Well, I write things," I said.

This seemed to impress them.

"Like motorcycles or horses?" the first Jim said.

"Sort of," I said. "Anyway, you shouldn't just shoot something when all you can do is hurt it."

We talked a while longer about everything and nothing, and then they said they had to go.

They started to walk to their bikes, and I was walking back to my car and wondering if I'd ruined a 12-year-old's afternoon when one of them yelled, "Hey, mister."

I turned around just in time to duck a dirt clod, and then another one hit me on the shoulder and exploded.

They got on their bikes and rode away as fast as they could, looking back to see if I was chasing them.

I started back to the car, watched all the way by the prairie dog, confident they had learned a valuable lesson.

Rocky Mountain News
January 26, 1994

Serves you right, you stupid,

self-righteous asshole.

LETTER FROM A READER

The Writing Class

NEW IBERIA, La. — Mrs. Myers' second- and fifth-period language arts classes at New Iberia Middle school have been assigned to write another composition, "describing your parents as people," due next Wednesday.

Mrs. Myers called me last week and asked if I would come and talk to them. She said I could talk about the assignment and what it is like to sit and write a composition almost every day. It sounded like a good idea — better than writing something else about the Sugar Cane Festival — but I was wary.

The last time I talked to an English teacher, she called to tell me it was wrong to quote people saying "could of" or "must of." She said they really say "could have" or "must have." I said anybody who had ever seen *On the Waterfront* knows that Marlon Brando said, "I could of been a contender."

Anyway, I told Mrs. Myers there wasn't much I felt qualified to talk about. The only thing I feel confident telling an English class is that no matter what happens they should avoid semi-colons. I have never seen a pause that was a semi-colon, unless maybe it was a couple of years ago when I went to a Garden Club meeting.

Mrs. Myers said I could talk about almost anything.

I said that left me almost nothing to say I couldn't talk about. Right after I said that sentence I wanted to take it back because it was awkward and most English teachers who received a sentence like that in a composition would make the student diagram it and then rewrite it, but that is what I meant. Mrs. Myers let it pass, so I said I would be there.

So last Wednesday, I was in room 217 at New Iberia Middle School. The last time I was in a school they made me take a test. The only test I plan to take is a urinalysis, and I don't expect to have any trouble as long as it is multiple choice.

Mrs. Myers introduced me. I smiled and made eye contact and said, "I ain't..." I stopped, smiled again, made some more eye contact and said, "I'm not..."

It was a long, rambling talk that started at story structure, went past the use of words that end in -ing and -ly, detoured all the way around punctuation, up around syntax, and ended somewhere around adjectives.

I asked if there were any questions.

A kid in the back row raised his hand.

"You ever talk to anybody who killed somebody?" That made them think of all sorts of questions. They asked me what was the weirdest and scariest and funniest stories I had ever done.

The problem was that the weirdest, scariest and funniest stories all involve words and situations that editors chop out, and I figured they were too young to hear about editors.

A girl in the row along the windows raised her hand and asked, "How do you decide whether you should write a story that's abstract or with a lot of detail?"

"Sometimes you analyze your subject, consider the context, and it becomes

169

apparent that it is appropriate to treat it in the abstract manner," I said. "Other times it just turns out that way."

A kid in the middle raised his hand and asked, "Do you use literary devices?"

When somebody says "literary device," I think of a black box with a lot of wires and knobs and gauges, and all it takes is one wrong move and it all goes up. They are dangerous. I said, "That all depends..."

A girl in the third row raised her hand and asked, "Does a story have to have a theme?"

If I remember anything, I remember that themes are one of the most important parts of a composition. Without a theme, you might as well not show up. I said, "Yes."

The abstract girl raised her hand. "Then what was the theme of that story you wrote a while ago with that headline, something like 'No use crying over spilled beer?' "

That was a column four or five months ago about a man who apparently drank too much beer and fell off a friend's roof and wanted to sue the friend. I had to think about it a minute. "That's abstract," I explained.

Both classes went by like that, and all I can say is that the students in Mrs. Myers' second- and fifth-period language arts classes could handle a story on the Sugar Cane Festival.

When I came back here, Scallan, the editor, was still mad about a story that was supposed to be done last Friday. Also, I didn't know what I was going to write for this Friday. I sat down and wondered whether I should write something abstract, maybe using a couple of literary devices, after I came up with a theme.

Then I decided what the hell and started typing.

The Daily Iberian
September 19, 1986

'Uh huh' answered Greg Lopez when asked if his job is interesting.

Greg visited Flood Middle School on Friday the 13th.

They were studying journalism, and got Greg to come in.

He was answering questions from how he got stories to which ones were his favorites.

Why does he do all these people stories?

Because this is his dream job.

COMPOSITION FROM A STUDENT AFTER GREG TALKED TO A CLASS

IN ENGLEWOOD, COLO., IN 1995

Watch Out for Sasha

NEW IBERIA, La. — When Sasha appeared in my life naked, I was at a bachelor party in the hospitality suite in a hotel in downtown Denver, Colorado, a week ago last Thursday.

And now I can tell you the rest of the story.

R.J., who is my oldest and best friend in the world, was sitting next to me. He is also an attorney, and when he met me at the airport he advised me to give him my airplane ticket back home, because I have a habit of misplacing things. Wallets, pens, jumper cables, car keys — a couple of years ago in St. Louis I misplaced the whole car.

R.J. stuck my airplane ticket in the inside pocket of his jacket, where a lawyer usually sticks the check, and we went to the bachelor party.

Right here, I should explain that the reason there was a bachelor party was because a friend of ours was getting married.

GREG, AGE 22, HIS FIRST JOB AT THE DAILY IBERIAN.

Anyway, Sasha did her bit and a little bit more. There is no need to describe this. Remember, R.J. is an attorney.

When she finished she worked her way around the room, collecting tips in her G-string. When she got around to our side of the room, R.J. naturally reached into the pocket that held my airplane ticket. He took it out and looked at me.

I shrugged. The ticket was for an 11 a.m. Dec. 13 flight to Houston, then to Lafayette. A week ago last Thursday, I was in no hurry to get home.

R.J. stuck it in her G-string. She pulled it out and looked at it. And then Sasha, holding my airplane ticket, winked at R.J.

That is how lawyers work it.

Sasha finished her trip around the room, and she was gone.

I know I am not the first person to be abandoned by a naked woman, but do you know how it feels when you bought her the airplane ticket?

By 11 a.m. the next morning I was at Stapleton International Airport. I told the woman at the counter that the ticket had been misplaced. She punched some keys on her computer terminal and shook her head.

My name didn't appear, she said. She punched some other keys on her terminal and she shook her head again. She said the reservations had been changed and I had flown to Lafayette at 8 a.m. that morning.

Sasha didn't even have time to go home and pack some clothes.

For the first time the realization of what had happened and the possible consequences hit me: If transporting a juvenile girl across state lines for immoral purposes violates the Mann Act, what is violated when you give an immoral girl an airplane ticket to cross the state lines for juvenile purposes?

I said, "Was there a girl at this counter this morning who didn't look like she was from southern Louisiana?"

The woman behind the counter said, "What did she look like?"

I said, "Anything I could tell you about her, I wouldn't have to tell you."

I told the woman behind the counter I would need a ticket to Lafayette Dec. 13 at 11 a.m.

The woman punched a few keys on her terminal and shook her head. She asked me to please wait and went back to talk to her supervisor. She came back a few minutes later.

"That flight is sold out," she said. "There was a bunch of people waiting for that one. Safeway had a bunch of people going to Houston. I think they had a motivational seminar up here or down there."

I didn't know whether to feel cheated or relieved — I mean, you worry about the things that can happen to a girl like Sasha on a plane full of fired-up grocers.

The woman said she could get me on a flight Dec. 14, but because it wasn't a round-trip ticket the price, naturally, would be higher. The round-trip ticket had cost $298. One-way was $215.

The difference, of course, is that you can't come back and complain.

I gave the woman my Visa — never pay cash for an airplane ticket, you don't know what can happen in the air — and at 11 a.m. Dec. 14 I left Denver.

And that is the story as far as I know it, although I still wonder about Sasha.

If you see a naked girl who doesn't look like she belongs down here, let me know.

The Daily Iberian
December 16, 1986

From what I remember,

it was a messy night that started early and ended late.

RAY LEGO

How to Handle Things

NEW IBERIA, La. — My friend Sweeney always knows how to handle things.

For example, there was the time a bunch of us were in Jackson, Wyoming, for a wedding, and another friend of ours, Scott, tried to jump over a brand-new Buick Park Avenue. He missed and went through the back window.

Everybody was standing around looking at the car and the shattered glass and trying to decide what angle Scott should have taken, and it was Sweeney who saw the piece of glass hanging out of Scott's leg. He talked Scott into going to the hospital and getting 14 stitches.

You can always count on Sweeney to decide it's better to cut the evening short than to bleed all over a tuxedo the next day.

And that's why I went up to Dallas last week, to spend a few days going to a lot of those Dallas places that are expensive because they are designed to look like they are run-down, and to soak up some of Sweeney's wisdom. Sweeney gave advice like, "Don't throw that can out while that policeman is watching," and "Remember, this is a nice restaurant, so don't break any glasses or tables or anything." When I left Monday, he said, "Don't drive too fast, unless you're in a hurry."

Roughly halfway between there and here there is a town named Zavalla, Texas, pop. 762. When 762 people live someplace, there has to be a reason, so I took a right at the flashing yellow light, went up over a hill past the Zavalla Cemetery, and down into the woods.

The pavement ends after about three miles, and after that the houses run out. The road is hard-packed dirt through a lot of pine trees, and every few miles there was a place where somebody used to live.

It was maybe nine miles outside of Zavalla when the tire went flat. The lug wrench for my car is on my back porch, where I was using it as a doorstop, so I started walking back to Zavalla, while the sun slowly went down behind me.

The pickup came from that dirction, and a man who looks like everything you have ever seen about old men who live miles away from towns like Zavalla stuck his head out.

"That your car back there?" he said. "Where's it made? Japan?"

"Yes, and I need a lug wrench for it," I said.

"Hop in if you want a ride," he said. "You can just call me Jackson, and that'll be $20."

Twenty dollars doesn't seem like much at 4:30 in the afternoon, nine miles outside of Zavalla, Texas, so I gave him a $20 bill and got in. He backed the truck off the road and pulled out going the other way. He asked me what it was I did for a living and where, and what made me think it was OK to drive a Japanese car.

He made a right, a left an maybe another right, and maybe six or seven miles later he stopped in front on an old house. It looked like the other abandoned houses along the road, except there was an abandoned Dodge Charger in the front yard, and three dogs were sleeping on the front porch. Jackson yelled, and a smaller version of him came around from behind the house.

Jackson told him what was wrong with my car and where it was manufactured and asked if they had a lug wrench that might fit it.

"You can just call him Jackson, too," he said. "Anything you got to say to one you can say to the other."

Jackson said he didn't know, but he expected there might be one around back, and he disappeared around the corner to check. Jackson leaned against the Charger and I sat down on the porch steps. One of the dogs came over, sniffed me, and collapsed right there.

"Do you two count in the 762 on the sign?" I asked.

GREG, AGE 7

"Me and him never went for livin' in the town much," Jackson said, and he squinted at me. "We don't care much for tourists, neither."

Jackson came around the corner from out back, carrying a rusted lug wrench, and he held it out to me.

"That'll be $15," he said.

"For a wrench?" I said.

"For a foreign wrench it is."

I gave him a 10 and five ones, and Jackson asked if I wanted a ride back. If it was going to cost another $20, I said I'd walk.

"Son, it's gettin' dark, it's easy to get lost, and nobody's going to pick up a stranger walkin' through the woods carrying a blunt instrument," Jackson said. "Besides, gotta pump some money back into the American economy, you know."

I gave him two more 10s, got in the truck, and we drove back to my car without saying anything. When we got there he shined his headlights on the front end of the car while I changed the tire.

Then he backed the truck off the road, pulled out heading the other way, and he stuck his head out the window and said, "We'd appreciate it if you didn't give us no publicity in no newspaper."

When I got home I called Sweeney and told him how I had taken his advice about not speeding if I wasn't in a hurry, and how I stayed calm, like he always advised.

"S—," he said. "I would of at least punched somebody."

The Daily Iberian
January 24, 1985

Of Falling Squirrels and Communication

DENVER — And so at seven Monday morning, I'm out in the back yard watering the black-eyed Susans we planted the day before under the apple tree, where nothing ever grows, but that's no excuse for not trying.

I'm thinking about how much I love this time of year and wondering how Kathleen forgot again to tell me to put suntan lotion on the space between the top of my shorts and the bottom of my T-shirt. I'm thinking about how important communication like that is in a successful marriage. I'm thinking this when I hear a sound in the tree and look up.

A squirrel lands on my chest.

Actually, the front feet are on my chest, and the back feet are on my right shoulder. Our eyes meet, and in that moment we each understand everything that is important about the other. And then with my left hand I knock him off my chest.

Let me say right here that it is not my intention to in any way glorify squirrels falling out of trees.

Anyway, I also must have yelled, because Kathleen comes out on the back porch with one of those looks like I woke up babies that haven't been born yet. This is one of the subtle forms of communication that arise from years of togetherness. Another is giving new goatskin work gloves last week for the anniversary.

"What's going on?" she says.

"I just slapped a squirrel," I say.

The way she looks at me, I can tell she is trying to figure out if I'm using another one of my colorful phrases from Louisiana.

I lift up my T-shirt and look down, where there is a scratch I'm sure I got wrestling with the dog.

"You mean a real squirrel?" she says. "He could have rabies, you know."

This is where we leave it and go to work. She calls twice during the day to ask if I'd called the advice nurse. That night, I tell her I'll call tomorrow.

Later that night, I'm brushing my teeth and rubbing some of her expensive face cream on the stripe on my back when I look in the mirror and see the tootpaste foaming and running out of the right side of my mouth. I rinse off the toothbrush. I go in and lie on my back next to my wife, who is reading another one of those books about women who are unhappy and living in New York.

"Did you let the dog in?" she says.

"Rrrrrr," I say.

"Are you sure?" she says.

"Rrrrrrrrrrr," I say.

She sits up and looks down at me, the toothpaste foaming and dripping down my chin. Our eyes meet. In that moment, we each understand everything that is important about the other.

It is great, and then it is gone.

"OK, OK," she says, and she marches into the bathroom and comes back with some kind of lotion.

She rubs it into the sunburned stripe on my back while I lie on my stomach, thinking how important communication is in a good marriage.

Rocky Mountain News
May 18, 1994

GREG AND KATHLEEN'S
WEDDING, MAY 1990.

Chapter six

A Guy's Life

Greetings, Greg:

It's a bit after 10 p.m., and Spooner, cup of soup in hand, just left for his cell. We visited

over a half hour — a rarity for him. I fixed some Top Ramen soup for us — and he had to have

some coffee with his so he left. We talked about movies 'n stuff mainly, but he also mentioned

a letter he had gotten today.

It seems a girl from his past (their people ran a hamburger joint next to the movie house in

Storm Lake) wrote him today. She'd seen the article!!!

We both sure liked the article, Greg. As noncommittal as Delmar is, he still was expressive

enough to state that he liked what you wrote. He said — tongue in cheek (I presume) — that

you made him out to be some kind of country bumpkin. I said, "Spoon, you ARE a country

bumpkin!" We both had a laugh at that, and I could tell he agreed.

You take care my friend. You're quite a spark plug, and I sure appreciate you in our lives.

Warmly, Habe Lawson

Baby-Faced Killer Grows Old in Prison

CANON CITY, Colo. — The Atlas of the World was opened to pages 102-103, northeast China, where Delmar Spooner spent the morning.

He sat on his cot, studying the world outside his cell in Four Mile Correctional Facility. He spends mornings here, serving a life sentence and waiting for lunch.

He has served 31 years for killing state patrol Lt. Hiram Short, and for 31 years the world has been the atlas. China is his favorite place.

"Right here," he said. "China. Some folks say this might be the cradle of civilization, where everything started that led to this.

"Assuming, of course, you believe what we have here is civilization." Spooner, 57, has been in the Colorado prison system longer than any other inmate. He was 25 in 1961 when he killed Short and Eagle County undersheriff John Clark and shot two other law officers because he didn't have a car registration or a driver's license and didn't want to go to prison.

He has lived what teen-agers Marcus Fernandez and Timothy White of Highlands Ranch could face if they are convicted in the killing of state patrol Lt. Lyle Wohlers in November near Georgetown. A preliminary hearing for White and Fernandez is scheduled for Tuesday in Clear Creek County District Court.

Spooner has his own cell. He has a black-and-white television. He has the atlas, a stack of *National Geographic* magazines and a copy of *The Power of Positive Thinking* by Norman Vincent Peale.

He rolled a cigarette. He uses tobacco sprinkled with water so it will burn slower. He closed the atlas.

He knows there are 254 counties in Texas, but he never has opened *The Power of Positive Thinking.*

"It just seemed like religion," he said. "I got nothing against it, but it just seems like the only thing religion offers is hope. It seems to me a fella can hope on his own, if he has a mind to."

He lit the cigarette.

His hair is slicked back the way he wore it in 1961, before life was a sentence. It has been 31 years since the newspapers called him a "baby-faced killer." He has bad feet from wearing shoes that were too small and from walking 24 days in the mountains after he escaped 11 years ago.

He smoked.

"Sometimes, I just sit and smoke," he said. "A lot of folks don't understand that smoking isn't just something you do while you're thinking about something else. I smoke for something to do all by itself.

"It keeps you from wondering about lunch."

He finished his cigarette.

He sat.

Lunch is at 11:30.

"Other times, I just wonder about things," he said. "My grandfather once claimed he forgot how to ride a bicycle, but nobody believed him. Some folks say it's impossible to forget how to ride a bicycle.

"I wonder if I'll ever find out if Grandpa was telling the truth."

Life in Storm Lake

Delmar Dean Spooner had an engine making noises and no car registration or driver's license.

A Marlin .22-caliber rifle and 1,000 rounds were in the back seat. A loaded P38 9mm pistol was hidden inside a tear in the upholstery of the driver-side door.

He didn't know where he was going but knew he didn't want to stay in Storm Lake, Iowa.

"Things weren't working out the way I wanted, so I figured it would be good to go someplace else and find a job and see the mountains," he said. "I was feeling pretty forlorn. I'm not exactly sure how I wanted things to work out, but I knew I didn't like the way they had so far."

He grew up in Storm Lake, and other children made fun of him because he was short. He never got into serious trouble.

His mother later testified that he never made friends, spent most of his time target shooting and acted "strange."

He graduated from high school, served in the Army and worked odd jobs.

He took the guns to Colorado for target shooting, he said. He wasn't sure what happened to his car registration. He never had applied for a driver's license.

Ten days after he got to Colorado, he was unemployed and two miles east of Kremmling when the engine started making noises.

He had the hood up when state Game and Fish Department officer Bob Hoover pulled up behind him. Hoover looked under the hood and said he didn't know what was wrong. Then Hoover looked in the back seat.

Hoover radioed for assistance, and Short and Grand County Sheriff Chancy Van Pelt both pulled up within two minutes. Hoover, Van Pelt and Short talked near their cars while Spooner waited next to his. Spooner thought he heard one of the men say "prison."

Spooner reached through the tear in the upholstery and pulled out the P38.

In his confession, he said, "I ordered them into the ditch by the side of the road. I then shot the officer in the brown shirt (Van Pelt), the state patrolman (Short) and the third man (Hoover). The third man started to run, and I hit him three to five times. I intended to hit them."

He put down the hood and drove west.

About 18 miles later, he came to a roadblock set up by Eagle County undersheriff John Clark.

Spooner drove around the roadblock, and Clark chased him. Two miles later, Spooner stopped his car and got out.

He emptied the gun, hitting Clark twice.

Short died of a single shot through his heart, and Clark died of a shot through the head. Van Pelt and Hoover both were critically wounded but recovered.

Spooner ran up a ravine on Yarmony Mountain, and more than 250 law officers and volunteers formed the largest manhunt in Colorado history.

The morning of the second day, he ran for a freight train on the Rio Grande Railroad tracks. He missed it by about 50 yards. A brakeman signaled to searchers.

As officers hiked toward him, Spooner dropped his pistol.

When they reached him, he said, "That's the way it goes."

He was taken to the Moffat County Jail in Craig because police thought he wouldn't be safe in Grand County. A man in the crowd at the jail yelled, "Lynch him," and another yelled "Get a rope." Spooner confessed that night.

"I figured between me having a gun and no identification for me or the car, I might end up in prison, and I sure didn't want that, so I had to do what I did," he told police.

He was charged with first-degree murder in the killing of Short, but wasn't charged for the other shootings. Spooner pleaded innocent. A Moffat County jury found him guilty of first-degree murder but decided he should not be put to death.

A juror told a reporter, "He just seems more mixed up than mean." Time for lunch

Lunch is beans, two slices of white bread and chocolate cake with white frosting. Spooner set down his tray at an empty table in the cafeteria. Hayward Lawson, who has served 19 years of a life sentence for first-degree murder, sat down across from him.

"I ordered a Big Mac and fries," Lawson said. "And I got the same thing you did."

"Why would you do that?" Spooner said.

Spooner never has seen a McDonald's. Beans are Wednesday, bread is white, 11:30 is lunch. Lunch is now.

"I was just having fun with you, Delmar," Lawson said. "You remember what fun is, don't you?"

Spooner put down his fork. Lunch stopped. He remembered.

"Well, I had some weenie roasts in my time," he said. "I'd call that fun. Around a campfire, out in the woods. But at those things, you always get too hot because you're standing so close to the fire, and you're straining yourself to hold the weenie over it. Then you finally get it cooked, and somebody probably forgot the mustard, so you had to eat your weenie plain."

He ate his beans. He ate one slice of bread. He ate the other.

Lawson interrupted.

"Delmar," he said. "Did you always think like that?" Spooner put down his fork. Lunch stopped. He remembered.

"Well," he said. "I used to steal things when I was a kid. It takes an optimist to steal, doesn't it?"

The daughter of one of the officers he killed wrote him a letter about 10 years ago, saying she had forgiven him.

He almost wrote her back.

"I was going to tell her I'm sorry about her old man, but I just never got around to writing her back," he said. "I am sorry. I mean, I am sorry, and I feel remorse and all that, but how many times can you say you're sorry?"

His mother was the last member of his family to visit, and he thinks it was in the mid-1980s.

He doesn't have any friends in prison except Lawson.

"You get to know a person in here, and then they go and get paroled," he said. "I've seen young guys come in here and tell me they can do five or 10, but no way could they do life. Well, in a lot of ways, it's easier to hope for something that's too far away, because then you don't really expect to ever get it."

In 1988, Lawson wrote to Focus, a volunteer group that helps prisoners and their families, and asked someone to visit Spooner.

Every other Friday since then, Charles Wolfers visits. Wolfers was an electrical engineer for McDonnell Douglas before he retired to Cañon City. He gave Spooner the atlas, the *National Geographics* and *The Power of Positive Thinking*.

Linda McConnell/Rocky Mountain News

DELMAR SPOONER HAS SPENT MOST OF HIS LIFE BEHIND BARS IN CAÑON CITY PRISON.

"It took so long for him to open up," Wolfers said. "But we've become friends. He has showed me he is honest about what he has done, and he is a feeling, thinking person.

"I mean, this is a man who knows how many square miles are in Alaska but doesn't know what the world right outside that prison is like."

On Sept. 19, 1981, his 46th birthday, Spooner walked away from Skyline Correctional Facility, a minimum-security prison in the Cañon City complex.

He wore prison work pants, a denim shirt and work boots with a notch cut from the heel. He had a beard down to his chest and hair down to his shoulders. He had 198 quarters he had saved and a can of Vienna sausages he had stolen.

Hundreds of searchers tracked the boots through the Sangre de Cristo Mountains to the area around Westcliffe. The first afternoon, they found the empty sausage can. He wandered around the mountains, lost and wondering whether he wanted to be found.

On Oct. 13, after 24 days of freedom and no food, he was spotted by two hunters who aimed their rifles at him. They told him he looked like the escaped prisoner. They asked him his name.

He said, "Mr. Smith."

They told him to walk in front of them with his hands in the air.

A mile down the road he said, "If I was Spooner, how much would you want to let me go?"

He still had 198 quarters.

He has read newspaper stories about the shooting of Trooper Lyle Wohlers.

Police say one boy panicked because they were in a stolen car and didn't have a driver's license. He has thought about what he would say to the boys.

"The only thing I could say is 'You shouldn't have done it,' " he said.

"That's all there is to say. It's too late for that, though, isn't it?"

He finished his cake.

He started back across the prison yard, back to his cell. If he had looked around, he could have seen the mountains he came to Colorado to see. He could have seen page 158 in the Atlas of the World.

He had said it is easier to hope for something that is too far away.

"The night after I got caught the first time, these people outside the jail were shining lights in at me so they could see me but I couldn't see their faces," he said. "I could hear them working the slides on their shotguns. I remember thinking at least I was safe in that cell."

He went back to his cell. He opened the atlas. He went to east and southeast China, pages 104-5.

Dinner is at 4:30.

"I wonder what it would be like to actually go to one of those places," he said. "I know they probably wouldn't be like I think they are, but I still wonder. What good is life if you can't at least wonder?"

Rocky Mountain News
January 17, 1993

The Leisure Suit

NEW IBERIA, La. — Harley Delahoussaye first wore the suit 11 years ago.

It is rust-colored polyester. The lapels you could pin a hubcap on. It went best with patent leather white belts and shoes.

It was called a leisure suit and it went out of style 10 years ago, but that didn't bother Harley.

"You can't buy suits like that anymore," he says. "They don't wear out, they don't stain, they don't fade. They're comfortable, too."

"That's why they call it a leisure suit."

Helen bought it for him, and he wore it to the interview that got him his job. He was wearing it the day he got a $25 a week raise. He had it on for just about every other significant event in his life during the past 11 years.

Helen has bought him several suits since then — tweed, wool, seersucker — but she couldn't convince him to get rid of this one.

Finally, she decided she had to just get rid of it.

Like so many other things man creates, the people who created leisure suits never stopped to think about how we were going to dispose of them. They give off toxic fumes if you burn them, and they won't decompose if you bury them. In fact, clothing drives are the only EPA-approved method of getting rid of a leisure suit.

Helen put it is a box with other clothes and dropped it off at their church.

Almost a month passed without any occasions special enough to require the leisure suit, until Helen's niece got married.

That morning, Harley came out yelling in his underwear, and Helen confessed.

"I couldn't believe she'd gone and gotten rid of it without telling me," he said. "So I've got to sit through a wedding in some uncomfortable suit. That's why they don't call them leisure suits, you know."

Harley had to settle for tweed.

The following Monday he called the woman who had organized the clothing drive and asked her if she remembered seeing a rust-colored leisure suit.

She said she remembered it, but it was gone. They still had some suits that were more stylish. Leisure suits hadn't been in style for more than 10 years, she said.

Harley told her the story behind his suit.

She called two of the other women who had helped to distribute the clothing. One of them remembered the suit and the man who bought it very clearly. The suit had been picked out while they were at Bacmonila Garden Apartments, by a man wearing a yellow shirt with brown sailboats on it.

Harley went to Bacmonila and knocked on the first door he came to. He asked for a man who wore either a yellow shirt with brown sailboats on it or a rust-colored leisure suit. It sounded like the suit and the shirt might match, so he could be wearing both at the same time.

A woman at either the third or fourth apartment he tried knew who he was looking for, and gave him directions to the apartment.

A man, maybe 65 years old, wearing jeans and no shirt, answered the door.

Harley introduced himself and asked the man if he had a rust-colored leisure suit

The man said he did.

Harley offered the man $5 for the suit.

The man shook his head.

Harley offered him $10.

The man shook his head again. He told Harley there were a lot of other suits at places like the Salvation Army that were just as good. For $10 he could probably get three or four different colors.

Harley told the man the story behind the suit.

The man turned around and went back into a room and came out with the suit.

He said he had gone through the pockets of the jacket and pants and there wasn't anything valuable Harley left in them. He said he was thinking about using it to do some painting. His wife wouldn't let him wear it when they went anywhere.

It went out of style five years ago, the man said.

"He was looking around like he expected somebody to jump out and say he's on *Candid Camera* or something," Harley says. "It took him a while to see I'm really serious."

When he did, he said Harley could have it for $20 or the jacket he was wearing.

The jacket Harley was wearing was a brown wool with pinstripes, something Helen had picked out. It had cost about $140. Harley figured it was only a matter of time until it went out of style.

Harley took it off, and they traded.

The Daily Iberian
January 13, 1987

Home Isn't Always Where the Heart Is

TOLEDO — "Steam Train" Maury Graham, the former King of the Hoboes, is talking about Albert "Slow Motion Shorty" Parker and trying to find his wife's keys.

Steam Train shuffles some of the papers on his desk in the dining room of his house on the south side of Toledo. Slow Motion Shorty, who also was a former King of the Hoboes, used to claim he was the only hobo who ever shook hands with Leo Durocher. The keys are missing because he borrowed them from his wife after he couldn't find his own.

It has been eight years since Steam Train came home, but some things don't just go away.

"They called him Slow Motion because he got hit by cars two or three times and fell off freights and was all bent over," Graham says. "Shorty's obvious. Before he caught the westbound, I remember one time we were ramblin' in Iowa and...

"That's the problem with living in houses — you gotta have keys."

Steam Train is 71, with white hair down to his shoulders and a beard halfway down his chest. He says he might hop a freight this spring. He said that last spring, too.

Right now, though, he has an artificial hip, no cartilage in one knee and sometimes still walks half a mile to watch the trains pass.

"So that time in Iowa, Slow Motion Shorty and me — did I tell you he used to say he was the only man in America who didn't have a Social Security card? — was sittin' around," Steam Train goes on. "Not doing nothin' but not worryin' about nothin' either, and I believe 'Big Town' Gorman was there. Big Town was the son of a man who built skyscrapers in St. Louis and graduated from college and then he roamed around...

"I could of swore those keys were in my jacket."

Steam Train grew up in Toledo, where he lived with his father, and took food to the hoboes at the rail yard. He was 13 the first time he hopped a freight to visit his mother in a sanitarium in Idaho. After that, he left every summer until he was 20.

He stopped when he got married. He and his wife raised two daughters, and he worked as a cement mason. After 35 years, their daughters were gone and his knees bothered him so much sometimes he couldn't work.

In 1970, he went to northern Michigan to camp for a week but the fishing wasn't any good, so he hopped a freight train. He tried to call home collect six weeks later but his wife refused to accept the call. She refused for six years, until he sent her a dozen yellow roses for their 38th anniversary.

Still, he didn't come home.

He roamed around Illinois, Indiana, Iowa and Pennsylvania. He washed windows, painted garages, cut grass and did other chores for money. He was elected King of the Hoboes five times at the annual National Hoboes Convention in Britt, Iowa.

Finally, the hoboes at the convention invented the title of King for Life east of the Mississippi River for him.

STEAM TRAIN GRAHAM

In 1981, he came home after 11 years, in slow motion because of the knees and a hip that had to be replaced.

"A lot of fellas, they kept going because they didn't have anything to stop for," he says. "I had to court her all over again, but at least I could come home to my wife."

Her name is Wanda and she calls him Maurice. Before she retired three years ago, she worked as a physical therapy technician and bought the house while he was gone. They will have been married 51 years in April.

For a couple of years after that, she would come home after work and there would be a note on the mantel. He would come back a few weeks or months later. He would have to court her again, but she always let him in.

The past couple of years, they have gone together in their motor home to the National Hobo Convention and anyplace else he wants to go.

"I took him back because of all the things that had happened before he left," she says. "I don't want to hear the stories about what he did while he was gone. That was something I just had to get over."

Anyway, it turns out he left her keys in her car when he went to speak to a group of vocational education students in high school, and his keys were on the coffee table under a postcard.

In the back of the garage he finds Slow Motion Shorty's bag. A social worker sent it here after its owner died. Inside, there is a Chicago Cubs jacket and letters.

The most recent letter is postmarked a couple of days before Slow Motion Shorty died:

"Dear Brother Shorty: Bless you ol' best pal, you can fool 'em. I got this new hip and if you could get a new heart maybe we could ride again. If we don't work it here, we will in heaven."

It is signed. "My own brother of the rails, river banks, creek banks, hoot owls and freight yards, Steam Train."

He puts the letter back in the envelope and puts everything back in the bag. He goes outside and pulls the door shut. The door knob comes off in his hand.

He looks down at the door knob, which is another problem with living in houses. It has been eight years, and some things don't just go away. And this spring, he plans to go out again.

He puts the door knob in his pocket.

"Now," Steam Train continues, "Where was I?"

The Detroit News
February 5, 1989

Barber's Art Cuts Many Ways

DENVER — Walt Young was cutting Edward Halfpenny's hair last week in the Upper Cut barbershop, and it wasn't clear whether he was talking about hair or art or both.

This is the kind of barber Young has been for 39 years on East Colfax, and this is the kind of artist he has become. It isn't a coincidence. He cuts hair and paints in his shop.

WALT YOUNG IS AN ARTIST AND BARBER ON COLFAX AVENUE IN DENVER.

The paintings are on display through July at Aum Gallery, and the haircuts are everywhere.

"So," Halfpenny said. "You think my ears stick out too much?"

"Nope," Young said. "If there's one thing I've learned, it's that your ears are your ears."

Young started drawing the people on East Colfax in 1985, when other people were complaining about the people on East Colfax.

"People were calling them things like 'undesirables' and stuff like that. And this was my way of saying they're just as desirable as anybody else," Young said. "A lot of them are dead now — alcohol. But living like that gives them this look...this feeling...If I could put it into words, I wouldn't have to paint it."

He hung the drawings on the walls of his shop. The subjects brought other people on East Colfax to see them. Young drew them, too.

Two years ago, a man walked in with a set of oil paints and asked Young if he wanted them.

"I don't know where he got them — I hope he didn't steal them — I don't know whether he knew what they were for," Young said. "That's the kind of street East Colfax is."

At any rate, Young started painting in oils. He added mountain landscapes, generally scenes of abandonment — barns and cabins that otherwise would be forgotten.

They are opposite anything you would see on East Colfax, but the feeling is the same. One is a barn near Marble with a stream running past it, and after Young finished the painting he caught four 14-inch rainbow trout. To Young, the feeling after catching the fish is the same feeling he gets after he finishes a portrait of someone.

"I don't want to paint something just because it's pretty," Young said. "I want to paint it because there's something more there, something else worth seeing."

Rocky Mountain News
July 12, 1993

He had the human touch that you don't find, not only in journalism, but hardly anywhere. The people he wrote about were the people other people wouldn't notice.

WALT YOUNG

Hope, Glory and No Regrets

DENVER — The tailgunner came into the room in the basement where the pictures and the models and the medals are, and said he had to make sure he doesn't forget to turn on Channel 4 at 4 p.m.

Bob Caron is 75 and lives in unincorporated Adams County, in a split-level house in a subdivision where none of the streets is straight. He saw the flash Aug. 6, 1945, over Hiroshima. The flash meant the atomic bomb had exploded, 80,000 people died instantly, and the 12 men on the Enola Gay accomplished their mission.

"Can't miss the First News Quiz," he said. "I can win $5,000 today. The people they've called haven't been home, but if Channel 4 ever calls I'll be ready."

He took the photograph that showed the world what the atomic bomb could create. The photograph is on the wall. On the opposite wall is a painting he did of the shoreline on Montauk Point, N.Y.

He didn't know the purpose of Special Bombing Mission 13 until it was history.

History says a 10,000-pound bomb was dropped from 31,600 feet and exploded 1,890 feet above the Shima Surgical Clinic.

It would change history, but it would not change him. "No remorse, no bad dreams," he said. "We accomplished our mission."

An exhibit on the Enola Gay, *The Final Act: The Atomic Bomb and the End of World War II*, was scheduled to open this month at the Smithsonian National Air and Space Museum. People from the museum flew the surviving members of the crew to Washington and interviewed them. The museum came up with an exhibit that questioned the morality of the decision to drop the bomb.

Veterans groups and 81 members of Congress demanded the resignation of the director of the museum, Martin Harwit, and he quit May 2.

The exhibit has been cut to include only the interviews with the crew and the front half of the fuselage of the Enola Gay.

No opening date has been set.

Six men on the crew still are living. They have heard the stories that what they did drove them to suicide. The stories are not true.

Caron got up and closed the door to the room.

"The wife doesn't like me smoking my pipe in the house," he said. "I don't care. If I'm going to talk about this, I'm going to smoke my pipe."

The mission

He grew up in Brooklyn and went to a high school for students who showed promise in engineering. He enlisted Sept. 8, 1943, trained at Lowry Air Force Base and was sent to the Boeing Plant in Wichita, Kansas. His job was to learn to operate the turrets in an experimental plane, the YB-29, the largest bomber ever built.

He was certified as a gunner and machinist, and sent back to Wichita to test the XB-29, modified from the YB-29. The commander was Col. Paul Tibbets. He met a girl named Kay at the public swimming pool, and they decided to get married on Halloween, his 25th birthday.

Late in September, Tibbets asked him to join a new composite group at Wendover Field in Nevada.

Caron reported Oct. 29, 1944.

Tibbets had a meeting the next morning in Colorado Springs and said Caron could fly with him. Tibbets had his driver drop Caron off on the edge of town. Caron hitchhiked on a semi-truck, a pickup and a wagon pulled by horses, and got to Wichita a day late.

He and Kay were married Nov. 1, 1944.

Back at Wendover, Tibbets told his men they should not speculate about their mission. They had 15 B-29s, modified from the YB-29. They took out the armor plating and the guns, except for the two guns in the tail, and Caron was assigned to teach the 14 other tailgunners to operate the tail turret and fire their guns at attacking planes.

They dropped fat, round casings filled with 10,000 pounds of ballast from 30,000 feet until they could hit a 300-foot circle.

After the bombs were released, they made 155-degree turns into a dive.

Among the men, a rumor started that a new chemical bomb had been developed by the British, and it would be their mission to drop it.

Caron spent his free time in the base library. He read an article about a cyclotron scientists had built in Berkeley, Calif., that could split atoms, creating a huge release of energy. It weighed 21 tons, but he thought if they ever could make one small enough to fit in a plane it could be a weapon.

Caron wrote Branch Rickey, president of the Brooklyn Dodgers, and said he was about to go overseas and wanted a Brooklyn Dodgers cap.

Just before Christmas, Bob Hope came to perform and referred to Wendover Field as "Leftover Field."

On April 12, 1945, Roosevelt died.

On May 8, the Germans surrendered.

On June 2, Caron's daughter, Judy, was born.

Tibbets and the crews flew to the Martin Bomber Plant in Omaha to pick up 15 B-29s manufactured to their specifications.

The foreman of the plant tapped Tibbets on the shoulder and pointed at one with the No. 82 painted on the nose.

"Take that one for yourself, colonel," the foreman said. "It was built on a Wednesday. You don't want one built on a Monday or a Friday."

Tibbets had an arrow in a circle painted on the tail of each plane.

Late in June, just before the men were told they would leave for Tinian in the Mariana Islands, the Brooklyn Dodgers sent Caron a cap.

On July 16, the first atom bomb was detonated near Alamogordo, N.M., in a valley the local people called Jornada del Muerto — The Journey of Death — and the scientists called Site S.

Tinian had been captured in July 1944. Someone decided it was shaped like Manhattan and named the roads after the major streets and avenues. The 509th moved into Quonset huts in the Columbia University area, where the Seabees had been until Tibbets asked for it.

Men on the base called them "Tibbets' Private Air Force" and threw rocks at their Quonset huts.

The 509th flew practice missions, dropping traditional bombs in the same fat casings, and making 155-degree turns into a dive.

The men were listening to American music on the radio when Tokyo Rose came on and said "Welcome, Black Arrow squadron with their pumpkins."

Tibbets had the arrows removed from the tails of his planes and replaced with a symbol on other planes on Tinian, the letter R.

Psychologists watched the men in the 509th play softball and drink in the enlisted men's club, and concluded the men in the 509th "probably were the most (psychologically) balanced in the Air Force."

At 2 p.m. Aug. 4, the crew was called into the briefing hut. Black cloths hung from the walls. Tibbets stood on a platform and said, "The moment has arrived."

The cloths were taken down to show maps of the primary targets, Hiroshima, Kokura, Nagasaki. Tibbets signaled to a technician to start a projector. The film got chewed up in the sprockets.

"The film you are not about to see was made of the only test we have performed," Tibbets said.

He drew a mushroom cloud on a chalkboard. He said a girl miles away, blind from birth, had seen a flash. He gave each man a pair of goggles with Polaroid lenses.

He told them the 155-degree turn into the dive was calculated to get away from the blast as fast as possible, but nobody knew how far away they needed to be.

The next morning, Caron's crew went to their plane, and a sign painter was just finishing the "Y" in "Enola Gay" in block letters on the nose.

The co-pilot, Bob Lewis ran to Tibbets' office and said "What the hell is this?"

"It's my mother," Tibbets said.

The night of Aug. 5, Caron read *Captain From Castile* and wrote letters to his parents and his wife. He said he couldn't tell them anything about the mission he would fly but they should save the newspaper clippings. At midnight, they went to the chow hut and were served Tibbets' favorite meal, pineapple fritters.

A physicist's worst nightmare

Floodlights shined on generals waiting when the crew walked out to the Enola Gay for Special Bombing Mission No. 13. One of the generals said the men would have all the hot dogs and cold beer they wanted when they got back. The crew posed for a photograph that would appear in newspapers around the world, Caron kneeling in the front row in the Brooklyn Dodgers cap.

A photographer gave Caron a K-20 camera, the military version of the Speed Graphic. He climbed the ladder into the plane, through the tunnel to the tail. He hung his rosary beads on his gun sight. The Enola Gay took off at 2:45 a.m., headed north-northwest.

In the forward compartment, Navy Capt. Deak Parsons, who had worked on the Manhattan Project, unscrewed a plug on the end of the bomb. He slid in a slug of uranium 235, then a gunpowder charge, then a detonator. He screwed the plug in.

In the tail, Caron fired 50 rounds to test his guns. He crawled into the rear compartment. The men were checking their instruments.

He sat on the scanner's seat.

Tibbets crawled back through the tunnel from the forward compartment and sat

Ellen Jaskol/Rocky Mountain News

BOB CARON, TAILGUNNER FOR THE ENOLA GAY, HOLDS THE PHOTO HE TOOK OF THE MUSHROOM CLOUD.

on the floor next to Caron. The colonel had 12 cyanide tablets in a cardboard box in his breast pocket. He wouldn't tell the men about them until one of their reunions.

The colonel turned to Caron.

"You figured out what we're doing today?" Tibbets said.

Caron remembered the rumor about the British chemical bomb.

"Is this a chemist's worst nightmare, colonel?" he said.

Tibbets shook his head.

Caron remembered the cyclotron in the magazine.

"Colonel, is this a physicist's worst nightmare?"

Tibbets squinted at Caron.

"You might call it that," Tibbets said. "I'd better get forward."

He started to crawl through the tunnel to the front, and Caron reached up and grabbed the cuff of his pants.

"Colonel, are we splitting atoms today?"

Tibbets backed out of the tunnel to look at Caron.

"We are carrying the world's first atomic bomb," he said. "You'd better get back in the tail."

Caron crawled through the tunnel to the tail and strapped himself into his harness. The sun rose. He was hot where it hit him, cold where it didn't.

He put on the Polaroid goggles and looked at the sun. It looked like a purple blob. He took them off and read *Captain From Castile*.

Tibbets came on the radio.

"Gentlemen, we are carrying the world's first atomic bomb. When the bomb is dropped, Lt. Beser will record our reactions to what we see. This recording is being made for history. Watch your language and don't clutter up the intercom."

They came over the coastline of Japan.

At 7:15, Tibbets came on and announced the target.

"It's Hiroshima."

Caron looked down at the villages, the smoke from factories, the people already out working in fields.

At 8:12, Tibbets told the men to put on their goggles.

Caron saw black.

At 8:15:17 a.m., 17 seconds past schedule, the bomb doors opened.

The plane leapt into the air from the loss of 10,000 pounds, then made a 155-degree turn into a dive.

The flash came 43 seconds after the bomb was released. The flash lasted one millionth of one second. Caron thought he was blinded.

Tibbets came on the radio.

"See anything, Bob?"

Caron opened his eyes.

"No, colonel," he said. "The turret's in the way."

Tibbets turned the plane 50 degrees to the left.

Caron saw a bubble expanding toward the plane.

He tried to yell.

It swallowed the plane.

"Flak!" Tibbets yelled.

"Here comes another one!" Caron yelled.

A second bubble swallowed the plane, and then it was calm.

Tibbets said the waves were air compressed by the explosion — the second had bounced off the ground — and there would be no more.

"Keep it short, and keep it clean," he said. "Bob?"

"A column of smoke rising fast," Caron said. "It has a fiery red core. A bubbling mass, purple-gray in color, with that red core. It's all turbulent. Fires are springing up everywhere, like flames shooting up out of a huge bed of coals. I am starting to count the fires. One, two, three, four, five, six. the mushroom shape that Capt. Parsons spoke about.... It's like a mass of bubbling molasses. The mushroom is spreading out. It's maybe a mile or two wide and half a mile high. It's nearly level with us and climbing. It's very black, but there's a purplish tint to the cloud. The base of the mushroom looks like a heavy undercast that is shot through with flames. The city must be below that."

"How's that ride back there, Bob?" Tibbets said.

"Better than the 25 cents Cyclone at Coney Island, colonel," Caron said.

"You can pay me the quarter when we land."

Tibbets turned the plane to circle the city so the rest of the crew could see. The other men gave their observations. Caron took photographs through the escape hatch.

The plane completed its circle and started back to Tinian.

In the movie *Above and Beyond*, Robert Taylor is Tibbets, and he says "My God, what have we done?" Tibbets has said he did not say that. Tibbets also has said he did say, "I think we've got this war won."

Caron thinks he might have said that but doesn't want to argue as long as somebody said it.

They were 363 miles away when Caron lost sight of the mushroom cloud.

He took off his chest parachute and used it for a pillow. He turned on his dynamometer and amplodyne for the warmth they created. He slept.

When he woke up, he finished *Captain From Castile.* The Enola Gay landed at Tinian at 2:58 p.m., the same generals waiting in the afternoon sun.

The crew was taken to a Quonset hut and told to sit in the chairs around a table. The generals stood behind them. When they finished telling what they had seen, they went to another Quonset hut for the hot dogs and cold beer.

Some enlisted men already had been there.

They went to the chow hall and got in line.

The answer to the First News Quiz is "Hope and Glory."

He and Kay moved here after the war because he liked it when he was in training at Lowry. They had two more daughters and a son, and now they have eight grandchildren and one great-grandchild. Caron was a design engineer for Sundstrand Corp. for 27 years until he retired, and Kay retired from cooking dinner.

Tonight is the night they go to Denny's.

" 'Hope and Glory,' " he said. "I ought to be able to remember that."

His photograph of the explosion was printed on millions of leaflets that were dropped over Japan the day after the bomb exploded. A plutonium bomb was dropped Aug. 9 on Nagasaki. Caron flew a bombing raid a day later and had the 85 combat points he needed to go home.

On Aug. 15, 1945, the war ended.

"I've told my grandchildren about being overseas," he said. "A lot of kids these days, it doesn't mean that much to them."

His autobiography, *Fire of a Thousand Suns,* published by WEB Publishing, was released this month. He sells autographed copies of the photograph of the mushroom cloud, the crew and the Enola Gay, plaques with his signature and commemorative caps. The Brooklyn Dodgers cap was stolen from his desk at work.

Tibbets lives in Columbus, Ohio, and he gets hate letters every year on the anniversary of the bombing.

Caron got an anonymous letter a couple of years ago, postmarked from San Diego, from a man who accused him of genocide.

He saved it and the piles of letters from men who were fighting on Okinawa when the bomb was dropped, thanking him for saving lives.

The Enola Gay was left in a corner on Andrews Air Force Base in Maryland until the early 1970s when it was taken to a warehouse and disassembled.

The exhibit at the Smithsonian will show only the fuselage.

Caron has not decided whether he will go.

"I don't go in for bleeding heart crap," he said. "I don't want to rewrite history. Let's just leave it at that."

The men on the crew of the Enola Gay have a reunion every two years. The 50th anniversary will be in Albuquerque at the National Atomic Museum.

The men don't talk about what happened, because they all were there.

Last year in Washington, he was eating breakfast with Tibbets in the coffee shop of their hotel, and he took a quarter out of his pocket.

"Here's that quarter I owe you for the ride," Caron said.

"I'll keep this," Tibbets said.

On Channel 4, Larry Green called a man in Longmont who wasn't home.

Caron turned off the television. His wife would be home soon. He sat back down and pulled on his pipe.

"No hope and glory for me today," he said. "But I'm still here. If there's one thing I've learned in life, it's that you have to be in the right place at the right time."

Rocky Mountain News
May 21, 1995

"Bottoms Up" to the Hilltop Lounge

DENVER — It was three in the afternoon, and Joe Muro and Roxie DeNuzzi were behind the bar in the Hilltop Lounge, in white aprons and red suspenders, wiping the black Formica.

Muro opened at noon, and DeNuzzi had just come in to take over. The only customer had been a radio advertising salesman who drove past for years and always wanted to stop for a beer. They lifted the ashtray in front of each stool and wiped the black Formica.

After 48 years, some people still don't set their beer on their coaster.

"Sarge switched to light," Muro said.

"Things change," DeNuzzi said.

They both are 78 and have done this since they opened in 1947, taking over for each other in the bar every day, and now it is sold.

The bar is brick and square, 20 feet by 20 feet, and it is set west of Sheridan Boulevard on West 48th Avenue. It has maple coolers with chrome latches, red linoleum, seven stools and five red-and-yellowed vinyl booths. Maximum occupancy: 28.

Muro left for supper.

"It'll be good for Joe," DeNuzzi said. "I don't want to quit, but there's all kinds of things I always wanted to do and couldn't. Things like...well, I can't think of anything specific right now."

DeNuzzi and Muro grew up across the alley from each other in northeast Denver, and after the war they got GI loans for this.

They built it themselves and named it the Hilltop Drive-In, and they made hamburgers and fries and had carhops. DeNuzzi says he invented the bacon cheeseburger one night. In 1959, they got tired of customers taking their carhops and marrying them, so they made it a bar.

Then Interstate 70 was built right in front, and people can't see the bar until they are past.

At 3:30, the regulars — Sarge, Al, Art, Terry, Chief — started to come in.

"The usual?" DeNuzzi said.

"Nah," Al said. "The usual light."

They have Michelob, Budweiser, regular and light Coors. They have some cans of Olympia for a guy who comes in Wednesday afternoons. They haven't had to mix a drink in two weeks, since the woman who likes tomato juice and vodka went to see her daughter in Utah.

DeNuzzi turned the crank on the cash register and set the beers back on the coasters.

Muro came back at six.

"Al switched," DeNuzzi said.

"What's going on?" Muro said.

DeNuzzi left, then the regulars did, and Muro wiped the Formica. Muro is married and has five boys. DeNuzzi is a bachelor. There have been doctor appointments, heart problems, funerals, but neither has taken a vacation since 1959.

The new owners plan to remodel and call it the Squeeze Inn.

"It's best for Roxie," Muro said. "We had a good place, never called the cops, but they had to go and build that highway. It's time to do the things we couldn't do, like... well, now the boys are all grown."

DeNuzzi came back at 9, and they stood behind the bar, wiping the black Formica. After 48 years, it glows.

"Things change," DeNuzzi said.

"Yeah," Muro said. "I just never thought it would be us."

Rocky Mountain News
November 29, 1995

The Longest Day's Journey

DENVER — On an afternoon 50 years after the Longest Day, three men sat around a table, seeing each other for the first time since the morning they waded onto Omaha Beach.

John Pellegren, Baynaird "Mac" McNeil and Harvey Seipp waded onto Omaha Beach with the 467th Battalion the morning of June 6, 1944. The story of D-Day has been told. This is about how the stories of three men are the same, and how they are different.

"Sammy DiPaolo — remember Sammy DiPaolo? — got shot right in the head, nicest guy you'd ever want to meet and then he's dead in the sand," Seipp said. "He was listed as missing in action. After the war I went up to Frederick just to let his mother know what had happened, that he wasn't coming back, and that he was a hero that day."

"You went up there, too?" McNeil said. "I did, too, just to let her know." "What else was there to do?" Pellegren said. "She needed to know what happened that day."

The 467th Anti-Aircraft Artillery Battalion was a self-propelled battalion that would suffer 20 percent casualties that day.

Pellegren, now 69 and living in Littleton, was a corporal with the headquarters battery. McNeil, now 75 and living in Arvada, was a sergeant with A Battery, first platoon. Seipp, now 70 and living in Golden, was a corporal with B Battery, second platoon.

They remember the smell of smoke and dead bodies and cows that day. They remember seeing the bodies of Germans with pistols that nobody touched because some had thin wires attached to them. They remember that they could not stop shaking and that the ground was shaking under them.

The LCT that had carried Seipp across the English Channel that morning couldn't get to the section of beach code-named Easy Red, because another LCT hit an underwater mine and blocked the way. While it headed for another opening, it hit another mine. The men went into the water and waded to an unfamiliar section of beach about 8 a.m.

Just after they got to the beach, mortars killed five men from Seipp's platoon, and an American half-track ran over another.

"The sergeant was giving an order, and he got hit right in the snoot," Seipp said. "That damn pillbox up there on the hill. I can still see that slot they were firing from, just a black line that you'd see fire shoot out of and somebody down on the beach going down."

McNeil landed on Easy Red about 8 a.m.

"They were aiming right down at us," McNeil said. "And then one of our gun sections got it. We knew it was out because it stopped shooting at us."

About an hour later, Pellegren's platoon was supposed to land on Easy Red but was dropped at the next section, Fox Green.

"I'd been so seasick for four days, I just wanted to get on land," Pellegren said. "Then we get there, and they're shooting down on us, and all you could see was that slot up there, and I'm still feeling more seasick and tired than scared, and we're just trying to get organized. And then the shooting from that pillbox finally stopped."

About 1 p.m., A Battery took out the pillbox, and the troops started to march single-file up the first exit.

McNeil's platoon reached the top of the bluffs late in the afternoon. Pellegren made it early in the evening. Seipp spent the night pinned down at the base of the bluffs.

"I ate an apple, the first food I'd been able to hold down for four days, dug a couple shovelfuls of dirt and laid down, and the next thing I know it's morning," Pellegren said.

"You got one of those apples?" Seipp said. "They were all shredded by the shrapnel by the time we got up there. It's funny, but I always wondered what they tasted like."

"Wonderful," Pellegren said.

The days after that were identified in relation to June 6 — D-plus-1 and so on. The 467th was not reunited before the end of the war. The platoons moved into Germany, fighting in most of the major battles until the Germans surrendered May 7, 1945.

Pellegren now is president of an architectural and engineering firm. Seipp owns a company that cleans septic tanks and sewerage lines. McNeil was a contractor and a factory representative in plumbing supplies and now is retired.

After the war, Seipp told people about what had happened June 6, 1944, and went to every reunion of A Battery.

"People need to know about what happened that day and why those boys died," he said. "It's important to understand what happened."

Pellegren didn't talk about D-Day until a neighbor convinced him to go to Normandy for the 40th anniversary, and since then he has gone to reunions of B Battery and read every book he can find about D-Day.

He is in Normandy for the 50th anniversary.

"For a while, I was sorry I had waited 40 years, but maybe I had to wait 40 years," he said.

"The first reunion, it was wonderful," he said. "After that, it was a lot of telling the same stories again, but it's still important to me to be with those people. That's why I'm going back again."

McNeil never had talked about it before.

"Maybe I missed something, but I wanted to get on with things," he said. "Even right now, talking about it for the first time with people who were there, people I haven't seen for 50 years, I feel like it's already time to get on with things. I don't know if anybody will ever really understand everything that happened that day."

A fourth man with the 467th lives in the Denver area but still refuses to talk about what happened that day.

Last week, a plaque recognizing members of the 467th was dedicated at the site of the pillbox.

That day 50 years ago, they were assigned to a mission, which became a battle, which became an historical event.

Today, there is no way to know how the individuals shaped the event, or how the event shaped the individuals.

There are only three men sitting around a table on an afternoon 50 years later, seeing each other for the first time since that morning.

"Looking back, I wouldn't take a million dollars for that day," Seipp said.

"And I wouldn't take two million dollars to go back," McNeil said.

"Yes," Pellegren said, "And I think I'm very glad that it has been 50 years."

Rocky Mountain News
June 5, 1994

A New Leg and a New Start

DENVER — Sgt. Hilbert Potter hopped on his left leg and dribbled the basketball until he was outside the three-point line.

Potter, 31, is at Fitzsimons Army Medical Center to be fitted for a prosthesis for his right leg, which was shot off by friendly fire two days before the end of the Persian Gulf War.

SGT. HILBERT POTTER LOST HIS LEG TO FRIENDLY FIRE DURING THE GULF WAR.

Glenn Asakawa/Rocky Mountain News

The old prosthesis cracked while he was playing basketball in the cold. Until he gets the new one, he plays basketball on one leg.

Potter jumped, and the ball arced through the net.

"Some people think this is out of my range," he said. "At first, playing was kind of like what happened to me over there that night — not sure what happened or what's going on. Now, I've learned to accept what happened, and to work around it."

Potter commanded a squad of six combat engineers attached to the 2nd Armored Cavalry Regiment. On Feb. 25, his squad was guarding 72 captured Iraqi soldiers behind the American line. But when it got dark, the Americans retreated to a defensive position about 400 yards behind his men.

At 1 a.m. the combat engineers left their prisoners and tried to get back behind the American line. They had just passed the forward scout units when their armored personnel carrier was hit.

"All I knew was the enemy can't hit you from the front when you're driving away from them," said Potter.

The driver apparently was killed, but Potter and the rest of his men were not injured. They crawled about 300 yards across the sand and lay in a circle to protect one another.

About 20 minutes later, they felt the ground rumble, and an American M1-A1 Abrams tank came out of the darkness. The tank stopped about 75 feet away. The 7.62-mm machine gun swiveled until it aimed at the men.

Two of his men stood up and yelled, "We're Americans, we're friendly," Potter said. "But the guy in the tank, he just had a scope that sensed the heat from our bodies. We were just shapes. He was probably just as scared as we were."

The machine gunner opened fire, killing the two men who were standing, Potter said. The firing stopped for about 15 seconds, then resumed.

Potter was hit once in the left shoulder, twice in the buttocks and at least twice above his right knee. Two other men were seriously wounded, each in the ankle and leg. One was not hit.

The tank turned and disappeared into the darkness.

Potter used his rifle sling as a tourniquet on his leg but could not see how seriously he was wounded.

"I kept kicking something with my left leg, and I thought it was a rock," he said. "We could feel the rumble of tanks all around us. We weren't on anybody's side then — it was like everybody was against us."

They were picked up by medics just after dawn, and Potter realized he had been kicking his right foot.

Two of the men returned to duty, but Potter and another wounded man are waiting to be discharged.

He lives in Louisville with his wife, Joy, and 6-year-old daughter, Amanda, and plans to earn a degree in physical therapy.

"My leg is gone, and it doesn't matter who pulled the trigger," he said.

"I'm getting a new leg and a new start. And pretty soon, I'll have my old jump shot back."

Rocky Mountain News
January 12, 1992

Women Can Still Break Your Heart

NEW IBERIA, La. — S.M. "Pete" Darby sits down in a spotless kitchen in the peeling white house where he lives alone, 73 years old and a retired carpenter.

"My wife died, it will be 11 months on the 10th," he says. "One day I come in here and she's sitting right where you're sitting, and she grabs my arm and tells me — it still sends a quiver through me — 'Pete, when I die, I don't want you to wear any mourning for me. I want you to go out and find a woman to take care of you.'

"When she passed away I put her away as good as a man can put a woman away, and for four months I didn't do anything. We were married 49 years, and when you're married that long to a woman as good as that, there's things you just don't forget."

And that is the way Pete Darby begins the conversation.

After his wife died, he spent a lot of time working in his garden and taking on carpentry jobs he could do at his house. Those were the same things he had done since he retired. He also sat around his house, doing what he'd promised his wife he wouldn't do.

"A friend of mine, his wife died before mine did, and he'd come over and sit out there and say, 'I've got nothing to live for.' I'd say, 'You got some beautiful kids and they love you.' He'd just say, 'I've got nothing to live for,' and it wasn't 90 days before he went up and joined her. Then after I lost my wife, sometimes I felt like that, too..."

After four months, his sister set him up with a blind date at Smiley's Bayou Club in Erath. He went and he met the blind date and a 22-year-old girl named Susan. Susan overheard him talking about finding a woman to take care of things around the house. One thing led to another and she moved in with him.

Everything worked out fine, as far as Susan and Darby were concerned.

Some people didn't see it that way.

"One time she had some people in Smiley's ask her, 'What are you doing with that old man? He's too old for you,'" he says.

"They were talking about me." Susan said, "That's my business and his business, and that man is good to me."

"And I was good to her — it's not the age, it's the treatment — but you know how young people are, you can't tie 'em down."

Susan moved out on friendly terms, and Darby kept going out. He goes to The Grey Goose in Delcambre on Friday nights and Smiley's Bayou Club in Erath on Saturday nights and Sunday afternoons. He drives an old Chevrolet station wagon and sometimes he has three or four women friends in it. When he came down with the flu and couldn't go out, a woman from Abbeville moved in to take care of him.

"When I was a young man I was on the bashful side," he says. "I thought if I asked a woman I might get the wrong answer. But there's no wrong answer, they either tell you yes or no."

During the week he works at remodeling his old workshop across the driveway to make a place for his grandson. He has flown more than 4,800 hours since 1950, but he doesn't fly anymore. He gave his garden to his neighbor, because his wife isn't around to put up what he raises.

He ran for sheriff of Iberia Parish two years ago, saying young people shouldn't be out drinking and hot rodding around until all hours of the night. He got only 237 votes, and if he feels as good in 1987 as he does now, he says he'll run again.

And he says he'll keep going out and doing the things he didn't do for 49 years.

"When my wife was living, if one of us wanted to go somewhere both of us went," he says. "Forty-nine years, and I never thought about going out. I never cared about racehorses or rooster fights. I might go to the rasslin' — my wife used to love rasslin' — but mostly I like to dance with the ladies.

"Sometimes I ask myself if I think I'm doing the right thing or not, but I can't come up with an answer. My wife told me to go out and find somebody to take care of me and that's what I'm doing. People who say I shouldn't be doing things like that, well they might be looking at my point of view from the wrong direction."

He has numbers written in different women's handwriting on the wall next to the telephone. He calls them, and they call him. Friday and Saturday nights and Sunday afternoons he goes out and meets them, but he says he's got to be careful.

"Women, they'll make you believe you can catch the moon with your teeth, some of them will," he says. "One of them even said that when my hair's all fixed up I got pretty hair. Oh yeah, you gotta be careful, though. They can still break your heart."

The Daily Iberian
March 8, 1985

Two Kinds of Fishing

NEW IBERIA, La. — The two men fished together whenever they could, which wasn't very often.

The man who owned the boat sat in the front and controlled the trolling motor. The other man sat in the back and went wherever the man in the front of the boat wanted to go. It didn't make much difference to him.

The man in the front of the boat often yelled at the man in the back of the boat, about the way he fished. The truth was, the man in the back of the boat wasn't a good fisherman. That didn't seem to bother him as much as it bothered the other man in the boat.

This morning the men fished in a pond surrounded by tall trees. They had come through a narrow canal, through the trees. When they came into the pond it was like they had discovered someplace, except there were Miller Lite cans and a Nacho Cheese Doritos bag floating in the water. Anyway, nobody else would come back there that day.

The man in the front of the boat was always telling the man in the back of the boat about the importance of setting the hook. Once, when the men were fishing a canal, he had set the hook so hard he had flung the fish over his head and onto the bank behind him. They had searched the ground until they found the fish, then thrown it back. Other times he had snapped the spines of fish, setting the hook.

This day they used electric-blue worms, which were rubber with speckles that glittered in the sun. Of course, they had lead weights so they would sink to the bottom where the bass were.

The man in the front of the boat knew all about worms and other lures because fishing was important to him. His wife would have a baby soon, and he knew that would require trade-offs. It also meant that eventually he would have one more person to go fishing with. Not that it made any difference, he didn't mind fishing alone.

Right after they came into the pond he set the hook in two small bass. Then nothing for several hours. The man in the back of the boat began to think maybe the two fish had come into the pond because they wanted to be alone.

When he fished, the man in the back of the boat tended to daydream. Once in a bowling alley he had met a guy who claimed to have the patent on the Dumpster. The guy with the patent had bought everybody drinks all night.

The man in the back of the boat was daydreaming about the guy with the patent. He wasn't sure he believed the part about the Dumpsters, but he admired a man who would back up a story with drinks.

The lilies in the pond drifted with the wind and the current. A raft of lilies would drift across the lake and another raft would drift another direction. That must have been how the continents drifted around on the face of the earth.

The man in the back of the boat was wondering about continental drift when the bass struck.

At first, the bass felt like it might have been an old branch or maybe moss. The man pulled on the line, the bass pulled back.

"Set the hook!" the man in the front of the boat yelled. "Set the hook!"

The fish started the fight, and that was why it got hooked. All the man did was reel it in, and when the fish was reeled up near the boat the man in the front of the boat scooped it up with the net.

The man in the back of the boat held it by its lower jaw and pulled out the hook. He hadn't set it very well.

It was 2 ½ pounds and beautiful, but only in the way all bass are beautiful. The truth was, as bass go it was fairly ugly. If it was a car, the man thought, it would be an AMC Pacer. He held it up in the sunshine and turned it, green and brown and yellow, then dropped it into the live well with the other two fish.

The man in the front of the boat seemed more excited about the fish than the man in the back. He just liked to see hooked fish.

They settled back to their fishing. Sometimes the man in the back of the boat would make different comments, the same way the other man tried different colors of worms. He would say things like, "What if your son turns out to be a daughter and she thinks fish are slimy and gross?"

The man in the front of the boat didn't say anything and kept fishing. By the end of the day, he would catch five fish, and the other man in the boat finished with two. Before they left they would throw back the fish they caught.

The man in the back of the boat would hold the bass in the sun, then drop it into the water and watch it sink. When it realized it was free, it would swim away. Chances are, it wouldn't hook itself again.

They would go home early because the man in the front of the boat would have to go to Lamaze classes that night. The trade-offs were already beginning.

For now, they sat there in the boat in the pond with the lilies. The one man daydreaming and the other man waiting for another chance to set the hook. That was what they both called fishing.

The Daily Iberian
May 14, 1984

Hobo Landry Still Has 23,800 Fish Hooks

NEW IBERIA, La. — During the 1950s Yarbro's Drugstore in Denver, Colorado, put thousands of fishhooks into a huge champagne glass and had a contest to see who could guess how many there were.

Hobo Landry was living in Denver then, but he hadn't started calling himself "Hobo" yet. Back then he was Roland, and he drove a delivery truck for drugstores. Yarbro's was on his route, and one day he made his guess.

He guessed 56,500.

"It just looked like there was a God damn lot of 'em," he says. "And I was right, except there was 56,582 or 83. I figure they just must of had a bunch of extra hooks they wanted to get rid of."

They gave him the hooks and the huge champagne glass — it didn't take him long to break the glass.

The hooks are shiny-gold, and at the eye they are bent at a 45-degree angle. They don't make fish hooks like that anymore, he says.

A woman who worked in another drugstore gave him hundreds of film canisters, the metal kind with screw-on tops. Every night after supper he counted out piles of 100 hooks and his kids put them in the canisters. During the day, nobody was allowed to go into that room.

It took months to divide up 56,582 or 56,583 fish hooks. After he had them all in canisters, he put them in a closet. The hooks are too big for trout, so nobody up in Denver wanted them.

He kept them in an old typewriter case, until the handle broke. Then he kept them in a cardboard box.

After his wife divorced him, Hobo moved back down here. He lived out in the swamp for a while and he started calling himself "Hobo." He had grown up with Wheel Louviere, so when Wheel's wife died about three years ago, he moved out here to the farm near Patoutville, to help out. He put the hooks in a shed behind the house.

Right now Hobo, 59, is wearing olive drab army pants, white rubber boots and no shirt. He has silver hair down to his shoulders and a silver beard that is halfway down his chest. When he lived in Denver, he grew a mustache and goatee like Buffalo Bill used to have. A barber in Denver used to trim them for free, just to help out. He hasn't shaved since Wheel's wife died.

The hooks are the right size for perch and bream, and Hobo says he knows a woman who caught a five-pound catfish with one. He gives them away or sold them for $1 a canister. He has sold several thousand to fishing stores, and the stores sell them for $2.

One woman bought some, gave away the hooks and saved the canister. They don't make film canisters like that anymore.

Hobo doesn't keep track of how many he has, so he takes me out to count them. He goes out the back door, past a white puppy, a black kitten, a white kitten and a black puppy. He goes through the gate, past the Shetland pony and her colt, through the back gate, climbs through the frame of the tractor shed he and Wheel are building, past the sow that has killed 13 of her 15 babies, past a mottled-gray bull, and through the back gate. Each gate Hobo has to lift up and kick to get it open — "Gotta fix this God damn gate one of these days," he says each time. Then he wades through weeds five feet tall, lifts up and kicks the door to the shed.

In the shed they also keep old boat propellers, old tires, pulleys, a red sweatshirt and all sorts of engine parts. The hooks are in the cardboard box, tied with rope around one way, then across the other. The cannisters are yellow with red lids, yellow and blue, all black, white and blue, white and red. There are 239.

He tells me to take one, and I pick out a yellow can with a blue lid. That leaves him with 238.

Then we go back to the house, and at each gate he says, "Gotta fix this God damn gate one of these days."

Lately, Hobo hasn't been doing much of anything.

"Every day it looks like it's gonna rain, so there's no use getting started on anything," he says. "I got some trotlines out — the hooks are perfect for that — but I haven't even bothered to bait 'em. With the weather the way it's been, mostly I just sleep. Drink beer, if we got it."

It is one of the backward things about this world that a man can have more than 23,800 fish hooks but no beer.

"Hell," Hobo says. "Those fish hooks'll probably be around after I'm gone. If you ever need any hooks, you know where to come."

The Daily Iberian
August 20, 1984

The Daily Iberian

HOBO LANDRY AND WHEEL LOUVIERE LIVE TOGETHER ON A FARM NEAR PATOUTVILLE, LA.

about Greg's shirts...

When Greg first started at the *Rocky Mountain News*, an editor took one look at his signature attire of Hawaiian shirt, black jeans and cowboy boots and said something about "not following the dress code."

Greg said, "I guess I just broke the code."

He started wearing Hawaiian shirts about 1989 after our first trip to Key West. When he died, he had 96 shirts in his closet.

Every morning, he would pick out a Hawaiian shirt, spray starch and iron it before he went to work.

Chapter seven

Western Life

Greg wanted to *understand*

the traditional ways.

DONLIN MANY BAD HORSES

There's Power in This Place

LITTLE BIGHORN NATIONAL BATTLEFIELD MONUMENT, Mont. — The two leaders walked away from their tribes, along the ridge where the battle ended.

All of their lives on their reservations they have been told June 25, 1876, was a day like this — hot and still and they could see until the ridges and ravines became wrinkles. Oliver Red Cloud, 77, is the great-grandson of the Lakota war chief Red Cloud. Dan Old Elk, 55, is the great-grandson of Curly, a Crow scout who led Lt. Col.

George Armstrong Custer and the 7th Cavalry to this place.

"Didn't your grandfather understand how strong we were on that day?" Red Cloud said.

"Didn't your grandfather understand that those ways had to end?" Old Elk said. "Now we are back, for this reason."

For this reason, all the tribes that were here on that day were back last week for the first time. They are the Crow, Arikira,

OLD AND NEW SHOW AT SUNRISE AT THE LAKOTA CAMP NEAR LITTLE BIGHORN NATIONAL MONUMENT IN MONTANA.

Northern Cheyenne, Arapaho and Lakota. More than 260 soldiers and attached personnel and about 100 American Indians died the last time they were here.

After 119 years, they came for the first time because they were invited for the first time.

For this reason, Donlin Many Bad Horses, keeper of the pipe for the Northern Cheyenne, sat on Battle Ridge and thanked the Great Spirit for the water and the plants and for bringing all the tribes together.

He opened the buffalo bag and filled the pipe with the sacred mixture. Three tribal leaders held out their disposable lighters.

"We keep the old ways that are important," he said later. "But we aren't stupid about it."

For this reason, a Custer stood at attention where the other Custer has a monument. Steve Alexander is killed five times a year in the Custer's Last Stand Re-enactment. In between, he is on a land survey crew for Consumer Power Co. in Jackson, Mich.

He wears buckskin, eats pemmican and hardtack, bows to women and calls them "ma'am."

"People say, 'You talk and walk just like Custer,'" Alexander said. "And the strange part is, I do."

And there also is the Real Bird Family Re-enactment of the Little Bighorn.

For this reason, Roger Kennedy, the director of the National Park Service, asked Bernard Red Cherries to introduce him to a group of elders. The elders spoke only Northern Cheyenne. Red Cherries moved his hands in the air to draw the shape of a dome.

"Washington," one of the elders said. "Aho."

"They said, 'Welcome back,' " Red Cherries said.

For this reason, Gerard Baker, the superintendent, went to his sweat lodge next to Little Bighorn River, a quarter of a mile from where Custer first saw the Indian camp. He is Hidatsa-Mandan. He built the lodge and covered it with canvas from old tepees, quilts and carpet.

"There's power in this place," he said. "Especially at a time like this. This isn't just a place where something happened a long time ago."

For this reason, the Crows killed a buffalo in their herd and took the meat to the Lakota camp.

"I got part of a haunch," Jimmy Low Eagle said. "When I get it home, I'll probably tell my mama somebody hit it with their pickup or something."

For this reason, Red Cloud and Old Elk walked past the signs that say "Stay On Road." They picked up dirt from the battlefield and rubbed it on their palms. They shook hands.

"It has been 119 years," Old Elk said.

"Yes, my friend," Red Cloud said. "Maybe 119 years is long enough."

Rocky Mountain News
July 2, 1995

Warriors Charge Battlefield Again

LITTLE BIGHORN NATIONAL BATTLEFIELD MONUMENT, Mont. — Just after dawn Monday, the warriors rode the path of Crazy Horse.

They rode out of the Lakota camp, past the Little Bighorn Casino and the Battlefield Convenience Center. They rode up toward the ridge. They rode toward where their tribe met Lt. Col. George Armstrong Custer and the 7th Cavalry, and then they came to the fence.

It is the path of Crazy Horse, but it also is a national monument.

"We had a discussion about cutting the fence," said Chief Oliver Red Cloud, great-grandson of the war chief Red Cloud. "But the people have finally been good to us here."

For the first time since Custer was killed here June 25, 1876, all the tribes who were at the battle had been invited back. This was the Lakota day on the schedule. About 800 came from the Pine Ridge Indian Reservation in South Dakota and set up tepees and tents in the field next to "Montana's Largest Casino."

They posted sentries, but the only problems were Crows who drove past and made war yells.

"The casino, though, it had power," Danny Two Horse said. "The casino reminds us we still must be on guard against powers that try to destroy our ways."

The leaders had led dances and prayers through the night to prepare for Monday's charge. Medicine men blessed the warriors, the horses and the ridge. The warriors prepared their dress.

Burton Barger, 37, goes to the mountains to hunt for eagle feathers, but he got the ones he wore in his hair in a trade for two snow tires.

"It is part of our culture to barter, too," he said.

When the warriors stopped at the fence, the young warriors of the tribe ran the rest of the way to Battle Ridge.

AT SUNRISE ON BATTLE RIDGE, JUST BELOW THE MASS GRAVES OF CUSTER AND SOME OF THE 7TH CALVARY, LAKOTA SPIRITUAL LEADERS CONDUCT A CEREMONY.

Dean Krakel/Rocky Mountain News

The night before, another ceremony had been held at the top of the ridge, at the obelisk that honors Custer and his men.

"I almost see George Armstrong Custer as the patron saint of Vietnam veterans for all the abuse he has taken," Bob Church, a member of the Custer Battlefield Historical & Museum Association, had said. "I don't know about you, but I don't want to see the Viet Cong flag flying over the Vietnam veterans memorial and Viet Cong doing a victory dance to celebrate some victory like Tet."

When the young warriors reached the obelisk, they touched it with coup sticks and ran away.

David Many Sticks, 13, explained the ceremony with the same kind of logic Church used the night before.

"Why are there white people here?" he said. "The white people lost."

The elders of the tribe spent the rest of the day talking about the generations that have passed.

Oliver Red Cloud, 77, was born eight years after his great-grandfather died. He has been chief since his father died in 1979. He never knew his grandfather, but he knew his grandfather would approve of the charge to the ridge Monday.

"When we go up to that ridge, we are not trying to re-enact the battle," he said. "The battle has happened. It was one battle, and we know what happened after it.

"No, today we try to regain what we had when we were going up to the ridge."

Rocky Mountain News
June 27, 1995

Clowning Around the Rodeo

DENVER — Leon Coffee was sitting in his dressing room before another National Western rodeo, trying to decide which hat to blow up.

He had packed the black powder, painted on a bigger smile and put on a blond wig to go out and be a clown. It is his 25th year as a clown and a bullfighter. He has busted 94 bones, died five times, collected enough artificial parts that he should be recycled when he dies for good and won't say how many marriages have been broken.

His knees were wrapped as tightly as he could in Ace bandages, and he wore size 56 overalls.

"That old straw hat," he said. "It's all busted up. 'Course, so am I, but at least I never run out of hats to blow up."

He works with another clown and a bullfighter. It is their job to distract horses and bulls after they have gotten rid of the riders on their backs and be entertaining about it. To do this, he has 27 hats, a squirt gun, a giant pink bra, shotgun shells packed with tissue paper and white powder and a family-size bottle of ibuprofen.

The family size lasts two weeks if the weather is warm.

"They thought I was trying to be funny when I tore the anterior cruciate ligament in my knee in San Angelo, Texas," he said. "It was a good fall. It's all timing."

He was born Luke Warm Coffee in Austin, Texas. His mother changed it to Leon when he was 2, but there was nothing she could do when he started riding bulls. Later, he decided he had a better chance if he started on the ground.

Now, some of his jokes are older than some of his body parts.

"That gag about how these guys are good at staying on, but they need work on getting off, I've used that one since I started," he said. "Like I said about timing."

Rocky Mountain News

LEON COFFEE

He stopped saying how old he is after he died.

He got hit by a bull on the left side of his head in 1991 in Kennewick, Wash. He died in the dirt. He was revived, but died four more times before the bright light he saw was a spotlight.

"This side of my face still don't work," he said. "I only talk with this side, smile with this side. Nobody notices out there."

His knees bend out like a stick in water, and the anterior cruciate ligament still is torn. He has scars of bull tracks on his back. He lost the feeling in the ring finger on his left hand when he ruptured a disk in his neck in October in San Francisco, and all of his fingers and one thumb have been broken so many times he can turn them sideways at right angles.

The other thumb he can't bend at all.

"It's like I heard a woman ask another lady if her hair was hers," he said.

" 'If I grew it or bought it, it's still mine.' "

Anyway, he would go out and blow up the straw hat. He would get laughs with the gag about the riders getting off, pretending to step in manure and walking like a sissy. He wouldn't be touched by a bull, although one named X270 would butt him around in a barrel and step on his hat.

Like he said, at least he never runs out of hats to blow up.

"I got me a saying," he said. "You don't retire from rodeo. Rodeo retires you."

Rocky Mountain News
January 12, 1996

George Kochaniec, Jr./Rocky Mountain News

VETERAN RODEO CLOWN LEON COFFEE
WORKS THE NATIONAL WESTERN STOCK
SHOW IN DENVER

Cowboy Buckles Down

TY MURRAY TAPES HIS HAND BEFORE THE BULL RIDING EVENT.

DENVER — Ty Murray is walking through the crowd in the parking lot Tuesday night before the 86th National Western Stock Show rodeo when he sees a man bending over to stare at his belt buckle.

The belt buckle identifies him as the Professional Rodeo Cowboys Association World Champion All-Around Cowboy and is big enough to say so. Murray stops. He is 22 years old but already has realized that one of the hazards of being the world champion all-around cowboy is walking into people who are bent over to stare at your belt buckle.

The man straightens and grabs Murray's hand.

"No, I mean squeeze it like the exact moment you're holding on to a big old bull, son," the man says. "I want the grip of a world champion. Three times."

"You want me to squeeze it three times?" Murray says.

"No, son," the man says. "You've been champion of the world three times. Remember?"

His right hand is half again as big as the left from all the years of holding onto the moment. It is attached to a right arm that has muscle on muscle and is hairless from having athletic tape ripped off it after every ride. The muscles bulged.

"That's it," the man says. "That's enough."

"Thank you, sir," Murray says. "Thank you kindly for wanting me to squeeze your hand."

Murray, who is expected to qualify to ride bareback and saddle broncs in Saturday's rodeos — depending on other riders' scores today and Friday — has been the PRCA All-Around Cowboy the past three years.

Last year, his $258,750 in prize money broke the record he set the year before, which broke the record he set in 1989. He was the youngest ever to win an all-around world title and is halfway to matching Larry Mahan's record of six.

In the meantime, he has a contract that pays him to wear the Larry Mahan Cowboy Collection.

Murray, who lives in Stephenville, Texas, walks into the dressing area and pulls down his Larry Mahans to put in his tailbone pad when the spotlights come on. It's a television crew for an independent station in New York. One of them says they are filming a documentary.

"First question," the man says. "Is it Cy or Ty, and aren't you a world champion?"

"Ty, sir," Murray says. "Like the thing some folks wear around their neck. And I was the all-around champion the last three years."

"So, tell me about the women."

"Which ones?"

"I mean the ones the other guys call 'Buckle Bunnies.' "

"All I can say about that is I try to do whatever I can to increase interest in rodeo."

His father breaks colts for a living, his mother rode bulls and his uncle was a world champion steer wrestler. He practiced riding the cover of his mother's sewing machine. He rode his first bull when he was nine and broke his jaw when he was bucked off the second.

He finishes dressing and tapes his ankle. The ankle is black and swollen since a bull stepped on it a couple of days before Christmas in Wichita. He goes back to the stables to see his bull, RK-7.

"I don't study 'em too much, because it throws you off when you think about it too much instead of just have a blank mind so you can read and react," he says. "That's why I don't have any superstitions, either. I just take it one jump at a time.

"The main thing is, you just got to hate to lose."

He stands on the bottom rail of the pen and looks at RK-7, who has a reputation for losing riders, then coming back to check on them. It is a brindle that stands at the back of the pen, away from the other bulls. It doesn't seem to notice Murray.

If human rules of behavior applied to bulls, after a ride all the rest of them would say, "He was a quiet bull, kept to himself..."

"One jump at a time," Murray says.

He is 5-foot-8, 145 pounds. He practices gymnastics and taught himself to ride a unicycle and juggle at the same time to improve his coordination. He lifts weights and stays away from the junk food that is sold at rodeos.

More important, he says, he makes an effort to think and act like he thinks a cowboy should.

He goes back to the dressing area and takes off his belt. He puts it in the cowboy boots he wears when he isn't riding. The buckle pokes him in the stomach when he rides.

He scored a 74 in the saddle bronc riding and a 77 in the bareback to place fifth and third.

RK-7 starts kicking before the gate is opened and the announcer can finish telling it who was in the saddle. When the gate opens, the bull slams Murray into the wall, then twists, then seems to jump straight backward.

Murray bounces off the dirt and is on his feet before the bull notices he is gone. He picks up his hat and walks back to the dressing area. He sits and stares straight ahead.

He doesn't move until he realizes he is staring at a woman's belt buckle.

"Ty, my name's Savannah, and we'll be at the Grizzly Rose tonight if you want some company," she says.

He looks up, his face blank. Read and react. He shakes his head.

"Thank you, ma'am," he says. "That bull that throwed me is all the company I'll need tonight. But thank you kindly for asking."

Rocky Mountain News
January 16, 1992

At Work in the Mind of a Cow

FORT COLLINS, Colo. — Cow No. 13 stood on the other side of the fence, trying to figure out what Temple Grandin was thinking.

Grandin is an assistant professor in animal science at Colorado State University. She is considered the world's leading designer of slaughterhouses and livestock holding facilities, with a third of the pigs and cattle slaughtered in the United States going through equipment from Grandin Livestock Systems. She is autistic.

None of this is a coincidence.

"Uh-oh," Grandin said. "We're four steps away. This could go either way."

Cow No. 13 tilted its head to the side, and Grandin tilted hers.

Grandin might understand what cows think better than anybody, because she has had to learn how she thinks. Her autobiography, *Emergence: Labeled Autistic,* published in 1986, is considered the most insightful and revealing look from the inside of autism. Instead of letting autism control her, she has used autism to make herself what she wants to be.

Cow No. 13 took four steps and laid its chin on the top rail of the fence, looking up at Grandin.

"See?" she said. "I understand what she's thinking. That's the difference between cows and people."

Autism is a developmental disorder that affects about one in 700 people, causing difficulty in communicating, repetitive actions and an inability to interact socially or to understand feelings.

Grandin, 46, was born in New York, five years after autism was identified. She screamed and clawed when her mother tried to hold her. As she got older, she could not bring herself to look people in the eye or to allow herself to be hugged, and when she did speak it was in a monotone.

She dreamed of a box padded inside, and she could climb in and close it. The box would hold her like a hug, but she would be in control. To get that feeling, she sometimes wore pieces of cardboard like a sandwich board.

Doctors recommended that she be institutionalized. Her father agreed, but her mother kept her in a public elementary school. She did poorly in such subjects as math and French but excelled in subjects that required creativity.

Her mother sent her to a psychologist who believed the cause of her problems was a trauma in her family life and tried to find the secret.

She was expelled from her first junior high school because she threw a history book at a student who called her a "retard." She was sent to a school for "special" students. Her IQ was measured at 137, but she could not pass algebra.

The summer after her junior year in high school, she stayed with an aunt on a ranch in Arizona. She watched cattle as they were herded into squeeze chutes, wooden panels hinged at the bottom to hold cattle in place while they were branded, vaccinated and slaughtered. Frightened cows calmed when the panels squeezed them.

She talked her aunt into squeezing her with the machine.

"It was the box I had dreamed about when I was a child," she said. "When it closed on me, for the first time in years I felt complete calm."

When she went home, she built her own chute with plywood, rope and pulleys.

The school psychologist tried to stop her from using it, thinking it was a symbol for a womb or a casket, or that she was having an identity crisis and thought she was a cow. To prove him wrong she started to study the effects of squeeze chutes.

This led her to try to understand animals and the way they think, which led her to understand the way she thinks. Her doctoral thesis was on the effects of enriched and impoverished environments on the development of pigs' brains. She has published more than 100 papers on animal behavior, humane treatment of animals and autism. Medical researchers are conducting studies on the effects of squeeze machines.

"All those years, I tried to find out the deep, dark secrets," she said. "And then I found out there aren't any."

Grandin has worked to make slaughterhouses more humane and efficient to reduce stress on the cattle, to cut down on bruising that ruins beef and to raise employee morale.

She has developed the idea of curved chutes to take advantage of cows' natural tendency to circle and to keep the animal from seeing where it is headed. She has worked to eliminate sights and sounds that frighten the animals. She has demonstrated that more humane conditions for the animals also raise the efficiency of workers and keep them from becoming brutes.

To do this, she has crawled through slaughterhouse chutes to see and think what cattle see and think, and she had herself dipped.

Plants that meet her standards get a "Stairway to Heaven" plaque.

"The ending of a life should be approached with respect," she said. "If there is no respect for the animals, it diminishes the person who is doing the killing."

At the same time, she has learned about herself.

She has learned to understand feelings.

"I love my mother, intellectually," she said. "But it's kind of the same way I feel that it's terrible for all of the bombing in Sarajevo. I know it's terrible that so many people are being killed, but what really bothers me is that I'm a builder and I see all those buildings being destroyed."

She has decided to be celibate because she knows it would be difficult to have an emotional relationship, and because if she married someone with autistic traits, they could be passed on to their child.

"To avoid being genetically irresponsible, I would have to marry someone I wouldn't like," she said.

She has no sense of social "signals."

"If I drop a glass and break it, and somebody says, 'Nice going,' I don't know instinctively whether they are being sarcastic or complimenting me," she said. "I've got what's like a collection of videotapes in my mind, and I run them to match up with what people say and the way they say it. I run them through my mind and compare them to figure out what people really mean."

TEMPLE GRANDIN IS THE WORLD'S LEADING DESIGNER OF SLAUGHTERHOUSES.

She read an article about antidepressant drugs 20 years ago in *Psychology Today* and recognized the symptoms they treat as some of her own. She went to a doctor and said she was depressed. She has taken the drugs since then, and it has given more inflection to her voice and almost eliminated nerve attacks.

"I don't have the nerve attacks, but there is a trade-off," she said. "The nerve attacks helped me to achieve what I achieved. Fixating gets things done."

Because she is autistic, she is a completely visual thinker.

If she wants to remember something she reads, she either has to turn it into images or take a mental photograph of the page and read it.

The first time she saw a draftsman draw a blueprint 25 years ago, she bought supplies and drew a blueprint of a slaughterhouse she visualized in her head, to exact specifications and architectural standards. She can visualize plans for a slaughterhouse and turn it around, looking at it from all angles. Sometimes, she notices parts she hadn't consciously thought about.

"You know that scene in *Jurassic Park*, where the dinosaurs are in the kitchen, and it looks real but it's really computer-generated?" she said. "I can do that in my head."

Her sense of right and wrong parallels most accepted beliefs, but it is based on logic.

"If you look at the theory of quantum physics, subatomic particles are moving around and being affected by each other, and I'm afraid if I do something wrong it will come back and affect something else," she said. "I'm afraid the steering linkage in my car might break."

At the same time, feelings that are considered "right" come naturally to her.

"The people who were so mean to me when I was growing up, if they said they were sorry today, I could forgive them completely," she said. "I would be cautious of them for a while, because I have learned I should. But in my heart, I really wouldn't hold any of the things they did or said against them."

She has learned to shake hands and look people in the eye. In classes at CSU and during talks, she has gone from reciting a script to speaking from a rough outline and answering questions. Most of her students and clients don't know she is autistic.

Still, she shows autistic traits.

If she is interrupted while she is speaking about a concept, she usually has to start at the beginning. Her description of events in her life are word-for-word, the way she described them in her autobiography. Answers to most questions somehow find their way back to her work.

"I owe so much to my mother, who saved me when my father thought I was hopeless, but I have come to understand that people think about things in different ways," she said. "I mean, people think a cow thinks like them and will be afraid of blood on the floor — they can't get past the red stuff, but actually they don't know what that is, and a little, swinging chain will scare them much more..."

She has a squeeze machine in her bedroom, upholstered and operated by an industrial compressor and a control box. She works every day and night. She can't remember the last time she did something for fun.

"My work is my life, and my life is my work," she said. "There isn't much else."

She is writing another book about autism, and one chapter will look at the connection between genius and autism. Albert Einstein showed signs of autistic behavior. She knows Einstein's cousin, who has one child who is autistic and another who is considered a musical genius.

"If we wiped out all of the genes that cause manic depression, Tourette's syndrome, autism, et cetera, we'd have a world of accountants," she said. "Maybe the reason there aren't more Einsteins and (Isaac) Newtons is they couldn't pass the GRE and couldn't get into graduate school.

"People find this hard to believe, but if I could just snap my fingers and not be autistic, I wouldn't."

The institution doctors wanted to send her to when she was a child now is the pig farm at Tufts Veterinary School. She went to Tufts to work on a study on the effects of the drug Naltrexene on pigs. She pulled her car over and sat alone.

"I got the heebee-jeebees," she said. "I...I got the heebee-jeebees. If I had gone into an institution, if my mother hadn't insisted on sending me to school, I might have never gotten out of there.

"I could have become what they thought I was."

Rocky Mountain News
March 5, 1995

From Cattle to Campaign Trail

PRITCHETT, Colo. — The cows walked across the prairie with Wes McKinley behind them on his buckskin horse, and it wasn't clear if he was talking about cattle or politics.

The land ran straight out to meet the sky at the edges, and the sun was up to eye level. Soapweed interrupted now and then. The colors were light brown to dark brown and everything in between, and above it the sky was so blue it looked like it might crack.

Out here, wherever you are, you are exactly in the center.

"Everything's smooth as can be, and then you get a maverick," McKinley said. "He'll decide to go thataway. Before you know it, they're all trailin'."

McKinley is 50 years old, and until he was picked to serve as foreman of a special grand jury investigating Rocky Flats and ended up being called a folk hero on national television, he was doing all he ever wanted to do. He has a mustache that hangs like an old rope and sideburns that frame his face like kitchen curtains. Now, he thinks he also should go to Washington and represent the 4th Congressional District.

"Work's workin' on the U-joints on the pickup," he said. "Why, if everybody just went where they're supposed to, where'd the fun be in that?"

He and some neighbors were helping another neighbor drive 161 head to winter pasture.

This morning, he had walked around in Wranglers, cowboy boots and a cowboy hat but no shirt. He hadn't shaved since he announced two weeks earlier that he is an independent candidate for Congress. His horse is named Little Sister, and he wrote a song about her mother he thinks will help people understand his stance on abortion.

And then a steer took off into the brush.

"Yep," he said. "More fun'n a goat rope."

And he took off after the maverick.

McKinley grew up 24 miles south of Walsh on the Cimarron River, on land his grandfather homesteaded in 1907, and for his first eight grades he went to a one-room, one-teacher sod building. They got electricity at home when he was 8. After he graduated from Walsh High School, he and a friend got in a pickup and went to see the Great Lakes.

He came back and graduated from Panhandle State University, the closest college to home, married his girlfriend from high school, Jan, taught advanced math at Pritchett High School, and he and Jan had three daughters. He quit teaching to check flow meters on oil wells and ranch and run the Kirkwell Cattle Co. with his partner, Dean Ormiston, and take people on cattle drives like this one for $1,200 a week. He and Jan live 18 miles south of Walsh, and their daughters are grown.

Jan was in Sterling this weekend doing graduate work toward her master's degree in library science, and he was here.

"We get pilgrims out here on the cattle drives — doctors, lawyers, teachers — they say their life's changed," McKinley said. "You got to get cactus picked out of your butt, it does things. You'd be surprised, the things that can change people's lives."

In June 1989, he got the letter from the federal court clerk. He called a lawyer in town to ask what a grand jury did. He drove his pickup 300 miles to Denver, and he was one of the 23 people chosen to hear what Rockwell International had done when it ran the nuclear weapons plant.

"I remembered Rocky Flats from when the old hippies used to demonstrate out there," he said. "I thought it was all taken care of."

Just then, Ormiston, his partner and best friend, rode up. Ormiston has the same mustache, a pony tail, rings on every finger, a 9-inch knife in a sheath strapped to his leg, and holsters on his belt that hold a .45 revolver and a gun that looks like a derringer but has a .45-caliber bullet in one barrel and a .410 shotgun shell in the other. They also run the annual Baca County coyote hunt, and Ormiston is the outlaw Black Jack Ketchum and McKinley is his partner Clay Allison in the re-enactment of the hanging of Ketchum every summer in Springfield.

"Wes's smart about things," Ormiston said. "Just for instance, he comes drivin' up in his pickup, and there's two halters dragging from the back. He gets out and sees them, he says, 'That's good.' I say, 'What's good about a couple ruined halters?' And old Wes says, 'Least I took the horses off.' "

Then a calf wandered off, and Ormiston took off after it.

WES MCKINLEY TACKLES CONGRESSIONAL RUN ON HORSEBACK.

Essdras M. Suarez/Rocky Mountain News

Once a month for 30 months, McKinley drove his pickup or took the Greyhound bus 300 miles to Denver to sit in a room in the federal courthouse for two to four days to hear testimony about what Rockwell had done. He understood nuclear weapons better than most of the other grand jurors because of his background in math. He was chosen foreman.

The grand jury finished with its hearings when then U.S. Attorney Mike Norton announced he had reached a plea agreement with Rockwell. The company paid $18.5 million, and no criminal charges were filed against individuals.

Federal law prohibits McKinley from talking about what the grand jury heard, but someone on the grand jury gave a copy of its preliminary report to *Westword*. The report cited careless handling and storage of nuclear waste, attempts to hide the truth and called Rocky Flats an "ongoing criminal enterprise." And then it was published, and then the national magazines and television shows did stories, and then the Justice Department was investigating the members of the grand jury for possible criminal charges for leaking the report.

He was talking about this when Charles Hoeffner, the owner of the cattle and the ranch and the only neighbor who doesn't have a mustache that hangs down below his chin, rode up. He grew up around here but went to Lubbock and had a rental car business. He came back two years ago and bought the ranch, and he also does the barbecues for the Kirkwell Cattle Co. trail rides.

"One thing you oughtta know about Wes, even back to when we were in Sunday school together, he says a fella's fulla chicken crap, you can take it to the bank," he said. "That fella's fulla chicken crap."

And then a heifer took off and Hoeffner did, too, and then he rode back and took off his hat and leaned on his saddle horn.

"One other thing I should of told you about Wes," he said. "I don't believe I ever heard him say a fella's fulla chicken crap."

When McKinley announced his candidacy to replace Wayne Allard last month, he said if he was elected he would to use his power to open the grand jury report on Rocky Flats.

The lawyer who advised the grand jury, Jonathan Turley, director of the Environmental Crimes Project at Georgetown University, told him if he is elected his opponents could try to keep him from being sworn in because he has the stated intention of violating the law.

Two weeks ago, the Justice Department said it wants to sue Rockwell for fraud because the company allegedly hid the seriousness of the problems at Rocky Flats.

McKinley still can't comment, and he was talking about not talking when Ormiston rode up.

"You know, I get elected, they might try and keep me off the congressional floor," McKinley said.

"On your horse?" Ormiston said.

By 3 in the afternoon, the sun had moved to the other side of the sky, the cattle were in their winter pasture, and everybody rode to the edge of a canyon that opened like an incision and got off their horses and threw rocks into it.

Ormiston took a bottle of Jack Daniels out of a saddlebag. He took a drink and wiped his mouth on his sleeve. He passed it around, and everybody else did, too.

McKinley sat on a sandstone rock. He built his home out of this rock, rocks that were used to build homesteader's homes and rocks that he cut. He knows where everything around here is and how it works and how to fix it if it doesn't. You could live your whole life here and never think things should be any different.

And then you could go someplace else and see how things are different.

"This land, you got to respect it," he said. "Just because you know some things doesn't mean you got the right to not respect it."

And that is as much as McKinley will say about the grand jury investigation into what happened at Rocky Flats.

On the way back, everybody let their horses run.

McKinley plans to start campaigning when the weather gets too cold to do this. He will drive a wagon train through the 4th district, up the east side of the state and then down through Fort Collins and Greeley. He will play his guitar and sing songs he wrote.

His campaign manager is Ryan Ross, who used to be Bryan Abas, who wrote the first story about the Rocky Flats grand jury report in *Westword*.

"I know some folks might think that looks controversial," McKinley said. "Like maybe I was the one that leaked the report. But I didn't, so I don't worry about it, just like I don't worry about it when he tells me I shouldn't play my guitar and sing on the campaign."

As an independent candidate, McKinley will have to raise his own support. He has gotten about $4,500 in contributions from people he knows. He figures he'll get more when he gets around to issues.

"I won't get the funding as an independent candidate, but I got one advantage in this campaign," he said. "I know this old boy, he's got a mule team I can use."

Back at the corrals, Hoeffner said he had a calf that needed to be castrated, so McKinley and Ormiston drove it into a chute. Ormiston took out his knife. McKinley held out his hand.

"That's what's wrong with politicians today," McKinley said. "Not enough Rocky Mountain oysters."

Hoeffner said he also had some Spam, and McKinley said thanks but he wanted to play guitar at the ranch house, so everybody loaded their horses and got in their pickups. McKinley got in Ormiston's pickup. About halfway there, Ormiston's .45 slid across the dashboard.

McKinley grabbed it.

"This is the kind of gun control I favor," he said.

He also is in favor of reduced spending and taxes, against the North American Free Trade Agreement and still hasn't decided where he stands on abortion.

He talks about how his 14-year-old daughter got pregnant, and the family considered abortion. They decided she should have the baby. She had a boy, now 5, who is being raised by McKinley's brother and sister-in-law.

"Anybody says that's an easy decision, they're wrong," he said. "We made the right decision — my brother and his wife always wanted a baby, and I got a grandbaby — but who am I to say what's right for everybody? So I'm against abortion, but I'm for keeping the government out of people's lives. That's why I want people to hear that song about that old mare."

Anyway, the ranch house is a double-wide mobile home on the land Ormiston's grandfather homesteaded in 1906. The carpet used to be green. A Mason jar on the kitchen counter is filled with anti-freeze and a couple of rattlesnakes Ormiston shot.

McKinley fried hamburgers and potatoes for everybody, and Ormiston took another bottle of Jack Daniels out of a boot in the toolbox in the back of his pickup, and after supper they both sat and played their guitars and sang.

McKinley sang the song about the mare and his daughter:

The two of them grew up together
They ran and played through all kinds of weather
Time goes on and, we know that nothing is forever
Only the land is

They would play and sing until quarter to 2 in the morning, and then Ormiston would do his coyote call, and McKinley would take out his pocket knife and get a raw potato and put salt on the slices he cut for everybody.

In the morning, McKinley would roll the Rocky Mountain oysters in flour and fry them with sausage and scrambled eggs. He would go and cut a pine tree for Christmas and take it home and put it up in time to take a photograph of it with his horse in the house before Jan got home from Sterling. He would work on the U-joints on his pickup.

It is starting to get too cold to be on the cattle trail, so it almost is time to get on the campaign trail.

Right now, though, it was still morning at the ranch house. He was wearing Wranglers, cowboy boots and a cowboy hat but no shirt. He was thinking about getting on his horse and doing the only job he used to think he ever wanted to do.

"You know, there's been folks who suggested I run a regular political campaign," he said. "You know, wear a suit, join a party, leave the horses at home. I admit, I thought about it a couple seconds.

"Then I thought, 'Nah.' "

Rocky Mountain News
December 31, 1995

A Special Delivery

STANDING ROCK INDIAN RESERVATION, S.D. — The road curved to meet the next curve, state highway 1806, and the semitrailer came on.

November, and everything on either side was a shade of brown. The land rose and fell out to the sky. Around another curve and up another hill to Wakpala, 31 houses on the left side of the highway, identical — window, door, window — except for the colors.

Henry Two Horse's house is pink, Peggy Hawk's is lime green, and Arthur Laughing Bear's is yellow, teal and brown because he was working construction off the reservation the day Lewis Trujillo came in the semi and gave away the paint.

"Now, 10,000 toys might not seem like a lot to some people," Trujillo said. "But that's how many more we still need if we're going to take toys to all 25 reservations for Christmas. You have to put these things in context."

Trujillo is 65, and he left Fort Collins at 4 a.m. the morning before to drive 624 miles to drop off the first of the 20,000 toys and three tons of candy for Christmas, tons of clothes for the winter, a computer and a toy horse. This is what he does. The organization he started 10 years ago is Night Walker Enterprises, and it will haul Christmas to 25 reservations.

A right turn onto tire tracks frozen in the mud, to Wakpala School, where 14 boys in grades 7 to 12 waited in front.

"Ten thousand toys means ten thousand kids," Trujillo said.

The school is brick, built in 1923. Prefabricated buildings have been added around it, one afterthought at a time. Trujillo drove his 1986 Toyota Camry, and Jim Cowen followed in the 48-foot semi, his wife, Beverly, next to him.

Trujillo got out, a man shaped like the letter "D," and he opened the back door of the semi.

"Fort Howard 2-Ply Bath Tissue," "Blue Thunder Stereo Speakers," "Cheerios," "Hiram Walker," it said on the boxes.

"Whiskey?" Paul Long Chase, a 10th-grader, said.

"No," Jeremy Gabe, a ninth-grader, said. "The things Mr. Trujillo brings aren't what it says on the box. Maybe there's even a toy horse in one, like last year."

At least two of the three T-shirts Zacheriah Tree Top, four, wore to kindergarten that morning — Kermit the Frog and Mountain States Auto Parts — were brought here last year by Night Walker. The crayons in the kindergarten class, the desks in the third- and fourth-grade classroom and the gold-plated faucets in the boys restroom came on a Night Walker semi. When a brushfire started last year, kids used the fire hose Night Walker had brought to keep it away from St. Elizabeth Episcopal Church until the trucks came.

It took him a week to load the truck for this trip.

Anna Two Horse, 78, walked up the road with an empty five-gallon gasoline can to fill with water to carry home to wash clothes.

"Two weeks ago, I said to my son, 'Lewis is coming,'" she said.

"But we didn't decide this was where we were coming until last week," Trujillo said.

"I know," she said.

The caretaker of the school, Dan Bleyle, came out and said the kids would be sent home after lunch unless he could get the furnace working. The furnace burns coal. He goes down in the boiler room every morning at 5:15 to shovel it.

HIGH SCHOOL STUDENTS AT STANDING ROCK INDIAN RESERVATION UNLOAD TOYS AND CANDY.

"You didn't happen to bring any fishing poles for the kids, did you?" Bleyle said. "And maybe a set of encyclopedias with all the letters?"

"Put it on the list," Trujillo said.

The need for fishing poles for the kids was realized when somebody noticed most of the antennas on cars were gone. Half of books in the library — textbooks, westerns, Time-Life collections — were brought here by Night Walker. The library has a 1964 set of World Book Encyclopedias, but volume D is missing.

Night Walker has taken 500,000 pounds of books to reservations.

A garbage bag filled with clothes fell to the ground and broke open, and Joe Strong Danny Yellow Fat, a senior, picked out a sweat shirt that said "Yale."

"You want to go to Yale?" Trujillo asked.

"They got work?" Yellow Fat asked.

Around another curve and down another hill, on the way to Fort Yates, a man stood in the road and waved his arms.

A 1986 Chevrolet Lumina had veered in front of a semi at the bottom of the hill. The driver of the car was killed on impact. It was the third fatal accident on the reservation in the past week.

A tribal police officer pulled up from behind and said the road would be closed for two hours.

"The average life span for a male on the reservation is 43," he said. "Unemployment runs 30 percent to 93 percent. The trick is to show people this isn't how life is."

Trujillo grew up in Creede. His grandfather had moved back to the traditional Ute country and changed the family name from Night Walker. Trujillo quit school when he was 15 and lied about his age to get into the Army. When his hitch was up, he sold sewing machines until the fighting started in Korea, and then he joined the Marines.

When he got out, he went to trade school to learn air conditioning and refrigeration repair. He had a business with five trucks. He had his first heart attack in 1972, then four more within a year.

"The doctors said to go home and get my affairs in order," he said. "I went fishing."

Within two months, he was fishing from sunrise until after dark. Within a couple more years, he was tired of fishing and repaired air conditioners donated to the Salvation Army. In 1986, he saw a documentary on television about the Rosebud Reservation and paid the Salvation Army 4 ½ cents a pound for clothes that would be sold as rags.

Now, Night Walker is the largest organization west of the Mississippi River to take reservations what they need. It is non-profit, and all the workers are volunteers. It has a scholarship program, and for American Indian students at Colorado State University, it has an eye-care program.

Every spring, Night Walker has an art show of works by American Indian students and brings them from the reservations to stay at the Holiday Inn and see CSU.

"The main thing is to get the kids a chance to see somewhere else," Trujillo said. "To see there are places that are different."

On Dec. 28 last year, somebody set fires in two trucks parked behind Night Walker's warehouse. One truck had been loaned by Coors, and about 25,000 pounds of clothes for the Crow Creek Reservation were destroyed. The other truck belonged to Night Walker, and it held the props for a haunted house a group operated to raise about $20,000 a year for Night Walker.

Police have no suspects in the arson.

To make up for the money it lost, Night Walker opened a store on College Avenue in Fort Collins that sells artwork by Indian children and adults.

"Maybe it worked out for the best, because it pushed us to open the store," Trujillo said. "That's what we want to do, to show people what these kids can do."

Back up the hill, down four miles of frozen tire tracks, then 19 miles up to Fort Yates, to the Tender Hearts battered women's shelter. The shelter used to be the Warrior Motel. A pickup pulled up, and eight men got out, and then two inmates walked over from the Fort Yates Jail with a sheriff's deputy behind them.

"This for the kitchen?" Jesse Taken Alive said.

"It's a tennis racket," Tim Murphy said. "For play."

Three hours later, when the semi was empty, Jim Cowen closed the door. He and Beverly volunteered for Night Walker in May and have made six trips to reservations. He had to get back to his job, to haul a load of wheat to Kansas City.

He and Beverly left for home in the empty semi.

"Maybe we can make Douglas (Wyo.) tonight," he said. Seven miles south of the Wakpala School, Trujillo turned just before the Grand River Casino, where a board painted white with black letters points to where Sitting Bull is buried.

The site is a stone bust of Tatante Iyotake, 1831-94, the greatest of Sioux warriors, who led his nation in the defeat of Lt. Col. George Armstrong Custer and the 7th Cavalry at Little Bighorn. He was killed near here by Indian police. The eagle feather on the bust was shot off again last year.

"Sitting Bull, best known American Indian, leader of 'hostile groups' for a generation, a powerful orator, a clever prophet," the plaque said.

A mile from the site is where the Gabes live.

Beatrice Gabe had asked Trujillo to come see the mobile home that had been delivered the day before. It was green and white, set next to the house where they have lived since 1957. The Army Corps of Engineers dammed the Missouri River and moved the families who lived on the bottom land to the ridge. They still are waiting for running water.

The kids were in school — the furnace had been fixed — and she had just come from Wakpala with four seven-gallon buckets of water to wash clothes and for the kids to take baths.

"Come in," she said. "Jeremy wanted you to see his toy horses. He already knows where he'll put them when everything's hooked up, and we can move in our new home."

Jeremy is a freshman at Wakpala School. The house is identical to the ones in Wakpala — window, door, window — except for the color. They didn't hear about the paint until it was gone, so it is the color of the years.

Trujillo followed her up the cinder blocks stacked for steps, through the front door with a plastic bag stuffed where the doorknob used to be, and she pulled aside a down comforter hung in the doorway to the living room to keep in the heat. Night Walker brought the down comforter two years ago. Eagle feathers, one for each male, hung from the ceiling.

"You know him and his toy horses," she said. "Ask him what he wants for Christmas, and he says, 'Same thing.' "

"What does Jeremy think about college?" Trujillo asked.

"Well, I'm not really sure, you know..."

Her husband, Chas, was disabled in a car accident in 1988, and he was in the bedroom. She works at the school when a teacher is sick. They had five boys, then adopted their daughter.

Trujillo tried to get Jeremy's older brother, Charles, to go to college after he graduated from Wakpala School last year, but Charles got a girl pregnant.

"You know, Jeremy could come down, stay with me, see what it's like," Trujillo said.

"We're going to Idaho in the summer to see his other brother," Beatrice Gabe said.

In the cupboards, she had dried wild turnips, corn and squash. She had bapa, thin slices of dried venison. In a drawer, there was a set of gold-plated silverware the actress Connie Stevens donated to Night Walker.

This afternoon after school, they will go down to the river to pick up wood to burn in the stove to warm the house.

"Now let me show you the new house," Beatrice Gabe said.

"I've been wanting to see it," Trujillo said.

She put on a goose down coat Night Walker brought the winter before last. The house was condemned in 1987 by Indian Health Services, because the foundation heaved. Regulations prohibited them from building a permanent home because they don't have running water.

Back outside, Gabe and Trujillo walked across the frozen mud to the mobile home.

"The girl that got killed in the accident, she used to go with my brother- in-law," she said. "Her little niece just died, day before yesterday, too. It will be nice to have a door with a doorknob."

She climbed the metal steps that came with the mobile home and opened the door. It is a 1972 model. A broken plate was in a cupboard, and the October 1987 issue of *Field and Stream* was on the floor in a bedroom.

"When we were told last month they would deliver our new home yesterday, I thought, 'Just in time for Mr. Trujillo to get here,'" Gabe said.

Trujillo would start back to Fort Collins from here, driving straight through, and the next day he would start loading the truck to go to the Crow Creek Reservation in South Dakota. He would take his wife to the Fort

Ellen Jaskol/Rocky Mountain News

A DELIVERY AT THE RESERVATION

Belknap Indian Reservation in Montana for Thanksgiving. This is what he does.

But first he had a question.

"We didn't even know we were coming until last week," he said. "So how did you know I was coming?"

"Oh," Gabe said. "Mr. Trujillo, you always come."

Rocky Mountain News
November 26, 1995

I see people who go through life who hold themselves back

from what's going on, but Greg jumped right in. I introduced him

to the Indian people and he just seemed to fit right in.

I haven't seen those people take to someone like that.

— LEWIS TRUJILLO

Strangers in a Wealthy Land

CARBONDALE, Colo. — The 6:35 a.m. Aspen Express moved down the Roaring Fork Valley, and the family in the back was trying to figure out the meaning of the word filthy.

There were six of them — three brothers, their stepfather, their cousin and her husband — speaking English because they think it is important to learn the language of the country they sneaked into. They had left their homes and run two miles in the night to get out of Mexico. They had left their three-bedroom apartment and walked half a mile in the morning to go to work.

The Aspen Express moved down the Roaring Fork Valley, up the pay scale.

"There is 'filthy Mexican,' " Juan said. "There is 'filthy rich.' "

"I look it up," Antonio said. "I do not understand."

There are 11 people in the family, and they are here with hundreds of other Mexicans who have come to Colorado illegally to work at ski resorts.

Last week, the Colorado State Patrol stopped a rented truck in Costilla County with 43 Mexican men in it.

Their cousins might have been on it, but they have no way to know.

The brothers — Antonio, Juan, Hector — and their stepfather, Jose, are on a crew building a $2.5 million, 10,000-square-foot house. Their cousin, Rita, is a maid in a hotel. Her husband, Pablo, washes dishes in a restaurant. The wives of Antonio and Juan, their mother and the three children stay in their three-bedroom apartment.

On the bus, two snowboarders wearing Crayola colors talked about shredding, and two men wearing Dallas Cowboys caps talked in Spanish about a soccer match.

"What is 'jet set?' " Rita said.

"Aviano grupo," Juan said.

"Ahhhh," Rita said.

Rita and Pablo and their two children came last week after a year in Los Angeles. Rita wore a coat she borrowed from Antonio's wife, and Pablo wore three sweatshirts he bought on sale for half price. The sweatshirts all said, "Somebody went to Aspen and all I got is this lousy sweatshirt."

The bus stopped in Aspen.

"One night, we went to one of these discos to see what all of this is about," Juan said. "Every time we go in the bathroom, American guys come in and say, 'You got any?' I say 'What?' and they say, 'You know, cocaine, man.'

"I say, 'We came here to make a good life, not a bad one.' "

Antonio came first, three years ago from their home in Toluca, outside Mexico City.

He is the oldest, 23, and he sent money for Juan to come a year ago. They sent money for their wives, their mother, their stepfather and their other brother to come. They are saving $1,600 to pay the coyotes to bring Hector's wife and their three children across the border.

The Immigration and Naturalization Service estimates there are 17,500 illegal workers in Colorado. Raids in the Aspen and Vail areas have sent 73 illegal workers back to Mexico since December. Antonio and Juan knew two of the men who were sent back — one has returned and lives in Basalt; the other still is trying to save $400 to pay the coyotes.

They walked to the house they are building and waited for the rest of the crew.

Antonio makes $16 an hour, because he has learned to cut the logs people like to use as beams in their new homes. It is almost 20 times what he made as a computer programmer for the telephone company in Mexico. It is $7 an hour less than the American who does the same job.

"We build these big houses, we want just what all Americans want," Antonio said. "A job, a home, a hot tub, a Toyota, a family."

Antonio's brothers and their stepfather make less because they have less experience. Taxes are taken out of their paychecks. They can't file for income-tax refunds because they made up the Social Security numbers on the cards they bought for $10 each.

Rita and Pablo each make $6.50 an hour, but they get paid cash.

"Some Americans we work with, they don't like us just because we are Mexicans," Juan said. "They say, 'You people take away our jobs.' The bosses, they give us the jobs because they know we work hard and shut the hell up."

A friend of theirs was paid $100 by a famous actor to teach him how to say dirty words in Spanish.

Another friend broke his arm and wrapped it in tape and molding for a door jamb for two weeks until he could afford to go to a doctor and get it set.

"A woman in Basalt, she will marry a man for $3,000 to make him legal," Antonio said. "That is not how we want to do it."

They were back at the apartment at 6:15.

The apartment is like all the others on the block, which is why they liked it. Kitchen and living room downstairs, three bedrooms upstairs, $1,400 a month. Their cousins live in one just like it nearby.

Rita and Pablo have two children, Teresa, four, and Guillermo, three. Juan and Angeles have a four-month-old daughter named Erin. Antonio's wife, Rosa, is five months pregnant.

Angeles had made carnitas and rice for Juan. Rosa had made menudo and refried beans for Antonio. Olivia had made carne y papas for everybody else.

The evening news was on television. They had bought a close-captioned television so they could study the words.

"We paid $3,000 to buy a double-wide trailer," Antonio said. "We pay $1,000 a month for three months, and the lady who sold it to us says, 'I didn't mean to sell it.' What can you do?"

They lost the money and moved into an apartment that looks like all the others.

When they first came to Colorado, they pretended to read newspapers on the bus so people would think they were Americans. They never went out in groups of more than two in case they were arrested by Immigration. They kept $1,000 in cash in case somebody was caught and sent back, but they used it to help pay the hospital $2,000 for delivering Erin.

They don't worry about Immigration now.

"The emigres, we have a saying about them," Juan said. "There are so many of us. We say, 'Vienen, bien. Me vengo patras.' They come, fine. I come back."

After supper, Rita and Pablo took the bus to Basalt High School for an English class. Erin slept.

The rest of the family watched a rerun of *Married . . . with Children,* studying the words at the bottom of the TV screen.

"That Al Bundy, what a guy," Antonio said. "You know something? Sometimes I already feel like an American."

Rocky Mountain News
February 4, 1996

The Team

LA JUNTA, Colo. — Dry Hollow Robin trotted around the corral with Andrew Allen on his back, practicing western-pleasure riding and something else.

ANDREW ALLEN AND DRY HOLLOW ROBIN COMPETE IN THE NATIONAL WESTERN STOCK SHOW.

Andrew is 16 and a Colorado Boys Ranch resident. Dry Hollow Robin is an appaloosa donated by a rancher. Both are in La Junta because they have a history of not doing what is expected of them.

Next week, they will become the first team from the Boys Ranch to compete at the National Western Stock Show, but at that moment Jim Kerr was trying to figure out what they were doing.

"You two might know what you're doing prancing around and laughing out there to get ready for the stock show," Kerr said. "But I'm teaching you, and I sure don't."

Dry Hollow Robin stopped and pawed the ground and Andrew patted his neck.

"I know, Robin," Andrew said. "Believe me, I understand."

Andrew lived in Indiana all his life before he came here, and the words he uses to describe that life might explain more than what he says.

"I was adopted at the age of birth, and at the age of 5 was sexually molested by a neighbor," he said. "At the age of 10, I began perpetrating. I also began to act out, primarily by setting fires. I had received placement to nine programs before I came here."

He came here two years ago. Each of the 80 boys who lives here has been a victim of abuse and has been through at least eight treatment programs. For most, the ranch is the last chance before prison.

The horsemanship program is run by Kerr, with horses and everything else donated, and the boys do all of the chores. The saddle-making program won first place at the state fair. The breeding program helps teach boys that sex doesn't have to be abuse.

Andrew chose the horsemanship program.

"One Sunday right after Andrew started, I got a call at home because he'd been missing all day," Kerr said. "I came out here, and Andrew was right where I expected to find him. He was out back there with this yearling stud colt, telling him his troubles."

Andrew learned to ride and he learned to listen to Kerr. Listening came harder. He got thrown off a colt every day for six weeks before he asked Kerr what he had meant about using a halter.

"I know all the words for what people did to me and what I did," Andrew said. "I know how to manipulate the system. I even know how to manipulate myself.

"With horses, though, I had to learn to earn their trust and to trust them."

He has done chores on ranches in the valley to buy riding boots, a western shirt, Wrangler jeans and a Garth Brooks compact disc. He borrowed Kerr's hat.

Still, he couldn't have competed at the stock show until a rancher from Pueblo donated Dry Hollow Robin.

One day last spring, Andrew and Kerr were grooming Dry Hollow Robin and Kerr said to the horse, "You and I, someday we're going to go to the stock show."

Andrew said, "Can I go, too?"

Last summer, he rode Dry Hollow Robin at the state fair. He watched 14 other riders go through the course. He left the gate and rode through the course in reverse order.

After the event, he didn't know what he had done. He was tested back at the ranch and was found to have a learning disability that never had been diagnosed.

"All my life, I never knew I could be good at something until this," he said. "I learned about more than riding on Robin. I wasn't going to let some learning disability keep me from doing what I was good at."

Now, he and Dry Hollow Robin work every day on western pleasure and hunter- under-saddle riding. He is the only person who rides and grooms him. They spend eight hours a day together, and Andrew doesn't see it as a coincidence.

"Robin and me, we've got a lot in common, the way we both came here and all," Andrew said. "He knows he can trust me. Only a weak person would do anything that would hurt anybody that trusts him."

For all of the words Andrew has learned, that might say more than any of them.

He and Dry Hollow Robin will ride Jan. 17 at the stock show. Andrew will wear a borrowed cowboy hat and ride a donated horse. Dry Hollow Robin will carry a rider who has learned about more than riding.

"You know when Jim didn't know what we were doing out there?" Andrew said. "You know what we were doing? Good.

"Because it's our secret."

Rocky Mountain News
January 9, 1994

A Champion Returns

DENVER — The woman was bent over, looking straight ahead, and Tuff Hedeman saw her just in time to stop.

It was Friday night at the National Western Stock Show rodeo, and Hedeman was here to ride a bull. He was here to ride in a rodeo for the first time since he lay in the dirt 13 months ago at the National Finals Rodeo in Las Vegas and couldn't move anything below his neck. The buckle on his belt said he was the 1991 world champion bull rider.

It is one of the hazards of the rodeo that never gets talked about, people bending over to read a belt buckle.

"Is that really you, Tuff Hedeman?" she said. "You're back?"

"My back's fine, ma'am," he said.

Hedeman, 31, from Bowie, Texas, went into a Tuff Shed to pay the $385 entry fee. He has $1,042,127 in career winnings and was the world champion bull rider in 1986, 1989 and 1991. To start the 1995 winter season, he brought his wife, Tracy, and their 3½-year-old son, Lane, to Denver. Lane is named after Lane Frost, the 1987 world champion bull rider who was killed in 1989 at Cheyenne Frontier Days.

"When I was lying in the dirt in Vegas, it felt like 10 minutes, so it must have only been five, but I thought these thoughts I never had before," Hedeman said. "When things are going right, it's eight seconds up there, but it doesn't seem like time at all because it's just you and the bull and nothing else. And then I'm lying there, thinking these things, like what if my son couldn't see me do what I do?"

Hedeman was the leading money winner when he hit the dirt at the National Finals Rodeo in 1993. He had a compressed disk between the fifth and sixth vertebra. Doctors used bone from his pelvis and a metal plate to fuse them.

"The doctor didn't say I shouldn't ride," he said. "Of course, he didn't say I should. Sometimes, it's like you just do what feels right."

Like at the finals in 1989, when he rode the bull eight seconds for the world championship, then rode the bull another eight seconds for Lane Frost.

The day of the deadline for entering the National Western, Hedeman drove 50 miles to a ranch. He stayed on three bulls. He went home and called Denver.

The fourth bull he would ride was Bull 2H on Friday night. It came out of the chute bucking to the left. Hedeman lay back, pulling on his spurs to get it to buck higher. Just him and the bull and nothing else. The judges gave him a 72, to tie for second.

Tracy came down from the stands, Lane asleep on her shoulder. He had not seen his father do what he does.

Hedeman lifted Lane into his arms. "He tried, honey," Tracy said. "Really."

"That's how it goes," Hedeman said. "Maybe next time."

Rocky Mountain News
January 15, 1995

Elders Recall the Bloody Day

NORTHERN CHEYENNE INDIAN RESERVATION, Mont. — It was a dawn much like this dawn, they said.

The sun came up over the creek where the sky reached the earth, the sky painted with brush strokes of orange and purple, and the sun was shoulder-high when it started.

They were here because of what happened the other dawn, Nov. 29, 1864, at Sand Creek.

"Maybe a little colder, the other dawn was," Donlin Many Bad Horses said. "There was ice on the edges of the creek. They were on the west side of the river, and the tepees faced east to show respect for the new day.

"And then it began."

The people who lived that day told about it to the people who live today so it would never be forgotten. Many Bad Horses, 57, was told by his great-grandmother, Plenty Camps, who was six years old that day. Ray Brady, 71, was told the story by his grandfather, Braided Hair, who was 34 at Sand Creek.

They have not read the books that have been written about the massacre. They have not been to Sand Creek. It is a part of their history, so it is a part of them.

The Cheyenne language doesn't have a past tense.

"The Army rifles started, and the horses ran past," Brady said, telling the story of Braided Hair. "He ran back in his tepee for his rawhide and threw it in the middle of them, hoping it would catch one, and he caught one."

Brady worked for the Bureau of Indian Affairs until his heart attack, and now he lives at the Wendell "Turkey" Shoulder Blade Senior Complex in Lame Deer, Mont. He also was a warrior for his people. In World War II, he parachuted into Normandy on D-Day with the 82nd Airborne Division of the U.S. Army.

"This horse, it was only green broke, trained only to drag tepee poles, so he had much trouble getting my grandmother on it," Brady said. "She was pregnant with her first child, my uncle, Charles Whistling Elk. When she was on it, he slapped it on the flank, and it ran up over the bluffs there. Dust was everywhere. And then a little girl this tall, she walked past leading an old man — I don't recall if it was the keeper of the arrow or the keeper of the sacred hat, but he had a bundle on his back, and it was his job to protect it. My grandfather was behind him, to protect him from the soldiers. He was hit on this elbow, but somehow made it to the bluffs. They made it to the bluffs, where the others were, possibly because of the power of the man my grandfather protected. I don't know why I don't remember if he was the keeper of the arrow or the keeper of the sacred hat."

Twelve years later, Brady's grandfather would fight at Little Bighorn in the battle against the 7th Cavalry and Lt. Col. George Armstrong Custer. Braided Hair would become a spiritual leader of his tribe. Later, he would take a Blackfoot scalp that would be the last scalp in the ceremonial bundle, the sacred hat.

Many Bad Horses is the ceremonial spokesman for his tribe, the keeper of the pipe. He has told his children what happened that day. After he talked about it this day, he would have a sweat lodge to honor the memory.

"Horses screamed," Many Bad Horses said, telling the story of Plenty Camps.

"The bluffs were too far for her. She ran toward the water. There is a bend in the creek there. The leaves were off the cottonwoods. The grass hung over the edge. She didn't know why she looked back, but when she did she saw soldiers with their bayonets...people dead but still running. She jumped in the creek and was able to hide under the grass that hung over the bank. She could hear the firing, the crying as the soldiers continued to make sure everybody was dead. She didn't know how many days she stayed under there — two, maybe three."

When the soldiers were gone, the Southern Cheyenne who survived walked south to their people in Oklahoma. The Northern Cheyenne who survived walked north to their people in South Dakota. They had lost their camps and their supplies, so it took most of the winter.

"When they got back to camp, they could say only, 'All gone, all gone. Soldiers,'" Many Bad Horses said.

In the Treaty of the Cheyenne and Arapaho of 1865, the government promised to pay reparations to survivors of the massacre at Sand Creek.

Every afternoon for the rest of her life, Many Bad Horses' grandmother walked the dirt path a mile and a half to the general store where the mail was dropped off to see whether the government had kept its promise. Many Bad Horses sometimes walked with her. Plenty Camps died in 1948 and is buried in the cemetery across the highway, a rock from the hills where she had come to live for a tombstone.

After she died, Many Bad Horse's mother went to the post office every day until she died in 1990.

"The government promised to make reparations," he said. "She believed them."

Braided Hair died in 1936 at the age of 106 and is buried in a cave on Muddy Creek. Brady is the only living person who knows where it is. He thinks it is time to tell one of his nephews.

He goes there sometimes to remember the stories his grandfather told him.

"That horse he caught for my grandmother, I never asked my grandfather what color it was," Brady said. "I will always wonder."

Rocky Mountain News
December 3, 1995

Chapter eight

A Sporting Life

He didn't show no airs.

The Boxer

DENVER — The kid has a left hand that causes problems for his opponents and a right hand that causes problems for himself.

Joe Garcia watched the kid work the heavy bag earlier this week in the gym next to Sloans Lake, training toward tonight's championship round of the Colorado Golden Gloves. The gym is the perfect size for his 23 boxers, which means it is too small. The heater blasts until air and sweat are the same.

Garcia, 69, has trained Golden Gloves fighters since 1947, and he is everything that never gets said about boxing.

"Sometimes, I want things that aren't mine, and suddenly they become mine," the kid said between punches. "I come here, and I fight it out of me."

"You keep your hands in boxing gloves, you stay out of trouble," Garcia said. "You don't, you've got me to face. Boxing is about more than fighting."

Garcia was born in Gilcrest and was 14 when he discovered he could do more with his hands than pick beets. He won his first match at Pickle Day in Platteville, then two Golden Gloves titles. He turned professional and was 22-5 before he was drafted into the Army.

When he got out in 1946, he signed to fight the No. 1 lightweight contender, but something had changed.

"I started to feel the punches," he said. "I had the No. 1 contender, and I told them to tear up the contract. Right then, I knew I had to get into training fighters."

His teams have won 13 state Golden Gloves titles, including the year he had 14 fighters in the eight championship matches. They won the national tournament in 1973 with 30 points, which still is a record. Ron Lyle, Larry Bonds, Danny Hermosillo, Sammy Ortega and five others won national titles.

He has trained more than 4,000 fighters, including most of the other trainers in the area, and will have as many as five in tonight's championship round.

Mike Quintana walked out of trouble and into Garcia's gym 32 years ago. He went 30-0 in the ring, then fought with the 1st Marine Division in Vietnam. He is 47, retired military, here every night.

"If you'd been in trouble or weren't working hard enough, he'd get you in the ring and bapbapbapbap," Quintana said. "Even today Joe could take just about any fighter who walks through that door."

Garcia was a machinist until he retired in 1987. He never married and lives in Commerce City with his cocker spaniel, Champ.

There have been kids who won it all and kids who felt the punches even before they landed. There have been kids who went on to become judges, state legislators and college professors. And there was the kid who didn't remember his trunks until he climbed into the ring and took off his robe.

At 8:30, after the fighters had left, he put on a pair of knuckle gloves and worked out on the bags.

When the bell rang, he shadowboxed, fighting the No. 1 contender in the world.

"A couple of years ago, I decided to stay home for two nights just to see what it felt like," he said. "The first night, it was terrible. The second night, I look at Champ and I say, 'Enough of this.'

"Now I know for sure I couldn't live without this."

Rocky Mountain News
April 4, 1992

JOE GARCIA TEACHES BOXER TOMMY CISNEROS, 24.

Ellen Jaskol/Rocky Mountain News

Capital 'P' Is a 'Z' Who's Mr. Baseball

DENVER — The man in the Colorado Rockies uniform sat alone on the bench in the home team dugout Friday morning, waiting for everybody else.

Don Zimmer, the bench coach for the Rockies, was here at 7:30 a.m. because the game started at 1:05 p.m. It was the first game in a new ballpark, but he didn't see any reason to change what he always has done. He walked around the warning track, checked the dirt in the infield, hit the padding on the center field wall, sat on the bench in the visitors dugout and sat where he will sit during games in his 47th season in professional baseball.

He pointed to the upper deck.

"That row of purple seats up there, you know, it has something to do with sea level," he said. "I never saw anything like that anywhere else. All the rest, it reminds me of someplace else.

"I mean in a good way, of course, but I never saw purple seats."

He took off his cap and rubbed his head, which is covered with a fuzz that

DON ZIMMER HANGS OUT WITH THE COLORADO ROCKIES.

Rocky Mountain News

looks like the result of 64 years of being rubbed every time he sees something new in baseball. The head is set on a body shaped like a capital P. He is a part of baseball there never could be a replacement for.

"That manual scoreboard is like Fenway Park, so I got to tell the guys to watch the way the ball comes off it," he said. "Right center is like Yankee Stadium. There's some Ebbets Field and Crosley Field and Polo Grounds and Shibe Park out there — every time I think of a ballpark, it reminds me of something good."

He and his wife, Soot, were married in 1951 at home plate at Dunn Field in Elmira, N.Y., after which he changed into his uniform and played shortstop for the Elmira Pioneers.

Since then, he has played, coached or managed in every major league stadium except The Ballpark at Arlington, Texas, which opened last season.

"You want to know something amazing?" he said. "This is the first time I ever was in the first game in a stadium. This might be one of the last things that'd still be the first in baseball for me.

"I almost wish I still chewed Red Man to be the first to spit here."

Four weeks ago in spring training in Arizona, on the bus ride from Scottsdale to Tucson, he had a transient ischemic attack, a temporary loss of blood to the brain. He spent two days in intensive care. He quit chewing tobacco and started walking around the field every morning at the stadium, since he was there anyway.

"You can talk about strikes and replacement players and all that, but there's more to life than that crap," he said. "I learned that. You can worry about that stuff, or you can just play baseball.

"This ballpark is about baseball."

He sat on the bench and waited for everybody else. Players came out of the clubhouse and went onto the field. Don Baylor, the manager of the Rockies, came into the dugout and stood next to him.

"How you feeling, Zim?" Baylor said.

"Like it's time to play baseball," Zimmer said. "Of course."

Rocky Mountain News
April 1, 1995

Spinks Loses His Teeth, Not His Cool

DETROIT — It is Tuesday night at Arietha's and Leon Spinks sets the usual in front of Charles T. Young.

Grapefruit juice and double gin, and when Young asks for a cherry, Leon puts one on top. Leon, the former World Boxing Association heavyweight champion, just got his bartending certificate.

"The customer's always right," Leon says. "And when the customer's right, nobody's going to be wrong. Right?"

The early shift at the post office on Fort at Trumbull has crossed the street to Arietha's, and Leon is mixing usuals. For atmosphere, Ron, who was a bartender here before Leon, took out every other light bulb. The late shift comes in at 11:30.

Leon still is thinking about when the customer is right when a woman at the other end of the bar shakes out a cigarette. He takes a Bic lighter out of his pocket, yells, "hold it" and jogs down to her. He holds out a flame.

They taught him that in bartending school.

Young watches Leon and lights his own cigarette.

"The thing about Leon is he isn't crazy like when he was fighting," Young says. "He gets personal with the regular customers. Me, I come in here every day, Leon yells, 'Hey, (expletive)!'

"Then he mixes me the usual, which right there is the point."

The point is that Leon doesn't tend bar the way he boxed, which means he doesn't make New York Mothers — vodka, gin, rum, triple sec and sour mix topped with amaretto — unless somebody orders one.

Leon comes back and takes a drag on the cigarette Young just lit.

"The customer's always right," Leon continues, "unless the customer does something crazy ass. Then I have to all of a sudden give him some common sense."

The idea of distributing common sense makes him smile.

Somebody stole Leon's teeth again.

He was in Las Vegas to be introduced in the ring before the Thomas Hearns fight last month and had some people up to his hotel room. After they left, his teeth were gone, he says. It was the fourth time somebody had stolen his teeth. His wife, Betty, has promised him four front teeth for Christmas.

"I don't know what anybody wants with my teeth, but they take them," he says. "I'm just having myself a good time, and then everybody leaves and I look around. Then I realize, somebody went and stole my teeth again.

"This is the kind of place where people don't care about things like that, though."

Arietha's is the kind of place where, when a woman lights a match to look for her cigarettes and accidentally catches her purse on fire, the man next to her throws it on the floor and the man next to him stomps it out.

Leon looks at the woman and shakes his head.

"You should have let me use my lighter," he says.

It also is the kind of place where, when it gets late, customers will ask Leon what happened to his boxing career.

He won an Olympic gold medal in 1976 and two years later beat Muhammad Ali to become world champion. He lost to Ali later that year and was knocked out by Larry Holmes in a title fight in 1981 in Detroit. He was 0-4-1 in his last five fights and retired last summer after Tony Morrison knocked him out 33 seconds into the first round.

During his career he also was arrested for driving without a license the wrong way on a one-way street, three times for drunken driving, and for other traffic, gun and drugs violations.

He won more than $7 million in the ring, but declared bankruptcy in 1986.

He is 35 and lives with Betty, his second wife, in a house they rent on Fenkell near Grand River, on the west side of Detroit. He wears a crucifix on a chain around his neck and weighs 198 pounds, which is about what he weighed when he was the champion. He was hired by Arietha DeLoach three months ago and hopes to get his own bar.

"This is the all-new Leon, and I don't like to talk about all that stuff like at least I got no taxes to pay. This side of the bar, I don't get in trouble like I did on that side.

Eric Williams/The Detroit News

LEON SPINKS TENDS BAR AT ARIETHA'S IN DETROIT.

"Right how, I'm just trying to keep everything cool and turn this into a good thing."

Tuesday night turns into Wednesday morning.

Two nurses from Detroit Receiving Hospital come in and order a beer between them and ask him to sign their napkin. "Don't forget to sign 'World's Greatest,' " one of them says.

Leon says, "I'll give you my autograph, but you ain't gonna tell me how to sign it." He signs it, "Best wishes, Leon Spinks," then signs three more for her niece. She gives him a $5 bill and tells him to keep the change.

Leon puts money for the beer in the cash register — "I wish I was this worryful with my own money" — and puts his tip in a glass that has a photograph of a naked man on it.

When it gets slow, he opens a Miller Lite and drinks it. He takes three puffs on a cigarette he lit two minutes earlier for a customer, empties the ashtray and grinds out the cigarette in it. He dances to the jukebox.

The things that made him the champion don't just go away.

"I keep moving back here," he says. "If I don't, I get all tight inside. Sometimes, it's harder to fight than fighting."

A couple of times people — mostly kids who come down from the suburbs and get drunk — have wanted to fight him, but he walked away.

A customer gives him a $100 bill, and he holds it up and says, "I ain't seen one of these in a long time." He takes a cigarette out of a customer's pack, pats his pockets and asks if anybody has a light. He dances to the jukebox, drinks another Miller Lite and mixes usuals until last call.

He is the all-new, certified Leon.

At 2:15 a.m., he yells, "All you (expletives) get moving!"

And then, Leon smiles.

The Detroit News
December 4, 1988

Touching Down in a Nebraska Town

PERU, Neb. — The tight end runs backward up the field, retracing his steps until he is surrounded by other players, where a tight end should be.

Lou Saban, the head coach of the Peru State College Bobcats, is watching films of his next opponent in his office in the basement of A.D. Majors Hall on "The Campus of a Thousand Oaks." He sits on the front edge of his desk so he can reach the buttons. He has spent the past 41 seasons trying to find the perfect place for a football coach, and now he can't find the remote control for the VCR.

He leans forward and punches a button, and the tight end is frozen.

"Right there," he says. "You think everything is moving in one direction, and it's going the opposite. So you run it back over and over, and there's always a moment when you see it there, black and white, and know exactly what to expect from the guy across the line of scrimmage, like it's written on his forehead."

He is 70, and the years have given him a wonderful forehead. It can go from Easter Island serious to creased with worry to all wrinkled with laughter. All of this has happened while he watched the tight end.

He takes a bite of a lemon-jelly-filled doughnut from Grannie's, the only restaurant in town since Ruboske's closed, and sets it back on a legal pad that is covered with arrows, Xs and Os.

He starts the tight end moving forward, but now he isn't necessarily talking about what is on the screen.

"You either see what's going on and make your move, or you're stuck like Xs and Os with no arrows," he says. "Everything happens for a reason. People look at it and might think they understand why somebody did what they did, but there's usually more to it than that, more..."

He leans back on the desk and smashes the doughnut with his hand. Lemon filling spreads out over the paper. It looks like a child's drawing of the sun.

"Now," he says. "How in the hell did I do that?"

Peru State is his 17th stop as a football coach. It has been 20 years since he left the Denver Broncos with half-loaves of bread falling like manna. It has been 41 years since the first time he turned down an opportunity to sell life insurance.

On the shelf he has the playbooks filled with the plays that were diagramed for Cookie Gilchrist, Floyd Little, O.J. Simpson, Ottis Anderson, Jim Kelly. Next to them is a stack of films of games he played for the Cleveland Browns in the 1940s. He sometimes tells his team this is a film of their next opponent, and it rolls until somebody notices that none of the players is wearing face masks.

The Peru State Bobcats are 6-3 and the seventh-ranked football team in the NAIA, the smallest college division. Peru, population 1,100, is a dot on the lower right-hand corner of the map of Nebraska, situated so Nebraska City won't look so lonesome.

Saban has two assistant coaches who also teach full course loads, and his defensive tackle just called to say he would miss practice because he has an oceanography lab.

"When you're out there on the sidelines or in here watching films, it doesn't matter where the hell you've been or why you left," he says. "At that moment, you're right there, coaching football. You are where you are, and all that other crap just doesn't matter."

He punches a button to start the tight end moving forward, knowing exactly what to expect.

Nicholas Saban came from Croatia and worked the mines in Leadville, Montana, Washington and California until he married Mary from his homeland and settled by the coal quarries of McCook., Ill. When their oldest son, Luka, was 14, Nicholas sneaked him past the union organizers.

Once, Luka packed so much dynamite in a hole, it rained rock on the town.

When World War II broke out, Luka joined the Army and volunteered for

Rocky Mountain News

LOU SABAN WALKS WITH PLAYER, JASON SEYMOUR, AFTER WINNING THE GAME.

intelligence duty in China. He took a 90-day crash course in Mandarin Chinese, one of the world's most difficult languages. He was assigned to work solitary night missions in China and Formosa.

When he came back, he was Lou, and a linebacker for the University of Indiana, then the Cleveland Browns.

He got his first head coaching job in 1950 at Case Institute in Cleveland, where he had to set a curfew so players wouldn't stay up too late studying.

He was named head coach at Northwestern University in 1955 and went 0-8-1. Before his second season, the athletic director asked him to meet at a coffee shop. The athletic director was late.

"I'd already ordered when he walked in, and he says, 'Sorry I'm late, Lou, but you're fired,'" Saban says. "So there I am, looking down at my sandwich, feeling like somebody had just picked up the knife off the table and stuck it in me. You learn.

"And you never look at a pastrami sandwich the same again."

He was hired as head coach at Western Illinois University, and two years later was Associated Press college coach of the year.

He was hired away in 1960 to coach the Boston Patriots of the new American Football League. He went 5-9 his first season, then started off 2-3. Walking off the practice field, he told team owner Billy Sullivan, "I got myself a couple of new tackles, and I think they'll make the difference."

Sullivan said, "That's nice, Lou, but you're no longer the coach."

He was hired the next year to coach the Buffalo Bills, a 1-13 team the year before. The Bills started 0-2 and were losing to the New York Titans at home when a fan threw a beer can on the field. More beer cans followed, until the coaches and players had to run to the middle of the field to get out of range.

The grounds crew counted 5,000 cans.

The next season, he paid $100 to get a HUD home quarterback named Jack Kemp off the waiver wire and won the next two AFL championships. He was named AFL coach of the year both seasons. He had gone from dodging empty beer cans to being sprayed with champagne, and then he quit.

He and his wife, Lorraine, had four children, and he thought they all would be happier if he was the coach at the University of Maryland.

"The Maryland job was one of the only times in my career I did something completely for my family," he said. "I figured it would be nice to raise the kids in the college atmosphere. And I did it for my wife, who never could understand why football made people do some of the things they did, why it made me do some of the things I did."

After his first season, the budget was cut, and he took a 10-year, $600,000 contract to be coach and general manager of the Denver Broncos.

The Broncos operated out of a quonset hut and had a future that appeared to be less permanent. They played in 34,000-seat Bears Stadium. The team's new owners, Gerald and Allan Phipps, had received offers to move the team.

"He came in here and put in place the organization you see now," Gerald Phipps says. "I used to go up there every Monday afternoon, win or lose, and put my feet up on his desk. I'd say, 'Why don't you try this?' Sometimes he'd nod, and sometimes he'd say, 'Gerry, that's the dumbest g——- idea I ever heard.'

"That's exactly what I wanted in my football coach, and I believe to this day he accomplished all you could ask of him."

The Broncos were leading Buffalo his first season, 14-13, with 1:21 to play when Floyd Little fumbled.

When Little went back to the sideline, Saban grabbed him and said, "There's a highway running east and west and one running north and south, and I want you to get the hell on one."

Buffalo kicked a field goal to take the lead, and Little started to the locker room.

"I got to the end zone, and said, 'Screw it,' and ran back on the field," says Little, who now owns Pacific Coast Ford near Seattle. "I told Fran Lynch to get the hell off the field, and then I told Marlin Brisco to throw the ball as far as he could. I caught it at the five, and we kicked the winning field goal.

"When I came off the field, Lou shook my hand and said, 'Kid, you got yourself another week.'

"There's that side of Lou, and there's also the guy who came up to me later, when he had gone back to Buffalo, and said, 'As long as I've got a job, my friend, you've got a job.'"

The Broncos became the first AFL team to beat an NFL team with a 13-7 win over the Detroit Lions in an exhibition game before the 1967 season. When a bond issue to expand Bears Stadium failed, he helped raise $1.8 million in private money to add 16,000 seats and a new name, Mile High Stadium. A new office and practice facility were built.

Then it all snapped with the shoulder of his quarterback, Steve Tensi.

The 1971 season, the Broncos opened against the Miami Dolphins, who would go on to the Super Bowl. Saban played conservatively. When the Broncos got the ball on their own 13-yard line with 2:19 to play, tied 10-10, he ran the ball and the clock.

"As the old saying goes, I'll take half a loaf if I can't get it all," he told reporters.

"It was just an old saying, like 'A stitch in time saves nine,'" he says. "I didn't think anything about it until I ran on the field before the next game and saw it. At first I thought it was a shame that somebody would waste food with so many hungry people in the world, and then I realized why."

It was half a loaf of bread, and he didn't need pastrami to tell him what it meant.

Fans threw garbage and eggs at his house, the postman left his mail on the lawn, and his children were taunted in school.

Barbara Saban, a psychotherapist who lives in Evergreen, remembers the nights she sat with her father until she fell asleep to the sound of the projector.

"I would look at stat sheets to try to pick out something he could use, or he would have me watch a certain player on the film," she says. "We all knew what he was going through — we saw the way people treated us just because we were related to him. He thought he could find the answer if he just could watch the film enough, and we wanted to be near him when it happened.

"To this day, the sound of a projector is still such a comforting sound to me."

After the ninth game of the season, Saban quit.

"You know what's the worst part?" he says. "I never had anything that was as tough — as physically tough — as Denver because I wanted to turn it around so bad, to just grab those guys by the face masks and drag them to win. But that wasn't the worst part.

"The worst part came later, when I found out that my kids and my wife hadn't told me what they went through, and I'm still not sure I know it all."

He was hired the next season as coach and general manager of the Buffalo Bills, a team that had slipped back to 1-13 with a disappointment at running back named O.J. Simpson.

"Before he came, I wanted out of Buffalo," Simpson says. "Then Lou came in. He made everybody play better because he was a great football coach, and he made everybody play harder because he was a great guy."

At halftime against Kansas City, Saban stood on a table and gave his pep talk in Chinese, and the Bills scored three touchdowns to win. Simpson led the league in rushing four of five seasons. They went 9-5 in his second season and to the playoffs in his third.

The Bills slipped to 8-6 in 1975. Lou gulped nitroglycerin for chest pains. There was nothing he could take for the Miami Dolphins or the Pittsburgh Steelers.

In 1976, the Bills started 2-3 and the general manager's job was taken away from him, so he quit.

He went to the University of Cincinnati as athletic director but left after 19 days, saying the program couldn't afford him.

He was hired five weeks later as coach and athletic director at the University of Miami, which had improved its record to 3-8 the previous season.

Two weeks later, he woke up in the hospital after a double-bypass heart operation.

Lorraine, who suffered from severe diabetes, walked with him every day after the operation. He talked about how they finally could raise the two children who were not grown in a college atmosphere. He went back to Miami a month later, and she stayed in Buffalo to pack.

The next day, he got the call.

"When she died, it made me think of all the things I had done and hadn't done, and there was a lot of guilt," he says. "There are still some things I just can't talk about. In the end, I decided there was only one thing I could do, which was what I had been doing all along, and that is to coach football."

A week later, he was back on the sidelines. He went 3-8 and 6-5. He remarried.

Joyce Saban is 20 years younger and understands there are things she can't understand.

Miami brought in a new administration after his second season, and the old problems came with them.

After his second season, a coach on his staff asked for a recommendation for the coaching job at Army.

The major general wasn't interested in the assistant and they talked about other possibilities.

"Maybe what you need," Saban said, "is an old Army man like myself."

He left Army after his first season, saying commitments had been broken.

He went to work for his old receivers coach at Northwestern, George Steinbrenner, and eventually was named president of the New York Yankees.

He left in 1983 to coach the University of Central Florida for two seasons, until the football program was de-emphasized.

He and Joyce built a home on four acres in Hendersonville, N.C., where he planned to write his autobiography. The farther in the past he went, the more he realized he was missing the future. One day, Joyce brought home a chain saw and told him to cut out the dead trees.

Every day, there were more stacks of firewood.

"So one day Joyce goes out to see everything I've done, and she started talking about deforestation and the 'greenhouse effect,'" he says. "She said, 'You've got to get back into coaching.'"

He called a former assistant who was head coach at Martin County High School, in Stuart, Fla., and was hired as defensive coordinator. The last game of his second season, Martin County shut out South Fork High School, 19-0. When the teams were walking off the field he saw an official from South Fork and said, "You look like you could use some help."

He left after one season at South Fork to coach Georgetown (S.C.) High School, then left after one season to be head coach of the Middle Georgia Heat Wave in the North American Spring League.

After the league folded, he flew himself up to Peru State for an interview.

"People look at my age and all the places I've been and won't hire me," Saban says. "In the past, I've learned you take your opportunities wherever they come. I look at my age and all the places I've been and say that's exactly why they should, because I'm a better coach now than I've ever been."

The Bobcats won the national title last year, but head coach Tom Shea left to coach at University of Mary in Bismarck, N.D.

Saban has a one-year, $25,000 contract and 10 returning starters.

"When he took the job, I looked at him and said, 'You've never taken over a team that's a winner before,'" Joyce Saban says. "I said, 'For God's sake, don't screw it up.'"

He stands in the center of the field in the Oak Bowl for practice before Saturday's game against Midwestern State University in the NAIA playoffs. It is 11 degrees, with a wind that got a running start in North Dakota. It is a good day to be an oceanography major at Peru State.

Matt Hug, the linebacker supposed to take the tight end, misses his assignment.

"Did you make a mistake?" Saban says.

"Well, I..." Hug says.

"Did you make a mistake?" Saban says.

"Yes," Hug says.

"Good," Saban says. "Mistakes we can work on. It's when you won't admit them we have a problem."

The practice continues, and the mistakes are worked out like a cramp.

"I thought coach was some old guy they got because nobody young wanted to come here," halfback Mark Whitaker says. "Then in a game, he yells, 'They're killing me, they're killing me.' All of a sudden, I realize this is the guy on ESPN in those old-time NFL films.

"After that, I realized he's just like a young guy, except he knows a lot more."

Barbara Saban: "He doesn't have all the assistants he had other places, so he has to do a lot more. A lot more of the films, a lot more of the little details. That's exactly what he loves."

He lives in a one-bedroom apartment in Auburn, 12 miles south of Peru. Joyce stays in Apollo Beach to take classes to become a paralegal. She comes up for his big games.

He watched films until 2:15 this afternoon past closing time for Grannie's, but she made him a turkey sandwich and warmed up a mound of mashed potatoes.

"The other day, I drove out to the Missouri River and just sat there alone watching it roll on by," he says. "It's a mean river — ice and logs and everything else that's not strong enough gets pulled down. I just watched it and thought about how it would have been nice to have stayed someplace long enough so it would always feel like home.

"I thought about how good that would be, and at the same time how good it is to still be wanted as a football coach."

Tonight, he will go back to his apartment and watch more films. He will finish reading *Sleepwalking Through History: America in the Reagan Years.* He will warm up something that is brown in a dish in the refrigerator.

Right now, though, there is football to coach. The players move back and forth, retracing their steps. He stands behind it all and lets it unfold like a diagram.

He is where he is, which is exactly where he wants to be.

"I wonder," he says.

The players turn to look at him, then follow his eyes up to the sky. A flock of geese is flying south. He watches the geese cross over the Oak Bowl and disappear, arrows without Xs and Os.

"Beautiful," Saban says. "Do you think they ever wish they could just stay in one place all the time? Don't you wonder?"

Rocky Mountain News
December 8, 1991

A Different Shade of White

LEADVILLE, Colo. — Tom Sobal moved across the snow, above the world, where everything was a different shade of white.

He ran on snowshoes up from Leadville until he was in a snowstorm above timberline. He ran there because nobody else had. He stopped.

He was not breathing hard, which was good because there wasn't enough oxygen for a tree.

"Sometimes, I just stop," he said. "There isn't a mark in the snow in front of me. Do you know what it feels like every time I run, to discover a whole new world just for yourself?"

Sobal is the best snowshoe racer in the world, but the world never has looked up and noticed.

He is 6-foot-3 and 160 pounds, so when he runs he is shaped like a question mark. He holds the world record for a 26.2-mile snowshoe marathon, 3:06:17. He

TOM SOBAL OF LEADVILLE, COLO., IS THE BEST SNOWSHOE RACER IN THE WORLD.

is 36 and has not eaten meat in 20 years or had a haircut in 10, and he never has had a full-time job, driven a car, used alcohol or caffeine or lost a snowshoe marathon.

"There's some things people don't seem to understand about what I do," he said. "If this was just about running on snowshoes as fast as I could, I would think I was crazy, too."

The first time Sobal ran competitively was as a freshman at William A. Wirt High School in Gary, Ind., but he quit after the first meet because he thought he knew more than the coach.

He studied physiology at Earlham College in Richmond, Ind., and graduated with honors. He considered graduate school but decided to study physiology by testing himself. He moved to Pagosa Springs to work on a dude ranch and run.

When he got bored, he chased cows.

"I figured I was making them leaner," he said. "It was like my way of making the world a healthier place."

Seven years ago, he borrowed a pair of snowshoes because he couldn't run on snow.

"I was running 70 to 80 miles a week, but the first time I ran three miles on snowshoes I was sore for three days," he said. "It was great. Not many people understand that, and I got lucky and found another one up here."

Her name is Melissa Lee Sobal. Two years ago, they ran the 109-mile Iditashoe race in Alaska. He won in 23:50, breaking the previous record by more than three hours. When she crossed the finish line more than 40 hours later, she became the first woman to complete the race.

He is a bicycle mechanic. She is a massage therapist. In Leadville, that means they usually have time to train as much as they want.

They have a trailer, but most of the year they house-sit around town. They keep the thermostat set at 45 degrees. His clothes are tennis shoes, sweat suits and spandex he wears in layers.

"It's not always an easy decision to leave here and go to a race," he said. "It's not like I've ever won any money at it. Sometimes, even if I'm pretty sure I can win, it's just not worth the cost."

To get to the 1991 World Snowshoe Marathon Championships in Duluth, Minn., he got a ride with a friend. It was 10 degrees below zero the morning of the race, and the car wouldn't start. He hitched a ride and got to the starting line 10 minutes after everybody had left.

He put on his snowshoes, slipped on ice and cracked a rib, and went on to set a course record and win by seven minutes. The grand prize was a $25 gift certificate to the Ground Round Bar and Grill. He gave it away because the Ground Round Bar and Grill didn't sound like a place for a vegetarian who doesn't drink, and he started to hitchhike home.

Since then, he has lost a snowshoe race for the first time, a five-kilometer sprint last spring up Aspen Mountain.

"That was good," he said. "Losing is the only way I'll find out how good I am."

He and a friend's burro, Maynard, also are generally considered the world champion burro racers.

He has not won any more recognition for burro racing, but at least when he's training, people don't stop their cars to ask if he needs a ride.

"I ask people what I can do to get more people involved in these sports, if I'm doing something wrong," he said. "They say the only thing I did wrong is to pick sports that people think are too hard."

Maybe someday the world will look up and notice.

For now, he has discovered a world just for himself, a world where everything is a different shade of white.

"Maybe I'm missing something," he said. "I have to admit, there have been times I've thought about that. Then I get up here, and I think it's everybody else down there who are missing something."

Rocky Mountain News
December 26, 1993

Greg jumped right in and said, "Take me snowshoeing."
I remember he was wearing cowboy boots and blue jeans, but he went out there and stomped around in the snow with me. It was great.

TOM SOBAL

The Baseball Fan

DENVER — During the seventh-inning stretch of the Colorado Rockies game Saturday at Mile High Stadium, Celia Thompson still couldn't do for the new home team what she did for the old ones for 39 seasons.

Thompson has come to every professional baseball game in Denver that wasn't on Sunday since 1954. And when the home team was behind in the seventh inning, she stood and turned around one time to bring them luck.

She did this for the Denver Bears and Zephyrs. Now, she will do it for the Rockies, except they were ahead of the Montreal Expos both games.

"It works, except when I forget," she said.

"So I have to stand up in the eighth inning and pretend like dum-de-dum-dum, I'm just kind of looking up at the fans when I'm really trying to save the game. I'm sure it'll work for these new guys, too."

Thompson sits in Section 108, Row 11, Seat 14, the seat directly in front of where she sat for Zephyr games. She has the box scores from the *Rocky Mountain News* for every game since 1956. She has come a long way from her days in Section 107.

In 1954, the first year she had season tickets, she sat farther down the first-base line in Section 107, and Sam Thompson sat in Section 109. He saw her and prayed, "Lord, if you want me to marry that woman, please do something to bring us closer together." Two games later, a season-ticket holder in Section 108 didn't show up, and she felt an unexplainable urge to sit closer to home plate.

On opening day 1956, he proposed, and they sat in Section 107 until he died during the '72 season.

"I sat next to an empty seat the rest of the season," she said. "I'd turn and say, 'Did you see that?' but he wasn't there. I know he saw it, though.'"

She sat alone in Section 108 after that, and she was the Zephyrs Fan Club, with Kathy Harman and Marie Taylor.

When Major League Baseball chose Denver, she didn't think she could afford Rockies season tickets. She didn't know what to do, until she realized she couldn't afford to not get Rockies season tickets. She worked extra hours taking care of two older women, telemarketing to raise money for children with Down's syndrome, and at her church day-care center.

She has had to adjust to more than just the new Colorado Rockies cap, jacket, sweatshirt, T-shirt, pennant and button.

"I think of all the people who couldn't be here today," she said. "Sam, Kathy, Marie who couldn't get season tickets for one reason or another," she said. "Sam couldn't be here for obvious reasons, but Kathy and Marie, that's really hard for them, sitting at home and knowing they're playing baseball here. That's hard, but the game has to go on, as they say."

She will miss her first Rockies home game today, because it is Sunday and she figures if the Lord would move her one section closer to Sam in the reserve grandstand, she can sit general admission in church one day a week.

Not even the major leagues can change the way she thinks about that, but she might be changing the way she thinks about the major leagues.

"I know this might surprise some people, but I think I might even like this more than the old Zephyrs and Bears games," she said. "I know it's kind of hard to take the change at first, but it's kind of like the time I got hit on the head with a foul ball and had to get four stitches in my head and was back here the next night. I didn't let that stop me from loving baseball — and I won't let a little change, either."

Rocky Mountain News
April 11, 1993

Back in the Starting Lineup

DENVER — The first elbow came 20 minutes into Calvin Natt's first practice as coach of the Montbello High School basketball team.

A player drove into the lane, faked left, jumped into the air, spun 180 degrees, threw a pass behind his head and crashed into an elbow. The player held his hand to his mouth. Natt pulled the hand away and looked down at it, checking for teeth.

For 12 seasons in professional basketball, Natt was the one with the elbow. "Not even blood?" he said. "Man, for a move like that, you oughta at least be bleeding."

Natt, 37, started Tuesday as coach at Montbello, taking off from his mortuary to try to help a basketball program recover. He replaced Albert Gale, who quit two weeks ago for "differences of philosophies." Gale had replaced Sayyid Abdal-Rahman, who was convicted last year on two counts of selling cocaine.

When Natt started at Montbello he went back to a world he didn't recognize.

"I walk the halls at school and see 6-8, 6-9 kids I have to look up to, and they aren't out playing on the team," he said. "Me, I had a teacher back in the fourth grade in Bastrop, La., Miss Inez Grant, who recognized something in the kid who won the stickhorse races and the sack races, and took me by the arm and pushed me to do something. I had parents who made me go to church with them and out to pick cotton, and if I didn't have those people...

"If I didn't have those people I could have been one of the baddest guys out there."

He came to the Nuggets in 1984 in a trade from the Portland Trailblazers. At 6-foot-6 and 220 pounds, he was shorter and less talented than most of the players he was assigned to stop. So when he stopped them, the difference was something inside him.

Julius Erving always refused to shake his hand.

"Not because I didn't respect Calvin and the way he played the game — you have to respect anybody did the things he did with what he had," Erving said. "But Calvin, he was so strong he'd leave your hand sore. He never did understand his own strength."

He also didn't understand his weaknesses, which probably shortened his career.

His first season with the Nuggets, he had bone chips and damaged cartilage in his right knee, so bone ground on bone. He averaged 23 points, eight rebounds and three assists a game. He went on to help the team take the Los Angeles Lakers to seven games in their only appearance ever in the Western Conference finals.

"I probably should have sat out more games," he said. "People tell me that, and now I realize that. But what people don't realize is that the things that made me successful in the NBA are the things that made it impossible for me to just sit out."

He injured the left knee the next season, then tore his Achilles' tendon in the first game of the next season. There was surgery on both knees, surgery to remove a blood clot and surgery to scrape off calcium deposits. Each time he came back, he tried to play like none of it had happened.

His contract called for a $50,000 bonus if the team won 53 games in 1988, but he refused to take it because he had played in only 27 games. He also turned down a playoff bonus his teammates voted him. He was traded in 1988 to the San Antonio Spurs, then went to the Indiana Pacers the next season, where his injuries conspired to end his career after playing 14 minutes in only two games.

He opened the Calvin Natt Family Mortuary two years ago. Growing up in Bastrop, he had worked after school at the mortuary owned by the father of a friend, mowing the lawn, then embalming and dressing. It says something about the way he played basketball that it served him as a recommendation when he became a mortician.

"Things have been good, people still remember me, but I've seen too many young bodies here," he said. "Once they get here, it's too late for me to do anything."

The things that made it impossible for him to sit out NBA games also made it impossible for him to sit out life.

CALVIN NATT COACHES THE MONTBELLO HIGH SCHOOL BASKETBALL TEAM.

In October, he crossed the street from the mortuary to be an assistant coach at East High School, so when the job opened at Montbello he was the natural choice. He watched videotapes over and over, working to learn the players' skills and names. Of course, this is a man who listens over and over to tapes of the sermons of the Rev. James Peters of New Hope Baptist Church.

He met his players before their game Tuesday against Manual, and they won 88-46. They won again Thursday at Lincoln, 110-46. They were 2-0 under Natt and 9-2 for the season going into Saturday's game against George Washington.

He got stacks of cards and baskets of fruit last week, but everybody knows better than to send flowers to Natt.

"No flowers," he said. "Nobody's going to send flowers to a guy who runs a mortuary. Anyway, I never really was the kind of guy you'd send flowers to."

Rocky Mountain News
January 23, 1994

Skiing's Bad Boy

CRESTED BUTTE, Colo. — Bill Johnson was driving his pickup up to the house he is building, and at one of the curves a small black case slid off the seat onto the floor.

The case was under the rags on the front seat, because he doesn't lock the truck. The truck is a 1984 Ford F-250, the first thing he bought after he won the downhill in the Olympics, and it was filled with boards and buckets for the house. The house started off to be 1,700 square feet and has grown to 3,200 square feet and is $100,000 over budget.

He picked up the case, opened it to check the gold medal, and reflected on what it has meant to him.

"Let's see, millions," he said. "One...two...Yeah, I was right."

Ten years ago in Sarajevo, Bill Johnson, then 23, became the only American to win the Olympic gold medal in the downhill. He had won one World Cup downhill race before that, a month earlier in Wengen, Switzerland. Going into the Olympics, he had said, "Everybody else is racing for second place."

The downhill, more than any other race, is a test to see who is willing to risk everything to win everything, and after he won he was asked what the gold medal meant to him.

"Millions," he said. "We're talking millions."

People called him arrogant and said he set a bad example as the only American to win the downhill, without taking into account that it might not have been a coincidence.

After the Olympics, he won two more World Cup races, had two back surgeries, crashed at 60 mph, broke a shoulder and tore up a knee, and retired from World Cup racing in 1990.

"When I won the gold, I'd accomplished everything I wanted to accomplish," he said. "What was left?"

He came to Crested Butte Mountain Resort three years ago to be the ski ambassador for the area, meaning his job basically is to wear a "Crested Butte" cap and be Bill Johnson.

By all accounts, he is good at both.

"I've got the perfect image," he said. "The Mahres (Phil and Steve, who finished first and second in the slalom in the 1984 Olympics), now they've got a bad image, being nice guys and boring. Me, I could probably walk into any ski resort in the world and get a job.

"But the people up here helped me one of the few times I needed help."

That was in 1981, after he had been kicked off the U.S. Ski team for being out of shape in July. He had never been popular with his coaches for questioning their methods and for having fun in his own ways. It also might have had something to do with his conviction for stealing a car when he was 16.

The next race for the U.S. team was in Crested Butte. He hitchhiked to Crested

Butte, went to the resort's headquarters in the Axtel Building and found the biggest office. He walked in and introduced himself to Edward Calloway, whose family owns Crested Butte and who found him a place to stay and eat while he skied well enough to force the coaches to take him back.

Rocky Mountain News

Now, he skis with anybody at Crested Butte if it fits into the schedule the public relations office and his mother in Mount Hood, Ore., make for him. He has sold the houses in Malibu and Lake Tahoe. He and his father-in-law, Dennis Ricci, have a construction business.

"You know how some people talk about how the good things that happen to them are a burden and make things more complicated?" he said. "Well, what people have to understand is that my life's a lot simpler, because now I just do the things I want to do."

One of the things he doesn't want to do is shovel snow, so the driveway that winds back and forth up to the house he is building is heated.

The house looks down on Crested Butte with views from every window, a Jacuzzi in every bathroom and a huge flagstone fireplace he designed.

He has done most of the work.

"I know people think I'm strong-headed," he said. "But some of that $100,000 is stuff my wife wanted."

His wife is Gina, and they met in Lake Tahoe in 1987, when he was there for knee surgery. They met through friends. Everybody else was dancing, so he threw away his crutches and danced.

They got married that year, and they had a son, Ryan.

Two years ago, they were at their home in Lake Tahoe, and each thought the other was watching Ryan. A friend had left the gate to the hot tub open. When Johnson found Ryan, he was unconscious, and two weeks later he was taken off life support.

People who know Johnson say he has mellowed since then, but Johnson says he hasn't.

"That's just part of life," he said. "When you're a downhiller, you look at death in a different way. It's just something you have to put behind you."

They have a son, Nick, who is 18 months old, and Gina is due in April.

Still, the things it takes to win the downhill don't just go away.

"Sometimes, I drive the Porsche over Kebler Pass," he said. "There's spots you can get up to 60, 70 miles an hour and spinning out in the dirt. In the Porsche, it's almost as much fun as downhill racing...

"Downhill racing, that's almost as much fun as stealing cars."

That night at The Rafters, drinking Coors Light from one glass and spitting Copenhagen juice into another, Johnson explained why he would win at pool.

He has won two pool tournaments here and also wrote the graffiti in the men's room above the urinal, which begins "Don't look up here..."

"The thing is, I don't know what failure is," he said. "I don't know what it is to not be good at something. What might bother some people is sometimes I get more specific."

Earlier this year he helped organize the first Jeep King of the Mountain Downhill for racers who have been retired for at least three years — he finished third last month at Aspen Highlands — and he plans more races next year.

He started playing golf three years ago and now is a five-handicap golfer.

"I figure it'll take eight years of playing 11 months a year to win the U.S. Open," he says. "When I get the time, that's what I'll do. Right now, though, I've got a family and a business and a job, and this might sound strange, but I've put those things ahead of achieving my goal."

And that is as close as Bill Johnson will come to admitting that anything in the past 10 years has changed him.

And then he cleared the table.

He went to the bar and ordered a shot of Grand Marnier, which is more specific, and drank it.

"Too many pansy asses," he said. "The Americans will be lucky to get one or two guys in the top 10 in the downhill in the Olympics this time."

BILL JOHNSON

In the morning, Johnson skied down the slopes at Crested Butte, where nobody recognized him. He was wearing goggles. He was 10 years past the gold medal.

He skied past the people he is ambassador for, to the bottom.

"This is really what it was all about, all along," he said. "People forget that, but I don't. It was about me, skiing."

He was thinking about this when a woman from Dallas said, "Bad Bill?"

"Yeah?" he said.

"You were bad, but you were great," she said.

"Yeah," he said. "I guess that's what it's all about, too."

Rocky Mountain News
February 13, 1994

Tucson Lenny

TUCSON, Ariz. — Tucson Lenny Rubin was walking into the Colorado Rockies clubhouse to do whatever it is he does, when somebody opened the door and smashed his cigar.

Whatever Tucson Lenny does, he has the cigar in his mouth. The cigar is fat and long, and Lenny follows wherever it goes. It never is lit, because when a cigar is lit, it smokes.

Everyone in Tucson knows Lenny, and Lenny knows the importance of a big cigar.

"See why I always gotta cigar in this business?" he said. "It's kinda like a blind man with a cane. You gotta look on the bright side of things, which is if I didn't have this cigar, there's a lotta times I woulda busted my face, see?"

Tucson Lenny came with Hi Corbett Field. He's worked here 28 years. He spends the games going in and out the doors under the stands, risking his cigar to take care of the facets of baseball most people never see, because they actually watch the games.

"So Rick Sutcliffe, Bert Blyleven and George Fraser, one year they tell me they need 42 feet of rubber surgical tubing and two funnels," he said. "I don't know what they want with 42 feet of rubber surgical tubing and two funnels, but I get 42 feet of surgical tubing and two funnels. They say thanks, Lenny.

"Then they cut up the surgical tubing and make slingshots with the funnels, and they're shooting water balloons from the area around third base into the other dugout.

"That's what I do."

Tucson Lenny, 66, grew up in Brooklyn, where he got his love of baseball and manner of speaking. He retired as a master sergeant after 20 years in the Air Force. He moved to Tucson in 1966 because it seemed to be the perfect place for someone named Tucson Lenny.

While the Rockies were playing the Chicago Cubs, he unclogged a drain in the locker room, got $200 for a money order for Rockies outfielder Chris Jones and picked up a stack of responses from players to mail to fans.

When the duck laid eggs next to the fence behind home plate, he covered them before every game until they hatched.

When Alejandro Gomez of the Oakland A's got married, he cooked the meatloaf.

"Got to pick up Don Baylor's shoes, real nice ones, llama, but they needed new soles and heels," he said. "How many guys getta drive around in their car with Don Baylor's shoes?"

The car is a 1963 Pontiac Tempest convertible held together by bumper stickers with his name painted on the side. The roof hasn't been up for at least 10 years, which is only half as long as the odometer hasn't worked. If he ever did decide to put up the roof it wouldn't show off the tiger-striped upholstery.

Anyway, he drove it to pick up Baylor's shoes, got the money order for Jones, mailed the stack of responses to fans and was back at Hi Corbett in time to see Rockies fans starting to leave because their team was losing, 12-3.

"I see a lotta distorted Rockies fans," he said to the clubhouse manager, Dan McGinn. "They must be losing."

Hal Stoelzle/Rocky Mountain News

TUCSON LENNY LOVES BASEBALL.

"You mean distraught Rockies fans?" McGinn said.

"No, I mean distorted Rockies fans," Lenny said. "How can you be distraught when you're watching such a wonderful ballgame in Tucson?"

Before that could sink in, he was gone.

He knows to get Perrier water for Gates Brown, six meatball sandwiches from Luke's restaurant for the California Angels clubhouse workers, and where to buy baby bathtubs for pitchers to soak their elbows.

He was getting orders for sandwiches from Rincon Market for the Seattle Mariners the next day when the game ended.

He had not seen a single play.

He had done what he does.

"See what I mean?" he said. "Where else could a guy getta opportunity to do this? Ain't baseball great?"

Rocky Mountain News
March 29, 1993

The Autumn of '72

NEW IBERIA, La. — In the autumn of 1972, in Billings, Montana, Mark Paloverde led his football team to the state championship. He broke every record there was, and sometimes he went back and broke them again. It all was done with a peculiar sidearm throwing motion that nobody but him could do.

It was a cliche that was coming true.

He got engaged to the prettiest cheerleader, got a college scholarship and got just about everything he always wanted. The local paper wrote stories about him, saying what a wonderful future he had and what a wonderful past he already had. He was 18 years old.

And you could go through your life and never have an autumn like the one Mark Paloverde had in 1972. And you could go through an autumn like that and go through the rest of your life wondering why it can't always be that good.

Some nights now when he starts drinking, he tells people about who he used to be in Billings, Montana. Some of them nod and say he must have been something to see, some of them tell him to drink another beer and go drain out another story. That's when he pulls out the newspaper clipping he keeps folded in his wallet.

It is brown and cracked along the folds, and it starts off, "Mark Paloverde, the golden boy with the magic arm..."

"One time that year I stopped and was watching some kids playing football in the park, and two of them were arguing about who was going to be me," he says. "That's how it was. They were arguing about who got to be me. They all wanted to grow up like me."

The college scholarship didn't work out, he says he never got a chance. The marriage didn't work out either.

He drifted down here, taking jobs where he could get them. Today he lives outside New Iberia in a trailer he rents. He worked a few months as a pizza cook, and now he works nights in a convenience store.

"We had this one play, 42 end split, and I guarantee you it worked almost every time," he says. "I'd get the snap and while I was dropping back I'd stop short and throw to the right sideline about 35 yards down the field — it was the receiver's job to be there when the ball was. You had to have a hell of an arm to connect on that pass, and I did. You would not believe how many touchdowns we scored on that one play alone."

He went back to Billings two years ago, when his father died. He went back to his school and saw the state championship trophy — it is the only one his school ever won — in a case. A picture of him throwing a football with that sidearm motion is next to it.

He went to a bar in his old neighborhood and told the bartender who he was. The bartender said yes, he remembered Mark Paloverde. Paloverde called up a running back, a defensive lineman and a linebacker from that team, and they came and met him.

One of them had a football in his trunk and they went out in the parking lot and threw it around. He called a 42 slant right. He threw with the same peculiar sidearm motion.

He connected with the receiver — it was the receiver's job to be there when the ball was — and he felt something snap. He kept throwing, even though the arm had gone numb. Nobody but him could throw it that way.

Then the one who used to be the running back said he had to get home for dinner, and the one who used to be the linebacker said he had to go pick up his daughter.

He came back down here and hasn't gone back since. There are things you just want to leave like they were, he says.

"When we won the state championship I was 9-for-11 and scored two touchdowns," he says. "There was nothing they could do to stop us. There's not many people who ever could say they could do the things I did on a football field."

Some nights when he starts drinking, he tells people who he used to be in Billings, Montana, in the autumn of 1972.

The Daily Iberian
January 14, 1986

Tigers' Kid Eddie Forester

DETROIT — Eddie Forester is sitting in a Tiger Stadium seat in his dining room, holding an autographed baseball, and something reminds him of the first time Ty Cobb fired him as his personal clubhouse boy.

Forester is 86 and worked for the Detroit Tigers for 53 years. He has on a Tigers cap he'll wear every day until he puts on a new one the day the baseball season begins. The only decoration in the house that doesn't say Detroit Tigers is a painting of a real tiger. The baseball is autographed by Ty Cobb.

It is priceless, but like all priceless things in this world, the stitches are coming loose.

"Ty Cobb, the kind of son of a bitch he was, somebody puts his shoes in his locker, and he tells me I'm fired as his personal clubhouse guy because they aren't perfectly straight," Forester says. "So then a couple of days later, he comes over and tells me to go and get him orange juice and a ham-and-egg sandwich. He says it better be the right kind of orange juice or I was fired as his personal guy, even though I hadn't been hired again.

"The only other guy who liked ham-and-egg sandwiches before games was that guy who could only hit home runs on Sunday...what was his name again?"

Forester gets up and walks to the back door to look at Tiger Stadium. He never has lived anyplace that he couldn't look out and see where the Tigers play. He carries his season passes from the 1988 and 1989 seasons in his shirt pocket, and he already has handed out 600 Detroit Tigers schedules for this season.

EDDIE FORESTER SHOWS HIS
BASEBALL MEMORABILIA.

Duane Belanger/The Detroit News

Right now, though, the owners have locked out the players while they negotiate, and he doesn't know if there will be a season.

"What'll I do if Opening Day gets here and there's no baseball?" he says. "It's just like a long winter that doesn't look like it's ever going to end. At least I've got memories."

Forester was hired to work for the Tigers in 1919 after he skipped school and waited outside the gate at Navin Field every day until Frank Navin asked him if he needed a job.

He started in the Tigers clubhouse, washing uniforms and running to the barbershop to place the players' bets on horses. His friends at St. Boniface did his homework, and he gave them autographed baseballs. Everybody called him kid.

After he got married, his wife baby-sat the players' children. The couple had twin daughters of their own — "the wife always claimed she could tell them apart, but I never believed her" — who grew up playing in the stadium. For vacations, they went to other baseball stadiums to check out the locker rooms.

After Cobb fired him the second time — somebody had crossed his bats — he went to work in the visitors' locker room for a couple of seasons. For about 30 seasons after that, he changed the numbers in the scoreboard. Then he was in charge of watching the stadium at night and letting the visiting teams into the locker room when they came to town.

He retired 17 seasons ago because he had injured his knee after stepping in a hole in the stadium and his eyesight was failing. He got a gold watch and six box seats for his dining room. Every season, Tigers chairman and chief executive officer Jim Campbell sends him a new cap and a season pass for two to any American League stadium.

"I was up visiting Mr. Campbell a while ago and Charlie Gehringer comes in and says, 'How are you doing kid?' " he says. "I'm 86 years old, and he still calls me kid, so it made me feel good. He remembers my name."

The knee has healed, and he has 20/20 vision since he got a left eye transplant eight years ago from a 55-year-old man who was killed in an automobile accident. The man's son and daughter visit him once a month. They talk for an hour, then say, "Well, we've seen our father and he's seen us."

He lives alone since his wife died 12 years ago, and his daughters married and moved to California. He says the woman he hired to clean his house stole the baseballs Babe Ruth autographed. He gave away most of the other baseballs and Birdie Tebbetts' and Mickey Cochrane's mitts.

Every day, three times a day, he eats at McDonald's and when he gets in his car to go, it reminds him of Mark Fidrych.

"I was just sitting there in my car after the game," he says. "I tell him the damn car's broke, that's what's wrong. So he fiddles under the hood and gets all greasy, and pretty soon he says, 'Start it up.'

"I don't know what he did, but it ran just like he pitched that year."

In McDonald's, they already know his order.

He starts to eat his hamburger, and it reminds him of Babe Ruth.

"So after the games, Babe Ruth, he'd always say to me, 'Grab some balls kid,' and we'd go to the hospital. He'd sign all the balls for the sick kids, and then we'd go out to eat. I'd order a hamburger, and he'd say, 'Kid, when you're with me, you eat steak.'

"I always did prefer hamburgers, though."

That reminds him of the story about Tris Speaker, who also made him eat steak, and that reminds him of the story about Al Kaline, then George Kell, then Frank Navin.

Until the season begins, the memories are all he's got.

He is back to Ty Cobb and the time somebody hung a sweatshirt backwards in his locker. All of a sudden he stops and takes off his Tigers cap.

"Charlie Maxwell," he says. "That was the guy who could only hit home runs on Sunday."

The Detroit News
March 11, 1990

Denny McLain — Still Fast with His Pitches

FORT WAYNE, Ind. — Denny McLain just missed his turn.

He is driving on Smith Road on a Thursday afternoon, talking on the car phone with Phil in Los Angeles for the movie on his life. He just finished talking to his lawyer in Tampa, Fla., and had started to tell the story about the time he lobbed the home run pitch to Mickey Mantle when the telephone rang and he missed the turn. He has call forwarding.

He looks at the missed turn in the rearview mirror of the Corvette, and there is more regret in his eyes than when he talks about any of the things Phil in Los Angeles wants to make a movie about. He checks his watch and the clock in the dashboard. He finishes his third Diet Coke in the last 45 minutes.

"I know another way," he says, and he steps on the accelerator. "It might even be faster. No, not you, Phil."

It is a year since he was released, after 29 months, on $200,000 bond from the federal penitentiary at Talladega, Ala. He doesn't know when or if he will have a third trial on federal cocaine, extortion, loan sharking and conspiracy charges.

In the meantime, he has organized a boxing exhibition in Sterling Heights between former *Playboy* bunnies, signed autographs around the country, been a partner in a nonalcoholic Australian wine distributorship, been hired and fired as director of promotions for the Fort Wayne Komets of the International Hockey League, set up Under the Gun competitions to find the fastest pitchers in 12 cities and collaborated on his second autobiography, *Strikeout.*

It is a year now, and he still is 29 months behind.

"Listen pal, when I was pitching, I didn't worry about who was hitting, who was catching me, who was playing shortstop behind me, how many people were in the ballpark," he says after he calls Brooks Robinson's agent and gets a busy signal. "Just let me go, don't bother me with the details. Details were what always got things screwed up.

"That reminds me, I better call Sharyn."

He and Sharyn have been married 24 years, and they talk on the telephone 10, 15 times a day. She was the one who noticed he had promised to be in Atlanta, Los Angeles and Phoenix at the same times on the following weekend. Tonight, on Interstate 69, the car will throw a rod, and she will drive out to wait with him for a tow truck.

He looks in the rearview mirror at a bank clock — you will never see a town that is as synchronized as Fort Wayne — and checks his watch.

"I knew I should have turned left back there," he says.

The car is a red 1988 Corvette that a dealer in Detroit lets him use for doing television commercials that play on his prison sentence. In one, he points at the license plate on a car and says, "I made that one."

He calls Jim Northrup, his former teammate on the Detroit Tigers, about appearing at a baseball card show, and a newspaper in Little Rock, Ark., about ads for Under the Gun. He makes two calls on the deals that are too new to talk about. And there always will be people who will give him another deal because he is Denny McLain.

And, because he is Denny McLain, there always will be people who will wait for him to screw it up.

"That's one of the best details I ever paid attention to," he says after he hangs up. "I changed phone companies, to the one where they drop a pin and you can hear it across the whole country."

He has just said goodbye to Brooks Robinson's agent when a kid in an orange pickup pulls up next to him at a stoplight. The kid — he looks like he was born about the time McLain first got famous doing everything fast — checks out the Corvette and guns his engine. McLain guns his.

The light turns green, and the kid squeals forward.

"Were we all that crazy when we were young?" he says.

Denny McLain steps on the accelerator and turns left. He has collaborated on two autobiographies and Phil in Los Angeles is supposed to call back this afternoon.

"I guess I'm certified," he says.

Free again

McLain's third trial has been delayed three times and now is scheduled to begin in mid-October before U.S. District Judge Elizabeth Kovachevich in Tampa.

Kovachevich currently is considering a request by McLain's lawyers that she disqualify herself because in June she was mailed, anonymously, the chapter of *Strikeout* that calls his trials a "masquerade of justice."

The 11th Circuit Court of Appeals in Atlanta overturned McLain's conviction and 23-year sentence Aug. 7, 1987, calling the trial "a classic example of judicial error and prosecutorial misconduct."

McLain's lawyer, Arnold Levine of Tampa, says he still is confident he can negotiate a plea agreement for time served. McLain says he would "plead guilty to the Lindbergh baby, say I put the iceberg in front of the Titanic, take credit for Hoffa" — anything except plead guilty to the drug charge to stay out of prison.

Assistant U.S. Prosecutor Ernst Mueller would not comment on possible plea agreements for McLain.

"All I'll say about that is the man did testify in his own defense at the trial, and the jury convicted him," he said. "This man is just a classic crook."

A few weeks after he got out, McLain was hired by David D. Welker, owner of the

Fort Wayne Komets, to play the organ at games and to be a partner in the Koala Kooler nonalcoholic wine distributorship. Welker fired McLain in March. McLain has sued, citing breach of contract, and Welker has filed a countersuit.

"Likable? He'll charm the hell out of you," Welker says. "But he thinks there's one set of rules for everyone else and one set of rules for Denny McLain. He can look you right in the eye and tell you something you know is not true and you'll believe him.

"You know, though, I'm still glad I got a chance to know him. I mean, he is Denny McLain."

Fat one for Mantle

Denny McLain was 31-6 for the Detroit Tigers in 1968, won the Cy Young Award and was the American League's Most Valuable Player. The next season he was 24-9 and won the Cy Young Award again. He also lost a $3,000 Russian white broadtail lamb Nehru jacket after he used it to wipe champagne on the floor of a bar and handed it to a woman, drank a case of Pepsi a day, placed bets from the telephone in the Tigers clubhouse and put out an album called *Denny McLain at the Organ: The Tigers Superstar Swings with Today's Hits.*

Late in the 1968 season, after he had won 30 games and the Tigers had clinched the pennant, Mickey Mantle came to bat in Tiger Stadium, one home run short of tying for third place on the all-time home run list. McLain called his catcher, Bill Freehan, to the mound. He told Freehan to tell Mantle the pitch would come down the middle.

Mantle watched the pitch go past for a strike.

Freehan went out to the mount again. McLain told him to tell Mantle to be ready. Mantle watched strike two.

Freehan went out to the mound again.

"I say to Freehan, 'What the hell is going on?'" McLain says. "'Tell him to be ready this time. This is his last chance.'"

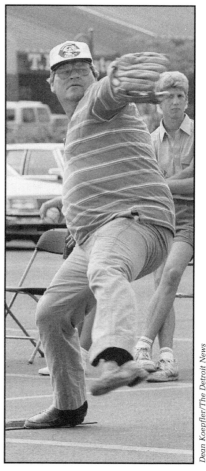

DENNY MCLAIN MAKES HIS PITCHES.

Dean Koepfler/The Detroit News

This time, Mantle smiled. He pointed at where he wanted the pitch. He tipped his cap to McLain after he rounded third base.

McLain knocked down the next batter.

"I don't see why everybody got so upset over one home run," McLain says. "I mean, it was a 45-mile-an-hour pitch but he still had to hit it."

Problems multiply

In 1970, he was suspended by baseball Commissioner Bowie Kuhn for 90 days for consorting with gamblers. After he came back, he was suspended for a week for dumping buckets of water on two sportswriters. After he came back, he was suspended from Sept. 9 to the end of the season for taking a gun on a two-week road trip to the West Coast.

He was traded to the Washington Senators later that year and finished 10-22. The next year he was traded to the Oakland A's, then to the Atlanta Braves, compiling a record of 14-29. He retired in 1973, when he was pitching for the Shreveport Captains in the Double A Texas League. He was 29.

Two years later, he published his first autobiography, *Nobody's Perfect.* The final chapter was "Life Begins at 30." It began, "...and if it doesn't, I'm in a whole lot of trouble — again."

After he was fired as general manager of the Triple A Memphis Blues in 1976, he owned a business that sold big-screen televisions, two walk-in medical clinics and a cypress mulch distributorship. The Internal Revenue Service was awarded $20,000 in payments, interest and penalties on Social Security and withholding taxes that had not been paid when he was with the Blues. Former partners, employees, banks and suppliers won at least six civil suits against him for bad debts.

He declared bankruptcy in 1977. His home in Lakeland, Fla., was destroyed by fire in 1979. In 1981, he suffered a heart attack.

He was a bookmaker — the only federal charge he does not deny — and during the 1981 football season made $150,000.

On March 19, 1984, after a 10-month federal grand jury investigation, he was indicted.

The prosecution called 67 witnesses to testify. A discotheque owner said he was physically threatened and forced to pay $8,000 interest in eight weeks on a $40,000 loan. Another witness, a convicted marijuana dealer, said he and McLain hid three kilograms of cocaine in a golf bag and flew it from Fort Lauderdale, Fla., to Newark, N.J.

"I'll be the first one to admit, I've been a stupid SOB," McLain says. "But that's all. Except for the gambling, my only crime is hanging out with a bunch of scumbags."

$160,000 on bed

"You want to hear the greatest story you ever heard?" McLain says.

It is 2:45 p.m. and he is walking to the Federal Building for his 4 p.m. appointment with his probation officer.

The story is about a real estate agent in Fort Lauderdale, who in July 1982, thought he was wanted on manslaughter charge. He asked McLain to find him a place to hide out. McLain asked Stan Myatt, who owned an island in the Bahamas, to check out the man.

It turned out the man was not wanted. McLain told the man he could hide out on Myatt's island. He told the man it would cost him $35,000.

The man showed McLain a suitcase full of money and asked him to take $250,000 and post bond for his brother, who had been arrested on drug charges. McLain said he wanted $35,000 to post the bond. The man counted $320,000 and gave the suitcase to McLain.

McLain flew the man to the island in his Cheyenne, then told him they couldn't get his brother out on bond. He told the man the price of the stay on the island now was $320,000. The man argued but finally agreed, and McLain and Myatt flew home with $160,000 each.

"So I get home and lay my share on the bed," McLain says. "Sharyn comes into the bedroom and sees $160,000 and says, 'I'm only going to ask one question. Did that money come from drugs?' I said, 'Sharyn, you know I wouldn't do drugs, but it probably came from drugs.' She thought about it a second and said to me, 'We can spend it better than him.'

"Now is that the greatest story ever, or what?"

When he walks into the U.S. Probation, Parole and Pretrial Services office on the third floor, the secretary is down the hall and the telephone is ringing.

He watches the phone ring three times before he answers it.

"Sharyn," he says. "It's me."

Pop and Oprah

McLain lives with Sharyn and their two youngest children, Tim, 19, and Michelle, 16, in a two-bedroom town house on the edge of Fort Wayne, in the kind of complex that is advertised as a lifestyle.

"We came to Fort Wayne because I thought I had a good deal, but that got screwed up," he says. "People say I'm crazy to stay here, that I'd do a lot more someplace like Detroit. I don't know, maybe someday, but right now this is a good place for Sharyn and the kids and me to put our life back together."

He gets a Diet Coke — he stopped drinking regular Pepsi in prison — turns on Oprah and sits on the couch. Sharyn comes out of their bedroom. She sits on the back of the couch and hands him a stack of certificates for Under the Gun participants.

He calls Phil in Los Angeles and starts to autograph the certificates.

"All of this keeps him busy," Sharyn says. "He needs to be busy or he goes crazy. I need him to be busy."

She is the daughter of Hall of Fame shortstop and manager Lou Boudreau. They met at a Babe Ruth League game in Harvey, Ill., when they were 15 and he threw a bat that hit her in the leg. They eloped to New Buffalo, Mich., when they were 19.

Seven months before he was indicted, she filed for divorce but let him move back in after he promised to be a "typical devoted family man."

"There have been a lot of good times," she says. "But all I ever wanted was for Denny to be a good husband. I always just want to live a typical life with him and the children."

For typical, she got collect calls from Talladega. While he was in prison, she sold his MVP and Cy Young awards and her diamond engagement ring to support their four children. She took two secretarial jobs and wrote letters to anybody in the federal government who might have been able to help with his appeal.

Anyway, Phil in Los Angeles still is waiting to hear something on the movie deal. McLain finishes signing the stack of certificates. Sharyn hands him another.

"I get $3 for my autograph at card shows," he says.

"You're home," she says. "Sign."

He glances at the huge clock on the wall and he checks his watch. He gets a Diet Coke from the refrigerator. He hugs Sharyn.

He is trying to pay more attention to details, but he still is 29 months late.

"Sharyn," he says. "Can I have a couple of dollars for gas?"

The Detroit News
August 28, 1988

Chapter nine

Snapshots of Life

Morning, another day.

Roosters brag. Fog you could drive a nail into.

Today's the day to get into somebody's snapshot.

Folks back in Ohio'll wonder who's in the sunglasses.

Some serious meandering to do.

Slow days.

GREG LOPEZ, THE DAILY IBERIAN, APRIL 28, 1983

The first robin was next to a puddle in front of the Conoco at Evans and Franklin, so Catherine A. Hurlbutt checked her rearview mirror and put on her brakes.

It was time for spring. The car is a Checker Cab with "Bird Ambulance" painted on her door. In a cardboard box next to her, she had one more pigeon from Cheesman Park that had tail feathers stuck together with Roost-No-More.

Hurlbutt is 82 years old, and one of the things she has learned is to always check the rearview mirror before she stops for a bird, even the first robin.

"Tweedle-dup, tweedle-dup," Hurlbutt said.

"Tweedle-dup, tweedle-dup," the robin said.

"My love of birds is my gift," she said. "I used to tell my parents I was going outside to hear the robin concerto, and now I have phonograph records of robins."

Other people can sing, others can cook, others have common sense.

"Beauties and abilities go away, but my gift always comes back."

At home, she took the pigeon out of the box and walked into one of the cages she built in the backyard.

In the cages, she had a robin, a goose, a duck, a bobwhite, two golden pheasants, two ring-necked doves, four crows, five housefinches, nine sparrows and 27 pigeons.

Her gift always comes back, but nobody else seems to want the pigeons.

"The pigeons, nobody misses once they're gone, so I eat them," she said. "I just boil them. Remember I mentioned cooking isn't one of my gifts?"

Rocky Mountain News
March 22, 1995

It is 6:45 on a Tuesday morning on a bus to Shipshewana, Ind., and "Big Daddy" Marshall Lackowski is playing "Roll out the Barrel" on the accordion, while his wife and oldest daughter serve pink champagne and doughnuts.

Shipshewana is where the flea market is.

Big Daddy, who bought a 10-foot dining table with tiger-paw feet the last time he led a group of people to Shipshewana, plays the accordion up and down the aisle.

He got his nickname when he weighed more and was in the seminary — before he got married and had seven children, including a son who plays bass and a daughter who takes turns with his wife, Mary Ann, on drums at festivals, weddings and polka masses. He is 51, still big, wears a cowboy hat and also is called "The La-Dee-Da Man."

The passengers on the bus, who had been sitting in their seats like eggs in a carton, clap and sing when Big Daddy starts to play.

"Roll out the barrel," he yells. "I hope this gets everybody in the mood for the flea market."

The Detroit News
July 7, 1988

Miss October, 1984, live and in the flesh, sat behind a table on the stage signing photographs of herself wearing a bathing suit. The men waiting in line — not all men buy *Playboy* just to read the articles — talked about what they were going to say to Miss October when they got their chance.

"I've gotten pretty good at listening to them," she says. "The men, they're so brave, joking with their buddies, until they're up in front on me. Then they're always real nice and polite."

Debi Johnson, the centerfold girl from the October 1984 *Playboy,* was at the World of Wheels car show last weekend in Lafayette. The show had all sorts of old and new cars, owned by people from the area, cars from *Knight Rider* and *Ghostbusters*, and "Bigfoot S-10," a Chevrolet pickup truck with huge tires that can drive over station wagons.

Debi Johnson is 5-5 and weighs 102 pounds, has brown eyes and blonde hair. Her measurements are 35-21-34, and if you want to find out anything else about the way she looks, you'll have to find the issue.

"One question I must hear 300 times a day, wherever I am. Everybody wants to know."

Then she pauses, giving a chance to figure out what everybody wants to ask the woman who was Miss October 1984. After all, the American male is supposed to be preoccupied with one thing.

"They all want to know, 'Do you get writer's cramp?' "

The Daily Iberian
March 5, 1985

I have been writing this column twice a week for two years now, and it occurs to me that there are some things I haven't told you.

There was the man who thought he had discovered an aphrodisiac that had something to do with burning manure and he was wondering if I knew any girls who would be willing to test it, the man who had developed a new and improved strain of bamboo but he couldn't talk about it because "they" were after him for it, and the woman who said her husband had died just to make her feel guilty about not wanting to go to Florida for a vacation.

There was the farmer who shot at crop dusters. Every time one flew near his property he would run into his kitchen, grab his shotgun and start blasting away at them. He wasn't sure if it was because they were moving or because they were too high, but he'd never hit one yet.

"But I've been practicing on birds," he said. "And I believe I'm finally getting it down."

Sitting at the kitchen table, he was telling me about how his wife called the sheriff's office on him and how he had told the deputies that whatever the planes were spraying was as bad as what he was shooting, when all of a sudden, he stopped.

"You gettin' this down right?" he said.

"I think so," I said.

"You sure?"

"As sure as I can be."

"Well," he said, and he reached under the table and pulled out a .22 pistol and set it in front of himself. "You better be damn sure. Now, like I was saying..."

The Daily Iberian
November 15, 1985

Right in the middle of the rinse cycle she sighs, hums a little, sighs.

"Well you're awful quiet today," she finally says, and then she reaches down and scratches her knee. "My second one was like that. When I married him I thought he was the strong silent type, then I realized he was just plain dumb."

She is somewhere past 30 and drinking a Mr. Pibb. Her hair is pulled back and in ponytails, and she is wearing a baby-blue T-shirt that for some reason says "Boom!" She sits in silence a few seconds, sighs, hums, then gives in.

"But you probably don't want to hear about all my problems," she says. "Lord knows I've had enough of them, though. But you probably don't want to hear about all them. Although it doesn't seem like I always meet somebody who's so easy to talk to in a laundromat."

"My washing machine's broken," I explain. "It fills up with water, but then it doesn't drain out."

"I'm surprised that hasn't happened to me," she says. "I don't know, things just always seem to happen to me more than others. If you don't want to hear about all this, just tell me to shut up. I'm practically always cryin' inside, you know, but I know nobody can tell that."

"Well," I say, "it is kind of hard to tell right off..."

The Daily Iberian
December 20, 1984

Because he read Aristotle this morning, Nick Psihas doesn't notice his cigar is not lit.

He walks down Veronica Street in East Detroit, talking about Greek philosophy, the cigar stuck in his mouth. His voice is as deep as Plato, and he hasn't shaved for three days. He is going to dinner.

Two boys playing catch in their front yard stop and watch.

"Aristotle says I am an outcast by choice," he says. "Page 211. In my own small way, I imitate Aristotle: I am an unknown."

Psihas, 57, was a professor of philosophy, theology and English at seven colleges and universities and is not an unknown around East Detroit. He lives in the basement of his mother's house in East Detroit and spends all his days reading philosophy or discussing it with anybody he meets. He also is a diagnosed paranoid schizophrenic.

He takes the cigar out of his mouth and looks at it.

The boys turn and run.

"Logical positivists, I bet," Psihas says, and he pats his pockets to find his lighter.

The Detroit News
May 21, 1989

Merlin Trahan, naked as the day he as born, sits there and says he's got nothing to be embarrassed about.

The sign outside says "Nude area, enter at own risk." Merlin Trahan is nude throughout this column, read at your own risk. He asks me if I want to get naked, I say I'd rather retain my objectivity.

So he sits there, 44 years old with a pot belly, wearing a watch, a graduation ring and cologne.

"There's really nothing to be embarrassed about," he says. "Now you can interpret that as either a good joke or a serious comment."

Trahan says he dresses only when it's cold or when he has to go to town. He usually undresses on his way home. Truck drivers blow their horns. If they laugh, Trahan says he's happy.

All he wants to be is naked, he says.

The Daily Iberian
April 23, 1987

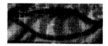

Back when Art Kapa and Wayne King were friends, they used to go into the woods to wait all night for Bigfoot.

King would shout something like "Uga-booga-booga," which he learned from Salish Indians who claim to communicate with Bigfoot, and Kapa would tell him if he had any sense, it would run the other way. King would open a can of sardines and throw it to bait Bigfoot, and Kapa would say he might as well throw crackers, too.

They would sit on lawn chairs and wait, but every time they ended up in arguments about Bigfoot that were so loud they would have scared it away.

The Detroit News
March 4, 1990

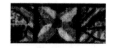

The dog lives a quarter of a mile from where Arthur Baudry and Allen Gonsoulin live.

More important, the dog lives on the road that led to the Food-n-Fun, where they used to walk to buy beer. It was one of the reasons they decided to make homemade beer last fall.

One day about a year ago, Baudry was walking home with a six-pack of Miller's and a 16-ounce can of pork and beans. He was about a half a block from the house when a car passed him, and the dog came around the corner, across the yard, jumped the ditch and chased it.

When the car was gone the dog stopped beside the road and waited for Baudry to pass — sort of the opposite of a cafeteria.

Baudry stopped, and he and the dog looked at each other.

"He was brown and yellow, but you know who he looked like?" Baudry says. "Jackie Gleason. Nothing against Jackie Gleason, but he wouldn't look good as a dog."

The Daily Iberian
June 30, 1987

Douglas Bruce was talking about how Colorado voters had one last chance, and his mother was talking about how some lucky woman will finally get a chance.

It was early Tuesday afternoon in the kitchen of the man who wrote Amendment 12. The latest polls had predicted Amendment 12 would lose. Bruce was predicting that there would be potato salad at the party that night.

"If people are too stupid to see the truth, what's right, there's nothing I can do for them," Douglas Bruce said.

"That's OK dear," Marjorie Bruce said. "Now people can see you have a nice side, too. Now you can finally find Miss Right."

He will try to find Miss Right after spending so many years telling everybody that he is right.

"They won't have Dougie to kick around any more," he said.

Rocky Mountain News
November 9, 1994

Twenty-eight years ago, Dave Hoover ran off and began a career that would lead to a billing as the last of the wild animal tamers.

A year later he was traveling with a one-ring circus, performing with three lions, when his truck threw a rod somewhere in North Carolina. He needed $300. He wired his father, asking for the money.

His father, who had invented the Quonset hut and who thought the circus was silly, wired back, "Be like Sitting Bull: Keep your arrows sharp and don't put money in show business."

It was the kind of advice you never forget, even if you never understand it, and 28 years later Hoover is still in the business.

He is standing next to his cat cages between performances in the Clyde Beatty-Cole Bros. Circus in New Iberia Monday, chewing on a cigar he will never light. His wife runs the circus dining hall and opens and closes the cages during his act, and she won't let him chew tobacco, so he chews cigars. Lion tamers always used to chew tobacco when they stuck their heads into the mouth of a lion, so they could spit if the lion started to close.

It is another tradition that has died.

Anyway, Hoover is talking about what it is like to walk into a cage with a gun loaded with wax-tipped blanks, a whip and a bentwood chair to make lions and tigers do a barrel roll across the cage, lie down next to each other and jump through a ring of fire. In the night performance a lion will spring at the car, bouncing him against the bars of a cage and stunning him before he can pull a gun and stun it with a wax bullet. He is billed as the last person in the world who does this for a living.

"I don't know, I guess I just like being the last one," he says.

The Daily Iberian
October 8, 1985

I wake up Tuesday morning, and the king is in my hotel room telling me what a good time everybody's gonna have.

I lie there with one eye open, wondering what to do. Sometimes the king is in your hotel room, and sometimes you're in his, and you want to be sure before you say something stupid. I close my eye and ask Phil what is going on.

"Mardi Gras," he says.

I open both eyes to see him standing in front of the television watching the king.

The people who ask all the questions let me come down here to do a story on how basic principles in American life are reflected during Mardi Gras. At least that is what I told the people who ask all the questions.

We get down there as fast as possible, and the first thing we see is a different king sitting on a float and waving to the people having a good time. He throws strings of beads, and they dive for them. It is the Rex parade down St. Charles Avenue.

He throws a string of fake white pearls, and a girl in fishnet stockings and a leotard in 35-degree weather dives for them. A man wearing an evening gown and a wig and a beard that goes back to Saturday bends down and grabs the beads at the same time as the girl.

They yank on them and the string breaks.

Fake white pearls roll everywhere on St. Charles Avenue.

"I spend three days trying to get beads like those," the girl in the fishnet stockings and a leotard in 35-degree weather says to the man in the evening gown and the wig and beard that goes back to Saturday. "And then you (bleeper) you go and break them, (bleeper). And it's probably the last chance I'll have to get any."

I take out my notebook and write: "People here exhibit a strong sense of history."

Day ends and night begins. It gets darker, and it gets drunker. It seems like the basic principles of American life are reflected less and less.

Midnight, inevitably, comes.

Mardi Gras 1986 is over.

Policemen make everybody go home, or least to one of the side streets. Street cleaners come down Bourbon Street, and there is nobody there to run up to the brushes and pretend to be shining his shoes like they usually do. All that is left is empty beer cans and crushed plastic cups and beads of every color, including fake white pearls.

I take out my notebook and write: "People here don't seem to be concerned with material goods."

The Daily Iberian
February 12, 1986

Tyree Guyton is painting green polka dots on the oil drums in the vacant lot across the street from his grandfather's house.

There are 18 oil drums, some partly crushed, stacked on each other and a tractor tire in front. It all was scattered in other vacant lots until Guyton brought it to this one, and it became art.

But like much of the art in this world, it didn't have enough polka dots.

"See the rhythm? Guyton says. "It's positive and negative, it's got a beat. That's what it's all about."

His grandfather, Sam Mackey, nods. He lived across Heidelberg when somebody lived in the house next door and three houses were on this lot. He is painting blue stripes on the oil drums.

He is 91, and he knows what he knows.

"Sometimes," he says, "a thing just needs some stripes."

The Detroit News
May 9, 1988

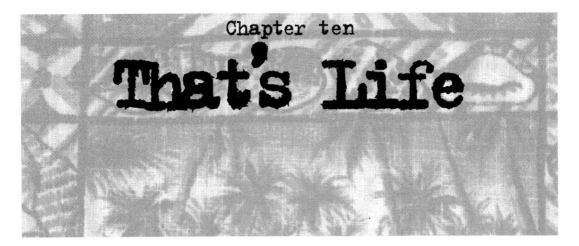

Chapter ten

That's Life

Dear Greg!

I have talked to you only four times, not in person but over the phone. The first time, I remember, was May 23, 1995, when you called me and asked if you were allowed to have an interview with my daughters who would be graduated the following June; and right that evening you came to my house for the interview. The next morning, you called me again and had the interview with me. Time flew by. When I knew that my wife was going to be laid off, I called you and asked if you could do anything to help, you said that you would do your best. Within 24 hours later, my family were introduced to the mailroom.

And now, you are gone. Everybody must die! But why did you go at the age you were supposed to make a lot more contributions to the society we are living in?

Dear Greg!

You are no longer in the world. But I know for sure that you still remain in our hearts, in the hearts of those who love you and in the hearts of those who owe you.

Lovingly, Minh Tran

(NOTE LEFT ON THE WINDSHIELD OF THE HEARSE
THE DAY OF GREG'S FUNERAL, MARCH 21, 1996)

The Sisters

THE TRAN SISTERS, (LEFT TO RIGHT) PHUONG, DONG, LINH AND LOAN, ALL HAVE A 4.0 GRADE-POINT AVERAGE.

Ken Papaleo/Rocky Mountain News

DENVER — Sixth period, American History, North High School, the teacher asked what made America what it is.

The two Tran sisters who sat at the two desks in the middle of the front row raised their hands. The two Tran sisters who sat behind them raised their hands. Ten months and 29 days ago, all they knew about American history was that it was their future.

Since then, one of them has missed one question on one test in American History.

Phuong Tran: "The concept of individuality is the theme that has dominated American history."

Loan Tran: "This theory is reflected in the concept of Reaganomics."

Dong Tran: "But many people do not seem to appreciate this."

Linh Tran: "Similar to the way many people continue to not understand Herbert Hoover."

And they all covered their mouths with their hands and giggled. Dong and Phuong are twins, 20 years old, Linh is 19 and Loan is 17. They came to the United States from Vietnam on June 30.

Saturday, they graduate with 4.0 grade-point averages.

"I speak for all of us when I say, 'Thanks a lot,'" Phuong said.

Their father, Minh Tran, graduated in 1965 from the University of Dalat in Vietnam with a degree in English. He went to the University of Saigon for his master's degree. He completed his thesis, "Transformational Generative Grammar Applied in Teaching English as a Second Language," and was waiting to present it when he was called into the South Vietnamese army.

Six years after Saigon fell, he was released from the "re-education" camp. He worked as a tutor. As a former officer in the South Vietnamese army, his daughters would not be allowed to attend a university, so he applied to leave the country.

He taught English to his daughters and his wife, Hoat, for an hour every night. Then they studied it on their own for two hours. Then the girls did their schoolwork.

"So many words have many uses," Loan said. "We still get a bad feeling when we hear the word 'file.'"

They were allowed to leave Vietnam a year ago and came to Denver because they heard it has good opportunities and weather. Minh Tran is a tutor and translator for Denver Public Schools. Hoat is a production worker for Denver Die and Molding Inc.

They live in a two-bedroom apartment a mile from school, the girls sharing one room. They go to Kmart and Cub Foods for fun on the weekends. After school, they go with their parents to Denver International Airport, where they all work from 4 to 9 p.m. at McDonald's.

"We have reached the place where the opportunities lie," Minh said. "Now it is up to each of us to uncover them."

So when the girls enrolled at North, they tried to take different classes. They didn't want anybody to think they had an unfair advantage because they are sisters. Because of scheduling problems, they all ended up in Jim Schrant's American History class.

"The first day for each new class, I give my students my home phone number," Schrant said. "Thirty years I've been doing this, and I get four, maybe five calls a year. These girls, they call four or five times a week.

"You hear teachers worry about whether they're reaching their students, and here's these four, whose only worry is whether they can reach their teacher."

Loan is the one who missed the one question in American History, and she asked to take the test again.

Loan: "For some reason I forgot Janet Reno is the attorney general. It was for extra credit. Mr. Schrant said there was no reason to take it again, because I got the other extra-credit question to receive 102 points, but I don't like to be the one who missed the question."

Phuong: "We all try to do our own share. It would have been nice to have a sister with me when people laughed because I didn't pronounce the word oil correctly. But we have to learn our own lessons."

Dong: "We also can share what the others learn in their different classes, because we have more textbooks available to us."

Linh: "Besides, we are all different. Dong is the quiet one, Phu is the one who is always asking questions, Loan is the active one and I am in between. For example, I like Rin Tin Tin, and Loan prefers Lassie."

Loan: "Lassie is cool."

Phuong and Dong want to study business, Loan wants to study medicine and Linh hasn't decided between business and medicine.

Phuong, Linh and Loan have been accepted to the University of Colorado. Dong was sick the day the advisers were at school, and she missed the deadline for her application. She will go to either the University of Northern Colorado or Metropolitan State College.

So they will go on, making America what it is.

Dong: "I would like to be with my sisters, but this is an opportunity to add extra experience."

Phuong: "And maybe someday we can go on a picnic in the mountains. I don't know what that requires, but it sounds nice."

Linh: "It really is very easy. All we have to do is work hard."

Loan: "Isn't this cool?"

Rocky Mountain News
May 28, 1995

The Miracle Has Already Happened

DENVER — Sara Leroux kneeled in front of her son's wheelchair Sunday morning, explaining why they were at Cherry Creek State Park and not sure either of them really understood.

They were at the back of the crowd, where the voice of the pope sounded like a guilty conscience, and Leroux pointed the wheelchair in the direction everybody else was looking. Blaine is 11 years old, mentally retarded and has cerebral palsy. Leroux is 42 and never had a feeling she would describe as religious.

She believes Blaine understands what she says, but it is the kind of belief she doesn't understand in other people.

"I just never could understand how this many people could do all this without any way to be sure they're right," she said.

"I think I do a lot of the things religious people do — treat other people right, be honest, all that. But when it comes to actually believing something without any proof..."

Leroux is divorced from Blaine's father and cleans houses. Blaine goes to school, where the teachers say he has the mental ability of a four year old. They live in an apartment a mile from Cherry Creek State Park, but she didn't think about going to the Mass until she saw a youth with cerebral palsy speaking at the vigil Saturday night.

"The TV was on just to have it on, and then there was this boy talking about how his belief in God helped him to overcome his disability," she said. "Something just told me to go. I'm not saying I heard any voice telling me what to do, but..."

They left at 6 a.m. Sunday morning, the rest of the crowd passing them on the dirt path to the Mass. Leroux told herself it would at least be a morning walk. She told herself she would go home if Blaine started to cry.

An Italian girl in a wheelchair yelled to them to stop.

"This girl, she told us she also had cerebral palsy, and she asked us if we were hoping for some kind of miracle," Leroux said. "I told her why we were going. She said, 'Ah, the miracle has already happened.'

"I'm still not sure exactly what she meant by that."

They sat through the Mass, and Leroux tried to figure out what things meant by watching the people around her. She turned the wheelchair to point in different directions to keep Blaine from getting sunburned or bored. She watched the other people, and she watched how they looked at Blaine.

When everybody else started to leave, she started to push the wheelchair back to the apartment.

"I know nobody else would understand this, but I think he really liked this today," she said.

"I might try to take him to something else, some kind of church, and see if he likes that, too. I know people don't think he understands any of this, but you just have to believe."

Rocky Mountain News
August 16, 1993

He Bought a Harley, Not a Lifestyle

DENVER — What it came down to, Ken Pernell says, is he was either going to get a Harley-Davidson or take a class at Colorado Free University.

He turned 44 in May, and since he was 22 the birthdays when both numbers are the same have bothered him. He lives in Littleton and is a management engineer, doing consulting work for small businesses. The last time he decided to do something different, he practically got eaten alive by mosquitoes in the mountains outside Boulder.

"There aren't many things left in today's society that have the mystery and power of the Harley," he wrote in his journal.

There was a nine-month wait for a new Harley, so he went through the classifieds and found a turquoise 1992 Sportster with a Fat Bob front fender for $10,500. There were others, but he liked the color. It was practically teal.

The guy who sold it said he was buying a lifestyle, but it didn't come with leathers.

"It isn't a way of life one just 'happens' into," he wrote.

And so on Friday two weeks ago, wearing black leather chaps and a jacket with a flame coming out of a wheel, he was in Sturgis, S.D., for the 55th Sturgis Rally. He called ahead, but the hotels within 70 miles were sold out. He went into a bar that had Budweiser on ice in a cattle trough. The first person he talked to sells real estate and lives in Westminster.

"They may seem to be all one type to the outsider, but under the leather they are individuals," he wrote.

He walked up Main Street. He bought a T-shirt for himself and three for friends. He saw girls with tattoos he could see only the top or bottom of.

He stayed that night in a campground two miles outside town. A guy let him use his pump to fill his air mattress. Some other guys yelled at women to show their breasts.

"There aren't many places left where you see such a sense of community," he wrote.

He heard shouts all night and tried to decide whether they meant something good or bad. The next morning, he asked a guy when they sleep. The guy said, "September."

He thought that was the funniest thing he'd heard since he got there, but the first guy he told it to didn't even smile.

"At the same time, outsiders must work to fit in," he wrote.

That morning, he watched some people getting tattoos in a booth under a tarp, then went to Mount Rushmore. He hadn't been there since he was a kid. That night, he got a room in Torrington, Wyo.

He was home with his wife and daughter by 10 a.m. Sunday. His wife already had mowed the lawn. He put a classified ad in the paper last week and sold the Harley last Saturday for $500 less than he paid for it. Now, he is thinking about taking a Spanish class.

"It is a way of life that is not for everybody," he wrote.

Rocky Mountain News
August 23, 1995

To Elvis

DETROIT — When Elvis was Elvis Presley, Cathy Jasinski was Cathy Bohannon.

ELVIS AND FANS.

The Detroit News

Now, Jasinski is 43, divorced and lives in a house in Taylor with pictures of Elvis in every room and an Elvis knocker on the front door. Her ex-husband got jealous. And now Johnny Seaton probably is as close as she ever will get to Elvis.

Wednesday night at Desoto's night club in Dearborn Heights, she tried to see how close.

"I know you aren't Elvis," she told Seaton. "But I used to pretend with my husband, too."

Seaton and two other Elvis impersonators, Julian Whitaker and Terry Mike Jeffrey, are in Detroit performing in *Elvis, a Musical Celebration,* through Sunday at the Fox Theatre. Jeffrey is the young Elvis. Whitaker is the Elvis who died. Seaton is the Elvis who still lives.

Not that it makes much difference any more.

The three Elvises went to Desoto's after their performances Wednesday night and their fans followed. The Elvises signed autographs, drank free drinks, posed for photographs and turned down propositions. The fans, including four members of the Friends for Elvis Fan Club, impersonated the fans who used to follow Elvis.

Elvis, hailed by his fans as the "King of Rock and Roll," died Aug. 16, 1977.

If Elvis Presley wasn't Elvis Presley, there is no way to know who the impersonators would be.

"They ain't the king," said Curtis Dykes, 53, a security guard whose boss makes him shave his sideburns. "But they ain't dead."

Seaton, 29, has lived most of his life trying not to be Elvis. He grew up in Beltsville, Md., recorded two albums of his own material and imitated Elvis only to benefit research in cancer and cystic fibrosis before he joined the show to develop his own career.

Elvis' life already has been done.

"Of all people, I wish Elvis was still alive so I could meet him," he said. "Also, I wish he was alive so I could be who I am."

Earlier Wednesday, he went to a McDonald's on Telegraph in Dearborn Heights and was recognized — as an Elvis — by Niki Maliszewski, 13.

"I never saw anybody who looked like somebody who looked like somebody famous before," she said. "Even though I was hardly born when the real Elvis died."

After a performance in Las Vegas, a woman — 18, maybe 19 years old — introduced herself and the man she had just married. She wore an orange blazer that she said Elvis had worn on an MGM movie lot. Seaton gave them an autograph and shook their hands.

The next night, the woman brought him roses and gave him a kiss while her husband watched.

The next night, she told him she had left her husband for him and cried until security guards dragged her away.

"I don't know that I'd want to be Elvis even if I was Elvis," Seaton said.

Whitaker, 40, started impersonating Elvis 25 years ago — before Elvis started to impersonate himself.

"If I'd been born a little earlier, Elvis might be sitting here right now, trying to look like Julian Whitaker," he said. "It's all in the way things work out."

Pat Patterson said things have worked out because of Elvis. She is 38, lives in Detroit, was co-founder of Friends for Elvis and was disabled in an automobile accident four years ago on her way to see an Elvis impersonator in Madison Heights.

Her husband, Joe, was hired for his current job as a bouncer at Nifty '50s in Southgate at a performance by another Elvis impersonator.

"See?" she said. "Elvis has been there at all the critical times in my life."

She goes to malls and anyplace else that might be crowded to get signatures on her petitions for an Elvis presidential medal of freedom and an Elvis U.S. postage stamp.

She and nine friends drove around Kalamazoo one day last summer, after it was reported in a tabloid, the *Weekly World News,* that he lives there. At each place he had been spotted, they left him an invitation to celebrate the 11th anniversary of his death, even though it wouldn't be an anniversary if he showed up. They had the party without him.

Wednesday night, she had her picture taken with the Elvises individually and together.

"I'm in Elvis heaven," she said. "All these Elvises all in one place, it fills a very big void in my life. I just don't see how some people can say they get Elvised out."

And finally, at midnight, Russ Weathers arrived.

Weathers, 27, lives in Inkster and impersonates Elvis part-time.

In a different world, he could make a living impersonating Julian Whitaker.

"This is the first time in my life I ever met a big-time Elvis impersonator in person," Weathers said. "It's hard to explain what this means to a guy like me."

The Elvis impersonators introduced themselves and shook each other's hands. They stood there, enough of them to play a game of bridge, and looked at each other. And all of a sudden one of them had a thought.

Johnny Seaton held up his beer, and Julian Whitaker, Terry Mike Jeffrey and Russ Weathers held up theirs.

"To Elvis," Seaton said.

Rocky Mountain News
January 18, 1989

Christmas Spirit at the Mission

DENVER — The hymn was *The Old Rugged Cross*, Charles Kenny on harmonica and Dorothy Kenny whistling, and David Hanner sat in the back row at the Volunteers of America Mission and hummed.

It was the Wednesday afternoon service. Charles Kenny is 75 and started coming here to play and preach 33 years ago, and Dorothy started after they got married. Hanner comes sometimes.

Hanner thought he remembered the tune. "My mom used to hum it," he said.

The notes rose and flattened like smoke from a train, coming out of the Kalamazoo Amplifier set on the floor.

The Kennys whistle and play harmonica and preach Wednesdays and the first three Sundays of the month, the fifth Sunday if there is one, and whenever somebody else can't come on the other days. He was a bus driver for the Regional Transportation District until he retired. One Saturday in 1972, she got on the bus at the corner of Forest Street and East Colfax Avenue.

Because it is the Christmas season, he wore a green and gold plaid jacket with a red tie and she wore red, and Hanner wore a dark blue down jacket with holes and stains.

"My mom, she'd be glad I was sitting here now," Hanner said.

There were 17 men and one woman in the chairs, the spaces between them like missing teeth.

Charles Kenny has played harmonica all his life and taught himself to play the saxophone. He joined a quartet when the old saxophone player got false teeth and had to switch to the trombone. The quartet wanted a name but not one that ended in "aires," so he came up with "Melodians," and then someone asked them to come to the mission.

The rest of the quartet quit after a couple of years because their wives didn't like them playing so much. Charles was playing here alone one day when the preacher didn't show up because he was out selling insurance. Charles spoke about the 14th chapter of the book of John, "Let not your hearts be troubled..."

Dorothy Kenny whistles because her father did, and she and her husband figure it is God's will that whistling and the harmonica go together like they do.

Hanner started coming to the mission for the free meal.

"My mom, though, she wouldn't be too proud of why I'm here," Hanner said.

The Kennys take requests, and they have played *The Old Rugged Cross* as many as three times in one service. A man named Sam played piano with the Kennys when he wasn't drinking, but they couldn't play *The Old Rugged Cross* because it made Sam cry. Sam died after he slipped on ice and hit his head.

Usually, though, the Kennys don't know what happened to the people to bring them here, or what happened to the people who don't come anymore.

The Kennys finished playing and started to pack up to go home. The other men and the woman got up for the meal. Hanner sat in his chair in the back row, humming.

"That song," he said. "It kind of sticks with you, doesn't it?"

Rocky Mountain News
December 24, 1995

What to Leave Behind

WEST GLENWOOD, Colo. — In the back bedroom, the closet that Russell and Mary Hawthorne kept closed for six years was open and empty.

Before the fire came within 500 yards of their home Wednesday, they had thought they never could leave what was inside the closet. They almost had to. After 14 firefighters were killed in the fire, they learned what they could leave behind.

"My son's things hadn't been touched since we closed that door," Mary Hawthorne said. "Young people shouldn't die. But now we know we aren't the only people who feel like we have felt."

Police told people who live on the west side of West Glenwood to be ready to evacuate at any time Wednesday afternoon. People packed the things they didn't want to leave. They didn't have to leave, but they did find out what things meant the most to them.

Rosemary Falligno packed her jewelry and her family photographs, except for the album covering the years she was married to her second husband.

Martha Drury packed photo albums and the wedding dress she wore 52 years ago last Monday.

Betty Robinson packed photo albums, needlepoints of each of the 50 state seals and three ceramic cats she had made. It wasn't until the danger was gone that she found out her husband, Richard, had taken the ceramic cats out of the trunk and put in the 32-inch color television.

"That's something that's still under discussion," she said.

The Hawthornes, both 68, moved to West Glenwood Springs in 1988 after their only child, Russell Jr., died of brain cancer. He was 29, mentally retarded and had lived with them all his life.

After the death, Russell Hawthorne sold his automobile glass business, and the couple moved to Colorado from Terre Haute, Ind., to get away from the house where Russell Jr. had lived all of his life.

The back room of their new home was where they put everything that was his.

"Mostly clothes and games," Russell Hawthorne said. "We were fortunate to have a little boy for 29 years. We were happy enough with R.J. that we never cared to have other children."

Mary Hawthorne doesn't remember how long she sat inside the closet Wednesday afternoon, but she finally decided to just close the door. She packed the photo albums. The couple waited but didn't have to leave.

On Friday morning when they knew the fire wasn't going to reach their house and that firefighters had died, she went back in the closet with empty boxes.

She loaded everything in the car — a neighbor came over and told her she didn't have to worry anymore — and took it to the Salvation Army.

"Other people's children died up there," Mary Hawthorne said. "I know how they feel. And I honestly don't know anything that will make them feel any better."

Rocky Mountain News
July 9, 1994

That One Wish

DENVER — Ken Rutherford stood on the sidewalk Monday, wondering whether he should try to climb a flight of stairs for the first time since half of his right leg and part of his left foot were blown off three months ago in Somalia.

He wanted to go to lunch at Nancy's Restaurant. He had a prosthesis on his right leg, a metal rod that led into a loafer, and a brace up to his knee on his left. He held the railing and lifted the brace onto the step, rested and lifted the prosthesis, rested and lifted the brace up the stairs to Nancy's.

At the top, a woman held open the door.

"Skiing accident?" she said.

"Land mine," Rutherford said.

Rutherford, 31, grew up in Boulder, played two seasons as a 207-pound walk-on nose guard for the University of Colorado football player and served 2½ years with the Peace Corps in western Africa. He earned a master's degree in international relations from Georgetown University and an MBA from CU. Then he took his lowest-paying offer, from the International Relief Committee.

The IRC, a worldwide organization founded in 1933 by Albert Einstein, assigned Rutherford to set up Somalia's only credit union. He was there for five months. On Dec. 16, he had an 8 a.m. meeting with the donkey cart operators who supply water to the city of Lugh, but when they were late he got in his Toyota Land Cruiser to check on a limestone operation.

Fifteen minutes down a dirt road, the land mine exploded.

"I just laid there, thinking about what a great life I had," he said.

"Except I hadn't walked down the aisle with Kim."

Rutherford was picked up by Islamic fundamentalists with machine guns, flown to Nairobi, Kenya, to have his right leg amputated, then flown to Geneva for a week of surgeries to try to save his left.

He was flown to Denver for more surgeries at Presbyterian-St. Luke's Medical Center. He had seven operations on his left foot, the first six to take out debris. In the seventh operation, doctors worked 12 hours to take muscle from his stomach to patch the hole in the foot, cover it with skin from his thigh and remove the bones of his fourth toe so they could sew the little toe to the third.

He works four to five hours a day, four days a week at Mapleton Rehabilitation Center. He has received letters from a leader of the Somalian National Army, Islamic fundamentalists he knew in Somalia and President Clinton. He went to a psychologist because he had nightmares, but the psychologist said they are a normal stage and he has handled everything so well he doesn't need counseling.

He hasn't decided whether to go back to the IRC or to get his Ph.D. in political science to teach and work on such issues as land mine proliferation.

He would like to go back to Somalia to say goodbye to the people and his life there.

All of that will have to wait until he walks up the aisle Sept. 10 at First Presbyterian Church — "a couple hundred feet, then a couple of steps up to the altar, then kneeling and standing up" — and marries Kim Schwers.

"Lying there after the explosion, looking at my leg and thinking about this, all I asked was to be able to walk down the aisle," he said. "I've still got a lot of work to go before I do, but already I feel like I owe so much. How many people are that lucky?"

Rocky Mountain News
March 30, 1994

Greg, I would like to express my appreciation

and gratitude for your companionship last week,

and more importantly, your article.

It certainly reflected my feelings and goal of walking

down the aisle. For that, I thank you.

KEN RUTHERFORD

Santa Gives a Briefing on Style

DENVER — The beard was white and made of real goat's hair, and Friday afternoon Carl Beck took it down from the top shelf in the closet in his apartment in northeast Denver.

It was the first Friday after Thanksgiving in 43 years that he wasn't somewhere being Santa.

He was giving everything to Paul Solano to be Santa.

"When they try to pull off the beard, be sure and say, 'Ouch!'" Beck said.

Beck is 77 years old and started playing Santa in 1951 because his sister had moved to Granby and her children didn't think Santa would be able to find them. He worked shifts at May D&F stores for about 15 years, but for the last 20 years he mostly went to day-care centers and parties, mostly for free. He has been the Santa on the front page of both daily newspapers in Denver.

He took out the red pants with fake fur trim.

"The right leg gets worn shiny faster than the other," he said. "I know a tailor who can just replace one."

He retired as a carpenter four years ago because of back problems. His wife died two years ago. They never had children.

He decided to stop being Santa after last Christmas because every year he had to lift a couple of kids who were too old to still believe in him.

"Your wife's name is Martha," he said. "A lot of Santas just make up a name for the children."

He also didn't want to end up like another Santa who used to go to parties he wasn't invited to.

"They're 'children,'" he said. "Not 'kids.'"

Every Christmas, he caught a cold or something else from the children. He wore wire-rimmed spectacles after one of the children poked him in the eye. He thinks another one of the children stole his wallet.

"If they say they want their Daddy back, give them an extra-long hug," he said. "I never did come up with a good answer to that one."

In 1977, he finished a party at a house and told all the children, "Ho, ho, ho, I'm off to the North Pole," and walked out the front door. The city had towed away his car. He walked a mile to a pay phone so he wouldn't have to explain to the children why he had to call a cab.

"I guess you won't be needing this," he said. "They don't like it most places anymore."

He put his pipe on the dresser.

He met Solano last year at a Christmas party at Solano's sister's house. Solano is 34 and is an aide in a nursing home, and he said he always wanted to be Santa. Solano fit the suit and Beck's idea of Santa.

Friday, Solano stood in the suit and beard and spectacles in the bedroom in the apartment in northeast Denver.

"And always remember," Beck said. "Children still believe in Santa. All you have to do is believe in children."

Rocky Mountain News
November 27, 1994

Castration Isn't a Complete Loss

DENVER — In the morning, the last sex offender to be castrated in the United States is the first person at the park to feed the pigeons.

He had the operation 23 years ago in Denver after he admitted he had sexually molested 400 to 500 girls under the age of 12. He lives in a small town in New England and agreed to be interviewed only if he and the town were not identified. He was talking Friday afternoon while Robert Enderson was in court in Boulder to decide whether he would be castrated as part of his punishment for sexually assaulting two children.

He is 65, retired as service manager for a tire shop, and at 2 p.m. Friday afternoon he had just come home from the park.

"Pigeons, they're a lot like little girls used to be," he said. "You're nice to them, they like you. The pigeons in the park, they've learned to trust me."

He was charged in 1971 with molesting 14 girls he had taken hiking, swimming and to movies with their parents' permission.

He won't talk about molesting girls or why he thinks he did it, but at a preliminary hearing in Denver District Court, he said, "If you release me, I'll just go out and do it again." He talked to psychiatrists and a Denver doctor who advocated castration of sex offenders. He decided that would help him stop molesting girls and keep him out of prison.

He was castrated Dec. 8, 1971, at Denver General Hospital.

"When you live a life like I led, it's a lot like a lobotomy," he said. "After that, I saw young girls like everybody else sees young girls. They're nice, they're pretty."

After the operation, he pleaded guilty to statutory rape and felonious assault of two girls — the prosecutor didn't press the other charges — and was given three years' probation.

He lived in Capitol Hill, worked at a service station and was in group therapy until he completed his probation and moved to a place where nobody knew him.

"My friends here, they think I'm lonely," he said. "They try to fix me up with old ladies. One of them, she said she'd go out with me as long as I didn't try and get fresh.

"I told her I wasn't that kind of guy."

He has tried to be friends with two young girls in his neighborhood, but when he attempted to give them candy bars they said their parents told them to not accept anything from a stranger.

"People now are so afraid of everything," he said. "They don't have to be afraid of me. There's nothing to be afraid of anymore."

He thinks sometimes about the girls he molested. The youngest would be in her 30s. Some might have young children of their own.

When he thinks about them, they still are young girls.

"I hope they're happy, married, with little kids of their own," he said. "I hope nothing I did might have hurt them as grown-ups. But to me, they'll always be my little girls."

Rocky Mountain News
August 20, 1994

Welfare Mom Finds Work Is Fun

DENVER — The envelope had her name in the window in the corner, and Yolanda Jones used one of the fingernails she had just glued on and painted red to open it.

She is 33, the mother of three, and she started her first job in November. She works for Big Brothers and Big Sisters Foundation, calling people on the telephone and asking for pledges. She earned $525 last year.

Now, she was opening her first W-2 form.

"Let me get this straight," she said. "They give it to me when I don't work. Then I work, and they take it away?

"What does the government need money for, anyway?"

Her grandmother is on welfare, her mother is on welfare, and 15 years ago Jones went from being a dependent child to being a welfare mother. She grew up in the Curtis Park Public Housing project, one of eight kids. When her son was born, she moved into the East Village subsidized housing.

"Taxes?" she said. "Why didn't they tell me about taxes?"

In September, a woman who used to live next to her told her about Volunteers of America's Brandon House, and she was accepted into the program. The program offers classes and counseling to help women make the transition off welfare. She is studying to get her general equivalency diploma.

"It used to be, whenever I'd get a letter with that little window with my name in it, it meant I made it to the first of the month," she said. "That's why February was my favorite month. Now, maybe I'll like one of the summer months best."

She heard about the job with Big Brothers and Big Sisters and took the bus to the offices. A woman gave her a form and said it was a job application. She asked if mowing a lawn could count as "previous job experience."

Now, she gets to work 45 minutes early every morning and does her nails every other day, even though the people she calls can't see them.

"I wanted to save my first paycheck, not cash it," she said. "Paychecks are all white. They're not as pretty as the government checks, but I kept it as long as I could before I had to cash it."

She still gets $312 a month in Aid to Families with Dependent Children. Her son is 15, and her daughters are 12 and 7. None of the fathers comes around.

"Even if they are gonna take money back for taxes, I want to keep right on working," she said. "Work is fun. It's easier than just waiting on a check to come."

At work, she gets an average of 22 pledges a day, while the average employee gets

12, her manager, Sandy Myers, said. A couple of weeks ago, she had only four pledges after two hours. She asked the woman who works next to her if that was what people mean when they talk about a bad day at work.

That afternoon, she got 20 pledges.

"This might sound funny, but it means something to have a job," she said. "To be part of something. I just wish somebody would have told me about this a long time ago."

Rocky Mountain News
January 31, 1995

Volunteer Rolls Out Hospitality

DENVER — Danny Melton hadn't had a smile since Sacramento, and then he got off at the Greyhound bus station in Denver where John Schrant was waiting for him.

Schrant is waiting to meet everybody on every bus, with a diesel voice and a hydraulic handshake. He is there to meet people who are happy to be there. He is there to meet people who think that the only thing worse than riding a bus is to get off at a bus station.

Melton was going on to Baltimore, and Schrant was just going on.

"The bus to Baltimore, it takes you a lot of wonderful places before you get there, although what's your hurry, seeing how we just met?" he said. "If you're going home to see your mother, though, you'd better get going, because it leaves in four minutes. And since we're on the subject, when was the last time you wrote your mother, son?"

"Salt Lake City," Melton said. "I'd like to stay and talk, but..."

Schrant took a postage stamp out of his wallet. "Be sure and tell her hello for Big John," he said. "And get moving, because it leaves in three minutes."

Schrant is 77 years old and is at the bus station six days a week to give maps, directions and advice to people who are going everywhere and nowhere. He does this six days a week, because Sundays he does it at Stapleton International Airport.

He doesn't get paid, but he also doesn't act 77 years old.

The advice is sort of like the bus to Baltimore, which takes you to a lot of places before you get there.

"Anybody who needs directions, get over here," Schrant says. "Anybody who doesn't think they need directions, you probably need them more than the other folks. And nobody needs directions to find Big John."

He taught for 40 years in Denver public schools, coached tennis and gave away pumpkin seeds to fight drug abuse. His motto was "Try a seed instead of a weed." He gave away 500 pounds a year.

Every other summer, he would take his wife and their five children on a freighter to another continent, to someplace where there wasn't anybody like him.

"So we were in Sevenoaks, England, one night, walking up and down the streets and looking for a place to stay, and finally I went into the police station," he said. "A fella in there said we could just stay there, and we slept on the floor of that police station. That got me to wondering what would happen to somebody from Sevenoaks, England, if they came to the United States and there wasn't anybody to help them."

In 1978, he told the manager of the bus station about his idea and was told he wasn't needed, which told him he was needed more than he had thought.

Fifteen years later, he has a desk in the middle of the station, and he was there when Marta and Melissa Melancon hugged goodbye.

"Has it already been a week?" he said. "It seems like yesterday you two were hugging in here."

The Melancons — Melissa from Denver, her daughter from Salt Lake City — had hugged in front of Schrant a week earlier when Martha came to visit.

A week later, the three were together again, saying goodbye.

They both hugged Schrant.

"Without you, This would seem like a...like a bus station," Melissa Melancon said.

"That's one of the sad things and the wonderful things about buses," he said. "Like everything else, they go both ways."

Schrant's wife died two years ago after 53 years of marriage, and he lives alone in north Denver. They had started Denver's first youth hostel in their back yard. Now, he figures he basically is doing the same thing by telling them where to get off.

He was telling a woman from Los Angeles why she was lucky to be taking a bus to Pittsburgh, when Paul Graner walked past.

JOHN SCHRANT VOLUNTEERS HIS TIME SIX MORNINGS A WEEK AT THE GREYHOUND BUS STATION IN DENVER.

"Where you from, mate?" he said.

"England," Graner said.

"And where in England would that be?" Schrant said.

"You've probably never heard of it — a little town called Sevenoaks."

Schrant had wondered about this moment when he started doing this 15 years ago. Now it was here, because he was here.

"Sevenoaks, England," he said. "I've been wondering when you were going to get here."

Rocky Mountain News
March 29, 1993

The Last White Spot

DENVER — Outside, the sun rose over the 7-Eleven to the east, all orange, gold, purple.

Inside the White Spot, the light fixtures and Naugahyde were orange, the Formica was gold, the woman at the end of the counter already was wearing eye shadow called "Violet Mood." It was morning at the last White Spot. You could tell, because Mary and S.W. Gregory sat at the other end of the counter, where they have sat and had their coffee every morning for the past 34 years.

"You come to think of this as your own personal seat," Mary Gregory said.

"You think if you didn't show up and sit here, they'd just pour the coffee here anyway," S.W. Gregory said. "Plus, if we did sit someplace else, what would the guys who sit next to me every day think?"

Sometime next week, the people here will find out whether the last White Spot, at Eighth and Broadway, the southeast corner of the Golden Triangle, will be torn down for a Taco Cabana. The city will decide whether to change the zoning for that area to permit a drive-through restaurant. At the same time, the owner of White Spot, Tony Clements, is trying to put together financing to buy the property and keep it going.

Dean Krakel/Rocky Mountain News

KIT GETTE, A WAITRESS AT THE WHITE SPOT FOR 20 YEARS, POURS A CUP OF COFFEE FOR CUSTOMER BOB HARRIS.

The Gregorys left, and in the afternoon Jack Selden sat down in Mary Gregory's seat, where he has sat and had his BLT sandwich for lunch every day for the past 22 years. He missed one BLT because his mother died. Another day, he came in and had ordered it before another waitress reminded him he had just been in and eaten his BLT an hour earlier.

"A while back, I thought about it, and I just did it," he said. "I sat in a booth. Now, at least nobody can say I didn't try to change."

The chain was started in 1946 by the late William Clements. He brought the

California coffee shop style of architecture to Colorado. By the time he opened his eighth restaurant, people were saying the same things about his chain they now are saying about Taco Cabana.

Three cooks have worked here for at least 25 years, three waitresses for more than 20, the manager for 25.

Now, White Spot is run by William Clements' son, Tony, and it is down to one restaurant in a drive-through world. It has added southwestern and stir-fry. In the back corner, they put in a non-smoking section.

Still, it is what it was, which is why people either come every day or they don't come at all.

Which is why Joe Lee came in as the sun was setting and sat in the seat Selden had just left, where he has sat and had his coffee and the special for dinner every evening for the past 12 years.

"I thought about sitting in a different seat one time," Lee said. "Meet some new and different people. But then I changed my mind.

"I know this might sound funny to you, but this here is my seat."

Rocky Mountain News
November 30, 1994

After 77 Years, She Still Has a Lot to Wonder About

DENVER — The woman sat at the kitchen table in the house in southwest Denver, the prescription bottles arranged shortest to tallest in the center, saying it wasn't her business to tell you how to write a newspaper story.

She had called earlier that day, just after the man who said he can swallow an oyster and make it come out his nose. He admitted he couldn't prove it still was an oyster. You tell people like that, "That sounds like something '9 Wants To Know'."

Then Mary Ricker called.

"I have lived to be 77 years old," she had said. "Don't you think there would be a story if you came to the house?"

At the house, she said she and her husband, Jack, had moved here in 1964 because it was almost exactly halfway between where they worked. She was a receptionist for the Davis & Davis law firm for 26 years, and he was the supervisor of the finance department at Harken Oil Corp. for 34 years. They were married 36 years.

Since he died, she is afraid living alone, she said.

"Is that what the story would be about?" you ask.

"At night three years ago, I heard noises," she said. "Up on the roof, so I called the police. It turned out to be squirrels, but that doesn't have anything to do with being afraid.

"It's just being alone."

He never missed a day of work or got home after 5:45 p.m. He died Jan. 12, 1977, at work while he was pulling on his galoshes to catch the bus home. There hasn't been a morning since then she hasn't looked at his photograph next to her bed and thanked him for the 36 years, she said.

"Is that what the story would be about?" you ask.

"Oh, no," she said. "He wouldn't like that, because everything was for Brian."

Brian was their only child, and he manages the business office of a chemical supply company in Englewood. He comes every Sunday at 3 p.m. He asks if there is anything she needs, but she doesn't want to be a burden, she said.

"Is that what the story would be about?" you ask.

"I would never want to make him feel pressured by me," she said. "Nothing would make me happier than if he was to meet a nice girl. But he has his life."

She almost is finished with the *Reader's Digest* version of *Little Women,* and she watches the O.J. Simpson trial on the television when they aren't talking about blood samples. She thought about learning to play bridge, but then she would have to find someone to play with. Some afternoons when it doesn't look like rain, she walks around the block and imagines the stories inside the houses.

"Is that what the story would be about?" you ask.

"Maybe," she said. "That I still have dreams. In 1937, I saw Charles Lindbergh in a Memorial Day parade and almost ran out and touched him, and I still wonder what it would have been like.

"I'm 77 years old. I have a lot to wonder about. You can't write a newspaper story about those kinds of things, though.

"Can you?"

Rocky Mountain News
May 10, 1995

The St. Patrick's Day Parade

DENVER — Kevin Fitzgerald looked up at Moby Dick and reflected on what he has learned in 10 years of building the biggest float in the St. Patrick's Day Parade.

He was in a warehouse in Globeville, and the members of the St. Patrick Benevolent Society were using chain saws to carve porpoises out of Styrofoam and painting things green and doing something that involved dropping pipes on concrete.

It isn't easy to carve a dream out of 384 cubic feet of Styrofoam. Still, you don't do it for 10 years without learning some things.

Nine years maybe, but not 10.

"I think we finally did it," Fitzgerald said. "I think we built a float that'll fit through the door to get out of the warehouse."

The St. Patrick Benevolent Society never runs out of hope or beer, which probably isn't a coincidence, and this year it is supposed to be St. Patrick meets Moby Dick. Fitzgerald and Scott "King Biscuit" Klune organize it. Tom Barlow, who just finished setting a world record by making a 22-foot-tall heart out of 1,500 pounds of chocolate, runs the chain saw.

There will be two queens this year because Fitzgerald and Klune asked different Victoria's Secret models.

"It's times like this you appreciate a friend like Biscuit," Fitzgerald said. "He's the perfect guy to have inhaling all those spray paint fumes in an enclosed space. If it wasn't for flashbacks, he couldn't find his car keys."

Fitzgerald is a standup comedian and a veterinarian. Klune owns Metro Chem Supply Co. They both are 44, single and do this because they can.

Ten years ago, they were just like everybody else with green tuxedos and nowhere to go. They went to New Orleans every year for Mardi Gras, so they decided to bring it here. Since then, they have won eight best float awards, which is another way of proving that hard work, determination and beer usually beats hard work and determination.

"This thing is bigger than all of us," Fitzgerald said. "But I always remember my grandmother, who has Irish Alzheimer's. She only remembers the people she hates."

They got 25 friends to pay $150 each, with the half that doesn't go into the float going to a good cause. This year it will go to fight Crohn's disease. Eventually, they hope to raise enough to reintroduce venomous reptiles — mambas, bushmasters, boomslangs and mangrove snakes — into Ireland.

And so they continue with the cause. They will toss 2,000 pounds of green Mardi Gras beads, 50 coconuts painted green, 150 pounds of rubber fried eggs and 50 pounds of rubber dog manure. They refuse to be deterred by anything like the ticket they got last year for playing James Brown as loud as he's supposed to be played.

This thing might be bigger than all of them, but with any luck it still will be small enough to fit under overpasses.

"The main point is to have fun," Fitzgerald said. "It's not fun unless somebody wakes up with a chalk outline around them."

Rocky Mountain News
March 16, 1996

Greg Lopez was very kind and gentle.

He liked people and people liked him.

What he could have done and what he would have

done! For me, the world will always be

one degree colder than it should be

without Greg in it. I hope he saves me a table.

KEVIN J. FITZGERALD

The Personals Ad

NEW IBERIA, La. — Single male seeking females for meetings, can be discreet. Anthony, P.O. Box 281, Erath, 70533

The ad appeared Friday in the classified section of *The Daily Iberian,* under an ad for a lost small black and white dog wearing an orange collar.

I wrote Anthony and asked him to call me. I said I wanted to talk to him about what he was looking for. I said I could be discreet, too.

I have been around long enough to know you have better chances if you are the lost dog.

He called Saturday night. He said he had just checked his box. It was empty, except for my letter.

"Just about any girl would do," he said. "The hard part is meeting them. I always had trouble meeting them."

He said he had already put ads in the newspapers at the checkout lanes in grocery stores, and he had answered some. He didn't have anything in common with most of the girls whose ads he answered or who answered his ads, except writing. The relationship has ended with all but two.

One is a teacher in New Orleans, and the other is a hairstylist in Brownsville, Texas. They're both 31, Anthony's age. They both sent pictures.

"They both look pretty good," Anthony said. "And you ought to read their letters — after you write a while, they get real good. I mean real good."

"We keep trying to make plans to meet, but nothing ever seems to work out."

Anthony said he would come here to talk to me.

I asked him to describe himself on the phone, like he would to a girl he was writing to.

He said: "Six feet. Two-hundred pounds. Hazel eyes. Kind of short hair, not real long, dirty blond. A mustache most of the time."

When he walked into the office yesterday afternoon, I didn't recognize him. He was everything he described, but he didn't look anything like the picture in my mind.

He had glasses, he hadn't shaved for a couple of days, he had the beginning of a belly. He wore a maroon T-shirt, white work pants, black canvas tennis shoes. He had on an orange hat from a pipe-coating company that has gone out of business.

There was something familiar about him, but it took me a minute to figure this out: Except for the T-shirt, he was wearing the same colors as the lost dog.

He said he operated a cherrypicker at the Port of Iberia, until the company shut down. Now, he is unemployed, living in Erath. He was married for nine years — "I met her when I was passing by her house on the way to the skating rink, and one of her brothers stopped me, and then we started talking" — until two years ago.

Now he goes to bars or rollerskating, hoping to meet girls, but things never seem to work out.

One was a girl a bar owner introduced, "but she was pretty looped up and probably doesn't even remember me."

One introduced herself at the rollerskating rink, and they went out a couple of times, "but then she moved away and got married."

One was a girl who worked where he used to work, and one night he went over to her house and asked here if she wanted to go to a movie. She said it was getting kind of late. "But it was only 7 o'clock, and shows to go on later, at 8 or 8:30, so I just figured she was just saying no."

There is one other girl he is trying to work up the courage to ask out. She is a checkout girl in a store in Erath. Anthony shops there.

"I went in there and got the stuff I needed — I really did need it, but I probably wouldn't have gone to that store unless she was working there," he said. "I was in line waiting, thinking about what I was gonna say, and then some people came up and got in line right behind me. So I just bought the stuff and left.

"One day I might just go there and leave her a note, if this ad doesn't work out."

He bought the ad in *The Daily Iberian* for a week. It costs him $12. It was extra because he had three words more than the minimum.

The "can be discreet" is what did him in, I said.

"You never know," he said. "I might get a whole lot of girls writing me. If that happened, I don't know what I'd do.

"I'd probably just take the first one and be happy with her."

The Daily Iberian
July 1, 1986

Together Like They Used to Be

DETROIT — Wally Duda and his band start to play *When You Wish Upon a Star* and Frank A. Borg bows to Ginger O'Kelly, hitches up his pants and holds out his hands.

O'Kelly, 70, just had her hair done the way it used to be done and wore the brown lace and satin dress like the ones she used to wear. Borg, 64 and 5-foot-5, wears a suit that is plaid down to his knuckles. They foxtrot.

It is Thursday afternoon at the Grande Ballroom in Westland and over it all a mirrored ball rotates and reflects the way it used to be.

"Nowadays, they say it's OK to just dance crazy, however you want to," O'Kelly says. "But I'm from the old school, where we danced right. This is just like it still should be."

Borg hitches up the pants, which also are plaid and also are too big.

"It's my brother's day off," he explains.

The Grande, named after the old Grande Ballroom in Detroit, is one of the last ballrooms in Metro Detroit and the only one that has afternoon dances. The dances, from 1 to 4 every Thursday afternoon, were started about 2 years ago. No alcohol is served — "most of us learned to dance during Prohibition anyway," Borg says — and they rarely have to check identification to make sure anybody is old enough to dance to Wally Duda.

Wally Duda has a mustache sharp as Saturday night, and he plays trumpet with Wally Lipiec on the accordion and Stan Melmer on the drums. He traveled with the bands of Elliott Lawrence, Bob Strong and Claude Thornhill. He is 62 and played at Detroit's Vanity, Graystone and old Grande ballrooms before they closed, when O'Kelly used to kick her legs over her head.

O'Kelly, who lives in Detroit, doesn't kick above her waist at the Grande because it wouldn't be proper for a 70-year-old woman, she says. She couldn't dance with her late husband because he had polio. Now, every week she gets her hair done and wears a dress like she used to wear.

"People tell me all the things I can't do because I'm too old," she says. "But this is something you can't do if you're too young."

She just finished a waltz with Jack Kane, 78, who is back from the hospital after an operation. One Thursday while Kane was lying in his bed in the hospital, he called the Grande and asked Wally Duda to play *Tenderly*. They left the phone on the snack counter and Kane listened from his bed.

Kane and O'Kelly used to dance together at the Graystone. And sometimes when O'Kelly is alone at home, she still kicks over her head. Anyway, O'Kelly and Borg jitterbug through *New York, New York*. After the song Chester Lojek stands up, cups his hands around his mouth and yells, "Who wants to dance?"

Lojek lost his eyesight to macular degeneration six years ago. He is 73, a retired salesman in real estate, car and insurance. He lives alone in Livonia and dances only to the slower songs when partners hold onto each other.

When Duda and his band start to play *Somewhere, My Love*, O'Kelly grabs Lojek and they waltz.

Somebody always wants to dance.

"This way, everything looks like it used to be," Lojek says. "I've never danced with a woman who isn't beautiful."

Lojek and O'Kelly waltz through *Always* and before he can cup his hands around his mouth and ask who wants to dance, A. Bubbles Maezes grabs him.

Maezes, who got her nickname when she sealed Daredevil fishing lures in plastic for Lou Eppinger Manufacturing Inc. in Dearborn, used to dance against doctors orders. She is 72, a World War II widow who lives alone in Dearborn. She has been retired for two years, since she had heart surgery.

She waltzed a couple of weeks after the operation. Then she two-stepped, then jitterbugged and polkaed. Now, she dances on her doctor's orders.

"The only thing is, I can't dress like I used to," she says, and she tugs on her sweater. "No plunging necklines now, because of the scar. Of course, it would plunge more than it used to, anyway."

Maezes and Lojek foxtrot through *Stardust*. She leads him back to his table and they sit down. She sits until Borg walks up, bows, hitches up his pants and holds out his hands.

Borg is divorced, lives alone on his horse farm in South Lyon and goes to Elks, Moose and Knights of Columbus dances, too. He prefers the women here. One time one of them slapped Borg. He had complained her girdle stay jabbed him in the stomach.

Now, he prefers women who don't wear girdles.

"I like to dance cheek-to-cheek, or as close as I can get at this age," he says. "Some people say it isn't as good as it used to be. Me, I say it's better."

Borg and Maezes jitterbug to *Opus 1* on a Thursday afternoon, just like it used to be.

And over it all, the mirrored ball rotates and reflects the way it still is.

The Detroit News
January 23, 1989

Bottle Man

DETROIT — The man has picked up bottles for as long as most people can remember.

He walks the streets on the west side of Detroit and carries plastic grocery bags full of clothes and bottles. He talks to himself about how someone named Charles wants to take him to Indianapolis for scientific experiments and about what phase the sun and moon are in. He smells of alcohol.

When he started to pick up bottles, they did not require a deposit.

Raleigh Chester, who lives on Temple near Trumbull, said he has tried to talk to the man but he probably would recognize only Chester's shoes because he always looks down at the sidewalk for bottles. Chester, 64, said the man's name is John, and they grew up together. Chester said the man was a sergeant in the U.S. Army in World War II.

"I remember, he came home after the war with his chest all covered with all these medals," Chester said. "The were all just a-glimmering, I remember. Old John — he wasn't old then, of course — he walked around looking like a Christmas tree.

"I still think about all those medals every time I see him."

One day last winter, Chester stepped in front of the man and held out two dollar bills. The man looked up until he came to the two dollars, then up until he came to Chester's face. Chester felt old.

The man looked down at the sidewalk and stepped around Chester.

The man used to carry the bottles in the lining of his overcoat. He put them in a pocket that had a hole in it and they fell into the lining. After a Tigers game, he looked like a sack of potatoes.

The coat dragged and finally wore a hole. Bottles fell out but he didn't always notice. Sometimes, he picked up the same bottle two or three times.

He got an Army coat and carries plastic grocery bags now.

Ruth Arlett, who lives on Bagley, said the man's name is Wally and she knew him in the 1950s when he lived two houses up the street from her. He was a mechanic and had a wife and nine children. They all moved away about 30 years ago, and she didn't see him until he came back alone.

Every morning Arlett rinses out the beer bottles her husband emptied the night before and leaves them next to her garage. They always are gone by the next morning. Kids take them, too.

"He's not bad, doesn't hurt anybody," she said. "Without him, there would be broken glass everywhere, popping tires and cutting up little kids. You don't see bottles lying around with him walking everywhere."

Ruby Willie, who lives two houses from Arlett, said the man's name is Douglas and he worked for Ford until he hurt his back. She and her husband used to play cards once a week with him and his mother. They stopped when his mother died in the early 1960s.

"One time, maybe two or three years ago, he comes walking up and I have a six-pack so I offer him a bottle of beer that's not opened," she said. "He opens it and pours it all out and puts the bottle in his bag and walks away. He might smell like alcohol but that's just from what's left in those bottles."

At 3:45 on a Monday afternoon, the man walked past a burned-out house where men sat on the front steps and drank beer. The men drink out of bottles in paper bags. They always sit there, as if there is no deposit on them.

When a bottle is empty, they take it to the party store on the corner and use it for a downpayment on tomorrow.

They turned one at a time and watched him come up the sidewalk. The man talked to himself about how they don't make anything like a '57 Hudson anymore. The men on the steps didn't say anything until he was past.

When he was 10 feet past them one of the men stood up and yelled, "Old goat! You're just like an old goat, picking up trash all the time! You want a bottle?"

The man didn't seem to hear.

"You want a bottle?" the man on the steps yelled again. He drank the last of the beer. He tore off the paper bag and held up the bottle.

The man kept walking.

The man was about 20 feet up the sidewalk when it hit his shoulder. It fell to the sidewalk and shattered. The man stopped and turned around.

The glass on the sidewalk glimmered, like medals from the war.

The man on the steps sat down and another man handed him a paper bag with a bottle in it. He took a gulp. The men on the steps laughed and watched the man on the sidewalk.

The man bent over and picked up the large pieces of glass one at a time and put them in one of his plastic grocery bags. He got down on his knees and picked up the small pieces. He has picked up bottles for as long as most people can remember.

When he was finished, he stood and walked up the sidewalk.

The Detroit News
November 27, 1989

Turtles and Parallels

NEW IBERIA, La. — The turtle is coming across the road, and Taylor says it is a good parallel to what life is all about.

"You get to thinking about it, that's all life is," Taylor says. "Trying to get across the road. Some go faster, some go slower, but we're all just trying to cross the road...

"No," he decides, "there's just no getting around some parallels."

There is the canal, the road, the yard and the house. Taylor is sitting on the front porch of the house. The turtle has come out of the canal on the other side of the road and is coming toward him.

He isn't sure when he started seeing the parallels, but it has been going on for a long time. He is 67 years old, retired, divorced. He lives alone in the house, three miles outside Jeanerette, and during the day he sits on the porch.

The parallels are everywhere.

The other day he saw a caterpillar inching down the sidewalk, and it made him think of the endless possibilities of life, he says. It made him realize that you have to keep crawling down the sidewalk anyway. It made him realize how things can be missed.

And today the turtle is coming across the road, and Taylor is sitting on his porch thinking about the parallels to what life is all about.

"Those birds over there on the line?" he says. "they're just like my son was. Paul, you'd try to get too close to him, he'd fly away.

"We got along about the same as most fathers and sons, I guess. Then one day, he must of been 19, all of a sudden he just left. I was still married then, and he called us from somewhere up in the northeast. He said he was broke and they'd thrown him in jail for sleeping in a park. He needed a hundred dollars to get out and another hundred dollars to come home.

"I said 'I'll send you the hundred to get out, but if you want to come back here you're gonna have to get back the same way you got up there."

He hasn't seen his son since, it has been 17 years. About two years ago he got a card and a picture of his son, a woman and two kids. In the card his son wrote that he and his family were living in Portland, Ore., and he was head of the service department of an automobile dealership.

By now the turtle is halfway across the far lane.

Taylor points to the weeds clogging the drainage ditch and says they are a lot like his cousin Arvey.

"You'd be all ready to go, say, duck hunting, and Arvey would come over and say he needed help real bad getting the roof fixed on his carport and then everything would get all screwed up," Taylor says. "Or another time, Arvey — his parents liked the initials R.V., but at the hospital when he was born they said R.V. had to stand for something — me and my wife and Paul were getting all ready to go down to Holly

Beach for the weekend, and he comes over and says if I could just come by and help him pull the engine out of his car he'd never be able to forget it. I didn't want to, but my wife said I'd better, so I end up spending the whole weekend showing Arvey how to rebuild the damn thing.

"He was just always clogging things up that way..."

He talks about the parallels between Perry, his second-oldest brother who could never stay out of trouble, and the clouds that look like rain. He talks about his mother, who raised three boys and a girl after his father died, and how she was like the giant pecan tree in the corner of the yard. He talks about Rossaman, his neighbor who moved in and started parking wrecked cars in his front yard, and how he is a lot like whatever it is that comes and digs holes in his yard at night.

By the time he is finished, the turtle is almost to the center of the road.

The only thing Taylor has never been able to see any parallels to is his wife, he says. Bees, hawks, foxes, roosters — all of them had similarities, but there was always something that didn't fit. It was something he has never understood.

"One day I come home from work, and there was a note," he says. "It just says 'I am leaving. You always think you know why I do everything, so maybe you'll know why I'm doing this.'

"I was never able to figure that one out."

He leaves it there.

By now the turtle is in the middle of the road.

The pickup truck appears down the road. Two kids. The driver sees the turtle, swerves and crushes it.

Right in the middle of the road.

Taylor has watched the pickup approach like he has been expecting it. There's just no getting around some parallels. He shakes his head.

"Damn."

The Daily Iberian
October 11, 1985

Charlie Home for Xmas

NEW IBERIA, La. — Charlie is coming home for Christmas, his mother says.

He said he'd pay her back as soon as he could. She bought his round-trip bus ticket and mailed it to him in Hollywood, Florida. It's worth $121 to have Charlie home for Christmas.

"He's so much fun, always happy, always laughing," she says. "Everybody's always happy when he's around. Even Robert."

Robert is her other son. He lives here and he comes over with his family every weekend. A wife, a son, two daughters. Charlie doesn't have a family yet. Maybe after he settles down, his mother says.

Their father is almost as excited as his wife. He retired after 43 years working for an oil company. Social Security gives them $346 a month, enough to pay the rent and the rest of the bills. They save what they can, and they spent it all on Christmas presents and Charlie's bus ticket.

Charlie will pay everything back when he gets back on his feet. He's between jobs right now. The last job he had, his boss expected him to do everything for not enough money, and since then he hasn't been able to find anything suitable for his abilities, his mother says.

He never found that job; each time he thinks he has it something happens. Four Christmases ago he worked in a department store in Lake Havasu City, Arizona, making sure nobody shoplifted anything. Since then he has managed a convenience store and a fast-food restaurant, sold used cars, mobile homes and a new candy bar with peanuts and a caramel center. Sometimes it's the boss, sometimes it's the hours (Charlie is a night person), sometimes it's the location.

It's always something, but when he finds it he'll do somebody a wonderful job and he'll pay everybody everything he owes, she says.

Robert is a year younger than Charlie. He works for an oil company, filling out purchase orders and checking inventories. It's the same company he's worked for for 12 years. It's not a great job, but when the company started letting people go the bosses called Robert in and told him he didn't have anything to worry about.

His wife is a secretary in a bank, and between them they make enough to pay the house note and put a little away for when the kids get old enough for college. Robert worries too much, his mother says. She worries about him worrying so much.

Robert and Charlie get along as well as most brothers, she says. Robert gets on his brother for not holding a job, but he just doesn't understand Charlie like she does.

"When I told Robert I'd sent the ticket, I thought he'd be all excited," she says. "He was happy, but he asked how much the ticket cost. When I told him, he just shrugged. Now what kind of Christmas spirit is that to have? Especially about his brother."

She shakes her head and starts a story about how much fun Charlie is.

One year when Robert was about 17 and Charlie was 18, Robert bought a used Ford with money he had saved since he was a little boy. One night he lent it to Charlie for an important date, after Charlie swore he'd drive slow and be home by 11:30. So at three o'clock in the morning Charlie comes walking up the front sidewalk carrying the muffler over his shoulder.

"I thought Robert was going to kill him," she says and she almost cries, she is laughing so hard at the memory. "His own brother, and Charlie looking like he was so sorry. He felt terrible, Charlie did. Robert did too, but he cooled off after a while, and his father helped him fix everything."

With Charlie around it was never dull. When he comes home he'll pick her up in his arms and swing her around, and she'll giggle like a little girl. It's always like that when Charlie comes home, and he'll be home for Christmas.

"Oh, I know Robert'll get over it when Charlie gets here and he starts making everybody laugh," she says. "He'll get over it, I know he will. You know how brothers are."

The Daily Iberian
December 13, 1984

Moralities and Unwatered Plants

NEW IBERIA, La. — A friend of mine met a woman at a New Year's Eve party, and something got started.

She called it a "relationship." He called it something else.

Whatever it was, it was over New Year's morning, as far as he was concerned. She didn't see it that way.

She asked him what they were going to do for lunch.

"I said, 'I don't know about you, but I'm gonna watch football,'" my friend says. "She said she didn't know much about football, but she was willing to learn. I said, 'Well, I'm going over to a friend's house and it's kind of small...' She said that sounded like it would be 'cozy.'"

They ended up watching the games at his place, and he says he didn't pay much attention to them. He was trying to find a nice way to end "the relationship," but every time he'd start to say something she'd ask him a question about football, like, "What's it supposed to mean when the referee holds both hands straight up in the air?"

He ended up pretending to fall asleep on the couch, and then he really did fall asleep. When he woke up, she was gone.

My friend says, "Whatever happened to 'The New Morality?' Wasn't it supposed to be OK to do things like that without having to get into a 'relationship' now?"

The next morning at work he was sitting at his desk, and at about 11:30 he looked up. She was standing there, waiting quietly.

She said she knew about a nice, quiet place that served club sandwiches for lunch. Somehow she knew he liked club sandwiches. It must have come up at the New Year's Eve party.

He said he was very busy and might not have time for lunch. She said he'd told her this was the slowest time of the year. She was right about that, too.

"All of the people in the office are looking at me funny, like I had been keeping some big secret from then," he says. "This girl I'd been meaning to ask out — I think she really liked me — is glaring at her, then at me, then at her. Right then I make a New Year's resolution never to get involved with a girl I don't know ever again, and I just want to get out of there."

Halfway through his club sandwich he glanced at his watch, and all of a sudden he remembered he was almost late for his plane to Boston. He apologized, left money on the table for the bill and rushed out. As he was walking away he said he didn't know how long he'd be gone, but it might be a long time.

She kept raising her voice as he got farther away, saying she'd call his office every day to find out when he'd be getting back, and she would miss him.

"Whatever happened to the 'Old Morality?' The one where the guy's supposed to call the girl and she's supposed to wait," my friend asks. "You've gotta operate under one morality or the other, it's only fair, you know."

That night he was sitting at home watching television when she walked in. He couldn't tell who was more surprised.

He said the trip had been canceled due to what he called "unforeseen circumstances." She said she'd come by to water his plants while he was in Boston.

She was glad about the unforeseen circumstances, because they meant he could come to her parents' house for dinner that weekend. They were dying to meet him, she said.

"I said, 'Don't you think, we're rushing this a little bit?'" my friend says. "And she said things just seemed to be falling into place so fast, that there was no use worrying about that."

He said, yes, there was something to worry about. He came right out and told her the truth about "the relationship," as gently as he could. She started crying and said all she wanted to do was water his plants while he was in Boston.

After a while she seemed to understand, he says. At least, she went home and she wasn't crying anymore.

The next day at work he felt terrible. She was a nice girl, and he kind of missed having her around. It always happens like that, he says.

He sat down at his desk and saw a note.

It said, "The next time you go to Boston, I hope all your plants die."

The Daily Iberian
January 10, 1985

Sweepstakes and Headaches

NEW IBERIA, La. — The first time Delores Rathman heard she won $10 million in the Publisher's Clearinghouse Sweepstakes was about 10 days ago, when her sister-in-law called.

"She was screaming, and at first I thought something bad must have happened," Delores says. "I couldn't get her to calm down and tell me what happened. When she finally told me I'd won the 10 million dollars, I started screaming, too."

When they both calmed down, Delores asked her sister-in-law how she knew. Her sister-in-law said a friend of hers had called and told her. She wasn't sure how her friend knew, but she must have known somebody in New York.

Still, Delores said she wouldn't believe anything until she heard from Ed McMahon himself.

Still, she called her mother and asked her to pick up the kids from school — with her luck, Ed would probably call while she was out. Delores is divorced with two kids, living with her mother in Jeanerette.

Within the next two days three friends called to congratulate her and ask her what she was going to do with all that money. One had heard the news from Delores's sister-in-law, one had heard it from Delores's other sister-in-law, and the other had heard from somebody who heard it from the person who had heard it from Delores's sister-in-law, but she wasn't sure which one.

"I didn't want to get too excited," Delores says. "But still, you have to wonder..."

If she did win, she decided she would buy a new house for her and her mother and the kids. She would pay for it with cash, even though it would be smarter to get a loan and use the money in the meantime. She didn't want to have to worry about making payments ever again.

She was going to buy a diamond ring, something she had always wanted, but just a small one.

The rest she was going to invest in something that was safe but would give her a good return.

People kept calling. Sometimes now it was the *Reader's Digest* Sweepstakes. Either one, it really didn't matter to Delores. Ten million is 10 million.

And 10 million to one is 10 million to one, which is what Delores figured were the odds against her winning the sweepstakes, including her mother and the kids.

Three or four days passed.

She was sick of hearing about the sweepstakes but afraid to leave the house.

She just wanted to shut out the sweepstakes and Ed McMahon, which is not as easy as you might think. One night she had a dream he knocked on the door, but it turned out to be the wrong address. She couldn't sleep, so she got up and turned on the television, and who do think was sitting there next to Johnny Carson?

A man who said he used to work with her brother called and said he'd been out of work for three months and if she would advance him some money to buy some food for his family and to get his car running so he could look for a job, he would pay her back out of his first paycheck.

She said she hadn't heard anything yet, so he said he'd call back in a couple of days.

A woman she hadn't seen since high school called and said that now she could afford to live someplace nice and buy some nice clothes and a nice car, and they ought to get together and go someplace nice for lunch.

A woman she didn't know but who knew her sister-in-law called and said she was planning to open a flower shop and said with her brains and Delores's money they could be a success. When Delores said she hadn't heard anything yet, the woman said Delores should just say no if she wasn't interested.

A man who used to play on her ex-husband's softball team called and asked her out.

By last Saturday, a week after she first heard she had won, Delores had given up any hope of winning $10 million. The telephone still rings sometimes, but she doesn't get excited anymore. Sometimes she tells people that Ed McMahon himself called and apologized.

She figures the odds against her being the subject of a rumor like that are also astronomical, so in a way she does feel fortunate.

She also feels fortunate in another way.

"I figure I came as close to winning as you can get," she says. "And after what I've been through, I hope I never do win anything."

The Daily Iberian
February 10, 1987

The Best Christmas Tree

NEW IBERIA, La. — The old man picked out the tree. The boy ran down the rows from tree to tree and picked out several, but the old man found something wrong with each one — it wasn't bushy enough, it had a hole in the branches, it wasn't tall enough, it wasn't straight enough. He wanted to make sure they found the right Christmas tree.

He explained to his grandson about how trees form rings, and how if you count them you can figure out how old the tree is.

"Grandpa, do people have rings?" the boy asked.

The old man stopped inspecting the tree, stopped a smile and shook his head.

"Then how do you remember how old you are?"

"Some things you just remember," he said.

They had driven 45 minutes to get to the Vincent Christmas Tree Farm near Kaplan to cut a Christmas tree, the old man said later. It's not like the old days when you went out in the woods, it's not much cheaper and it's a longer drive, but it's worth it to find the right Christmas tree and cut it down.

They found the right tree in a back corner of the lot. The old man looked it over and couldn't find anything wrong with it. Seven feet tall, bushy, with no holes in the branches. He knelt down and started the saw with short, slow strokes, making a groove.

The boy watched, he had never seen a tree cut down before. He thought this was the modern way to get a Christmas tree.

"Is this a better way to get a Christmas tree?" he asked.

The old man nodded.

"Why?"

The old man stopped sawing and though about it. "Well, in the old days..." the man would often say when the boy asked something like that. Then he would catch himself.

The old days were better, but there is nothing he or the boy can do about it.

"It's the best kind of Christmas tree because you get to pick out exactly what tree you want, and if you don't want one it will live until next Christmas," he said. "Besides, when you buy a tree at a grocery store you don't know what kind of mood the person was in when they cut it. This way you can be sure everything's right."

The boy grabbed the other end of the saw and helped. It was a pruning saw with a handle like a bow, but it wasn't made for two people. Still, they began to saw through the trunk of the tree — the amount of effort each put into the strokes was about equal — cutting through the rings.

Two-and-a-half years ago, the old man had retired with a pension after working for the government for 42 years. He had a serious heart attack, but it was nothing to worry about as long as he watched himself.

By the time they said he had to retire, he had worked his way into a comfortable position, people respected him.

During that time there were years he couldn't remember how they got a Christmas tree. He would come home after work and it would there, already decorated.

They kept sawing. Thirty-four years ago his son, the boy's father, had been born. Now the old man kept telling him to slow down and appreciate things more, but his son didn't listen. They never do, the old man said.

He and the boy had cut through the center of the tree, and each stroke met less resistance. The old man's breath was coming in short puffs, the strokes became slower, and the boy slowed his own. The amount each was putting into each stroke was not equal.

When the old man was the boy's age, there was no place to buy a Christmas tree. You didn't have any choice back then, he said. You had to look until you found a good tree, then you cut it down. There always were enough good trees.

Back then he always was in a hurry, but it was so much easier in those days, he said. There never was very much to go around, but it was always enough, he said. It was like you see in Christmas specials on television. The old days.

Now all these years later it is important for him to pick out the Christmas tree every year, he said. It's funny, the things that become important.

Before they were finished sawing the tree fell and broke itself off. They picked it up and started back to the car. He carried the tree at the base, the boy carried the tree near the tip.

The best kind, the old man said.

The Daily Iberian
December 6, 1984

Charles and Charlie

NEW IBERIA, La. — For 18 years, Allen Charles opened his front door every morning and caught his dog, Charley.

It was the only trick Charley had ever learned and he taught it to himself as a puppy. He would come out of his bed in the garage, run across the yard onto the front porch, jump up on a chair, then onto the table next to the front door. When Allen opened the door, he was waiting.

Of course, catching a 40-pound dog the first thing in the morning probably is a better trick, but over 18 years, it is the sort of thing you come to expect.

"I don't want this to sound corny and I don't mean to say it was like having Bernice — that was my wife — around, but we always got along just fine together," Allen says. "I mean I didn't go around talking to him, because I don't believe dogs can understand what humans are saying and the other way around. But I do believe we got to understand what each other was thinking."

Allen got Charley a few weeks after Bernice died. He was 55, living alone in the house on Dale Street. His kids, grown and moved to Lafayette, said a dog would be good company.

Charley grew to be about the size of a retriever, brown with black and white spots like a beagle, and always looked like a sorry hound dog.

When Charley was 11 years old, Allen retired from the oilfield. Most of the places Allen went allowed dogs — "I don't know whether that tells you something about the way I treated myself" — so they were together most of the time. They spent most of it walking up and down Dale Street or sitting on the front porch.

About a year and a half ago it seemed like Charley got old all of a sudden. Some days he didn't eat anything, sometimes he missed doorways and he was stone deaf. Allen took him to the veterinarian, who said it was just old age but Charley didn't seem to be suffering.

Allen never figured out how but every morning Charley was waiting on the table by the front door.

Last summer they had been in Lafayette all day on business — it included getting a new bed for Charley — and Allen stopped at Burger King to get them both a hamburger. Drive-thru was backed up, so he decided to go inside. He didn't want to leave Charley alone so he put him on his leash and went in.

A kid in a Burger King suit ran over and said only seeing-eye dogs were allowed.

Allen said he could see fine but Charley was almost completely blind, so he was his dog's seeing-eye person.

The kid thought about it and said it was all right as long as Charley didn't sit in a booth.

Allen ordered to go.

About three months ago, they were at his son's house for a barbecue and Charley was sleeping in a corner, behind Allen.

"Somebody came over and wrinkled up their nose and said something," he says. "I think they said, 'That poor, poor animal. When dogs get old like that they just can't control themselves. They shouldn't be around people, though.'

"I stood up and said to all the people there, 'Excuse me everybody, but us old men just can't control ourselves sometimes and I apologize if I offended anybody.'

"And we left."

One morning a couple of weeks ago, for the first morning in 18 years, Allen opened the front door and Charley wasn't waiting. He started toward the garage and Charley came walking out. They met halfway, and Charley followed Allen back to the front porch.

That morning Allen decided to have Charley put to sleep the next day. The next morning he decided to put it off until the next day. He spent the day sitting with Charley on the front porch.

"I know this sounds corny, but I just wanted to spend a little more time with him," Allen says. "I figured I owed him that. Besides, I'm getting older myself — too old to start over with a puppy, anyway."

Allen is 74 years old now and is in perfect health for a man that age, his doctor tells him. He has thought about moving in with one of his sons in Lafayette but he isn't sure what he will do even now. Whatever he does won't have anything to do with what happened to Charley.

The next morning he decided to call the veterinarian as soon as the office opened and make an appointment. He went to the front door and opened it. Charley was on the table, lying still.

The Daily Iberian
March 10, 1987

Another World

DETROIT — In the morning, the sun comes up behind Walter Rybiski, and he waits for it in the darkness on East Grand Boulevard.

He sits on the front porch of the Witman Adult Foster Care (AFC) home until he sees the sun's reflection in the windows of the AFC home across the boulevard. He is 57, a paranoid schizophrenic. For 12 years here and 27 years in Northville Regional Psychiatric Facility, every sunrise has been reflected.

And some mornings, when there are no clouds and it is the middle of summer and he hasn't taken his Thorazine, the reflection in the windows is like somebody staring at him.

"It looks like my father when I was wrong," he says. "I hear voices. It makes me go back inside."

The ambulance screams up the boulevard. A century ago, when Detroit's most prominent citizens lived in the mansions on the boulevard, men weren't allowed to sit on the front porches in their shirt sleeves. Now, there are about 250 more mentally ill people on East Grand than in Northville, the state's largest psychiatric hospital.

The day begins to blush. The windows across the boulevard turn purple, then red, then fade into the day. Rybiski stares at his reflection.

The ambulance goes back down the boulevard, its siren silent and Rybiski stands up to go inside to borrow a cigarette.

"It's going to be a good day, I think," he says.

Joe Gray walks down East Grand and waves at the people on the porches.

They sit apart, silent, as if somebody took away the words and left the punctuation.

Today on the boulevard, a resident of an AFC home will be sent back to Northville after he takes off his clothes and runs down the sidewalk, and two in nursing homes will die of natural causes.

A man in pajamas tries to hitch a ride up the boulevard, then crosses and tries to hitch a ride the other way.

"I don't take my lithium and, man, I'm king of the world," Gray says. "Now, I take it, and, man, I'm king of East Grand Boulevard."

Gray is 42 and built like an avalanche, and he spends his days on the telephone at the Chandler Haven AFC home or visiting friends from Northville, He charged $3,800 to call a talk line in Seattle and $6,000 introducing himself to people in Honolulu and Iraq. The telephone companies let him off with a warning when he told them he was manic depressive and lived in an AFC home.

Joe Adams comes down from the porch of his rooming house, and the two Joes hug.

"Remember the time I'd been in seclusion and Elvis Presley died?" Gray says. "No clothes or nothing because I'd acted like I hung myself, and I come out of seclusion and the first person I see is Joe. He tells me Elvis Presley was dead."

L-O-V-E is tattooed on the fingers of Adams' right hand, H-A-T-E on the left. He says he was a cocaine addict and served two years in Jackson State Prison for armed robbery before he was diagnosed as a paranoid schizophrenic. His arms are lined with scars from his initiation into the Outlaws motorcycle gang, which later kicked him out because he didn't have a motorcycle.

They walk to the Payless Market on Kercheval, and Adams borrows a dollar from Gray for cigarettes.

"That's what I hate about seclusion," Adams says. "People were always dying while you were in there. Ed Sullivan died while I was in."

Gray and Adams talk about the death of Elvis Presley while they walk back up the boulevard to check on a watermelon in Harvey Majeske's garden.

A 72-year-old man who makes only right turns walks past.

"Last year, I got put in the hospital before the watermelon I wanted got big enough," Adams says. "The year before that, somebody stole it."

Majeske, 86, is hoeing. He grew up on a farm, then worked 39 years on the farm at the Wayne County facility for the mentally ill. He came to Chandler Haven 27 years ago and tended other people's gardens until a home burned 12 years ago and the remaining lot became his garden.

"It's just like it was on my father's farm and the county farm," he says. "Sometimes, it seems like no time has gone by. Other times, it seems like it's all gone by."

Mary Mylonas walks up with a pack of cigarettes and a bag of potato chips, and taps Majeske on the arm.

"I just got a new statue, Harvey," she says. "Come on."

Mylonas, 52, charges 25 cents to walk a half a block to Payless. People a block away stand on their porches and yell her name when they need something. Some days, she earns $3.

She uses the money to buy statues of the Virgin Mary.

"They're all Mary," she says. "I had two daughters I had to put up for adoption — they'd be 28 and 30 years old, and they probably have children by now. Me, I've got my statues."

Her boyfriend, Ray Markel, is in the swing on the porch. She gives him the cigarettes and goes inside to deliver the potato chips. She comes out cradling six statues.

She stands them in a row, tall and short, brunette and blond, smiling and sad.

"That's nothing," Markel says. "You know that statue, the Spirit of Detroit, the guy holding up the sun? That's me."

Markel, 52, lived at Hitt Home when he first asked Mylonas whether she wanted to share a pizza he had ordered, Feb. 1, 1976. They would get married, but somebody said people who live on East Grand Boulevard aren't U.S. citizens.

Everybody leaves the swing on the porch for them.

"You know what else?" Markel says. "Remember when Alaska and Hawaii became states? I knew it before it happened."

Majeske kneels and looks at the statues, one at a time.

Mylonas taps his shoulder.

"Would you like a statue, Harvey?" she says.

Mylonas always gives away her statues, but Majeske never has found one he likes. He looks each one in the eye. He goes back to a blond who is smiling with her arms open.

He picks up the Virgin Mary he has chosen.

"She looks like the woman that used to mop my room at the county farm," he says.

Majeske leaves with his Virgin Mary and his hoe, and a woman runs up the sidewalk, chased by seven other residents.

"You're looking at a waitress," she says.

"Will you make $20 a week?" Wally Domzalski asks.

The woman is 27, lives two houses up in independent living and hadn't worked since she had a nervous breakdown two years ago. Her family and the other people in the house told her she should apply at restaurants. She started work immediately.

Eleven people follow her home.

"I already had one grouchy customer," says the woman, who asked that her name and where she works be withheld to protect her job. "I was just nice. I got a $2 tip."

"Twenty-five dollars a week?" Domzalski asks.

She promises to buy fried chicken for everybody.

Walter Rybiski comes in and holds out two cucumbers.

"Congratulations," he says. "Harvey must be taking a nap."

The day begins to wear off.

After supper, Domzalski, Adams and Danny Sculley walk to Payless for a pack of cigarettes and three quarts of Milwaukee's Best beer, $1 apiece. The medication they took this morning has faded and it's too early for the dose that will put them to sleep. Domzalski owes Sculley $1.57 and four cigarettes, Sculley owes Adams $2.14 and Adams owes Domzalski $1.11 and two packs.

Adams buys.

"I owe 17 people money and 14 people owe me," he says. "I'm $3.27 ahead."

They walk single file to a burned-out house on East Grand, around to the back steps.

Rybiski is waiting. This afternoon, he was awakened from a nap by voices talking about disintegrating crime and lasers, until he realized two men were arguing next door. It was a good day.

"I like to sit with people who don't make me talk," he says. "It doesn't gum up your thoughts that way. I have a lot to think about."

When he was 17, he stabbed his father twice in the leg with a kitchen knife. Rybiski didn't see his father again before 1967 or 1977 — he is sure a Democrat was president.

Seven years ago, he left the boulevard and moved in with his mother, who got him a job bagging groceries. When he didn't show up for work one Monday, his boss went to his house and found him sitting on the front porch, badly sunburned. His mother was inside, dead of natural causes for at least two days.

He moved back to East Grand Boulevard.

"Everybody I know is here," he says. "Everybody who knows me is here. I personally know the guy who is the Spirit of Detroit."

The four men stand on the back step like a measure of music in the shadows and the smell of urine. In February, Rybiski almost lost two fingers to frostbite holding his beer. The quarts go back and forth.

"I'm going to see mother in Florida in February," Sculley says.

"I just got upped on Thorazine," Rybiski says.

"Another month, I'll be eating watermelon, boys," Adams says.

"Beats the hell out of Haldol, I'll tell you that," Rybiski says.

"You don't think she'll make $40 a week?" Domzalski says.

"Six years since I saw her," Sculley says.

Rybiski drinks the rest of his quart.

In three weeks, he will be sent to Northville after he refuses to take his medication and tries to smother himself with a pillow.

Right now, though, he borrows a cigarette from Domzalski, and Adams lights it.

"Got to get up early in the morning," he says.

Excerpted from *The Detroit News*
September 24, 1989

Living for the Moment

DENVER — The Daytimer said it was the time of day to go for a walk, so Ted Lesser and Barbara Butler came out of the townhouse in Aurora to go for a walk.

They live in the townhouse. They are married. They met two years ago in a support group for people who have had brain injuries, and now it was the time of day to go for a walk.

It was a pastel morning with a top and a bottom and sides.

"Everything seems so new," she said.

"Again," he said.

Butler is 52 and Lesser is 57. They had gone to an air show the day before. She remembered seeing a helicopter, because she always wanted to ride in one, and he remembered a lot of kids laughing.

They stopped to look at a crocus that had poked through the dirt.

"It's joyous," she said. "That's a word I've started to use."

"It's perfect," he said.

She organized fund-raisers and walked out of an office building five years ago and slipped on ice. He was a major in the Army and remembers driving on Loveland Pass in 1970, not wearing a seat belt, and a car pulling off the side of the road in front of him. When they met, they both were divorced with grown children, living alone and leaving their apartments only for groceries and support-group meetings.

They moved out of the way of a man on a bicycle.

"Not even wearing a helmet," he said.

"But it looks like fun, anyway," she said. "We're going to try to start riding bikes again."

She took an adult-literacy program to learn to read again, and she has started Teddy Bear Tales in the extra bedroom, printing personalized books and letters. He doesn't read, because he can't remember what he just read. They have rented the movie *A Fish Called Wanda* three times this month and laughed just as much the third time.

They stopped to watch a mother pushing her child in a stroller.

"Look at that, just living for this moment," she said. "That's how we all should be."

"That's how we have to be," he said.

They both work as volunteers for the Brain Injury Association of Colorado. She arranges speakers. He talks to people who live the way they did before they met and talks to high school students about how not to turn out like them.

They stopped to look at the leaves budding on a cottonwood.

"Living for the moment is joyous," she said.

"Because you can never get anything back," he said.

They came back to the townhouse.

The Daytimer said he would make some calls that afternoon and write to the maker of a butter substitute because an advertisement showed people on in-line skates without helmets. The Daytimer said she had a doctor's appointment. For lunch they would have turkey, because last week she cooked a 24-pound turkey.

They stopped to look back at the morning.

"We'll have to do this again," he said.

"I think we already have," she said. "But let's do it anyway. It's joyous."

Rocky Mountain News
March 17, 1996
(Greg's last story)

We will always remember Greg Lopez.

Greg cared and was interested

and wanted to know about us and

what "brain injury" meant

and the effect it had on people.

Greg Lopez was a beautiful person

and will always be remembered and loved.

BARBARA BUTLER AND TED LESSER

Goodbye

Excerpt from Greg's final column in New Iberia, July 10, 1987

A couple of years ago I met a man who said he was a descendant of George Washington. He counted greats through all of the fingers on his right hand and all but one on his left before he came to grandson. At the time he was in a cell in the city jail — he threw a rock through a store window because he didn't have a place to sleep one night — and we never got a chance to talk about that or anything else.

Someone told me he was crazy.

I thought about this a while and decided if he was crazy he would have said he was George Washington, and that was the general rule I followed with this column.

That is a run-on sentence, which seems like a fitting way to end this.

Goodbye.